## Praise for *Werewolf Pa*

"What Denny Sargent has put together is a us(
tive practices within a framework that brings balance oı ınınu սռս _ _ y
spirit through the ritual embrace of the primal forces within. It's a continuation of a historic current with modern magickal beliefs incorporated that produces a cool transformation and brings peace to folks trying to live with their inner ferocity."

—Joshua Gadbois, also known as Rufus Opus,
author of *Seven Spheres, Goetic Grimoire,*
and administrator of Applied Hermetics

"Magickal rituals are much more potent when performed by a group…Thus, solo werewolf magick experiences are greatly enhanced when working within a pack, and progress is accelerated. Mr. Sargent's research has convinced him of the existence of numerous group werewolf rites and festivals in the ancient world. His goal is to reintroduce these into the modern world. The path offered is that of reclaiming who we truly are and sharing the journey with like-minded individuals."

—Tony Mierzwicki, author of *Hellenismos*

# WEREWOLF
# PACK
# MAGICK

———— )( ————

© Denny Sargent

## About the Author

Denny Sargent (Aion 131, Hermeticusnath) is a writer, artist, and university instructor. He has a bachelor's degree in education and a master's degree in history and intercultural communications and has been involved in international education most of his life. He has written several university textbooks and sets of international curriculum.

In the magickal world, he has been an initiate of or an accepted member of a number of esoteric traditions and groups including, but not limited to Welsh Traditional Craft, Church of All Worlds Church of the Eternal Source, the Typhonian OTO, Nath Tantrika Lineage, the Grove of the Star & Snake, Voxas Rimotae, the Voodoo Spiritual Temple, the Shinto Kamisama and Priests, the Horus Maat Lodge, and Coven of the Mystical Merkaba. Denny has written for a number of magazines and anthologies in the United States and Japan, and has written books and articles on Paganism, Western occultism, spells, folklore, magick and tantra extensively. His published books include *Global Ritualism, Myth & Magick Around the World, The Tao of Birth Days, Your Guardian Angel and You, Clean Sweep, Banishing What You Don't Need, The Book of the Horned One, Naga Magick,* and *Dancing with Spirits: Festivals & Folklore of Japan.* He was a coauthor for *The Book of Dog Magic* and *The Magical Garden.* He has had three limited edition grimoires published as well: *Liber Sigil A IAF, Liber Phoenix,* and *Liber Eos.* He is Elder Guardian of the Horus Maat Lodge and has edited and written parts of two books for the LodgeHML: *The Compleat Liber Pennae Praenumbra, The Horus Maat Lodge Book,* and *The Grimoire of a PanAeonic Magickal Tribe.*

Denny lives in Seattle where he gardens, tutors adults with autism (including his son), travels internationally as much as possible, and has a wonderful dog named Faunus. More information can be found at www.dennysargentauthor.com and on Instagram at @dennysargentauthor.

# WEREWOLF
# PACK
# MAGICK

)(

## A SHAPESHIFTER'S BOOK OF SHADOWS

## DENNY SARGENT

Llewellyn Publications
Woodbury, Minnesota

FIRST EDITION
First Printing, 2022

Cover design by Kevin R. Brown
Interior art by Llewellyn Art Department
Interior photographs by Denny Sargent
Self-portrait by Denny Sargent


Llewellyn Publications is a registered trademark of Llewellyn Worldwide Ltd.

**Library of Congress Cataloging-in-Publication Data (Pending)**
ISBN: 978-0-7387-7035-2

Llewellyn Worldwide Ltd. does not participate in, endorse, or have any authority or responsibility concerning private business transactions between our authors and the public.

All mail addressed to the author is forwarded but the publisher cannot, unless specifically instructed by the author, give out an address or phone number.

Any internet references contained in this work are current at publication time, but the publisher cannot guarantee that a specific location will continue to be maintained. Please refer to the publisher's website for links to authors' websites and other sources.

Llewellyn Publications
A Division of Llewellyn Worldwide Ltd.
2143 Wooddale Drive
Woodbury, MN 55125-2989
www.llewellyn.com

Printed in the United States of America

## Other Books by Denny Sargent

*Werewolf Magick*

*The Book of Dog Magic*

*Global Ritualism*

## Acknowledgments

Many thanks to all my friends and loved ones who who gave me moral, magickal, and sometimes physical support and help. I am indebted especially to Peter, Craig, Phil, Kineta, Damien, Karen and Robert B., Lori, Mitch, Jeffrey, Ken, Shellay, Tony M., and many others. Also thanks to members of the Horus Maat Lodge, Horizon OTO, and other circles.

I am deeply indebted to all the werewolf magick fans who brought amazing power to the workshops, rituals, and events I led, and to all who expressed enthusiasm for this wild work. I also acknowledge the astounding werewolf Facebook groups where I and werewolf magick were accepted and embraced. Finally, I acknowledge all wildlife organizations and people who are saving and supporting wolves and other wild kin of Gaia. Please contribute to the saving of our wild animal brothers and sisters!

Full D 12/2020
Self Portrait

*"For the strength of the Pack is the Wolf,
and the strength of the Wolf is the Pack."*
—Rudyard Kipling, *The Jungle Book*

# Dedication

I dedicate this book first and foremost to the souls of all our fellow wild beasts in the wildness who face genocide. May we remember they are kin so we may reunite more consciously with Mother Earth. I also dedicate this book to my pack who miraculously appeared when called by wildness to join me in the werewolf magick rites, shapeshifting, howling, prowling, and partying under the full Moon Mother amidst the vibrant woods. I am so grateful that this primal magick that I once did alone is now shared with deep feral wer friends and my wolfish dog Faunus who is an important part of every rite. The advice from my pack made this book so much better than it would have been and I am grateful that we howl as one. AWOOO!

# Contents

# Activities, Rituals, Spells, and Rites

# PREFACE

)(

I was at PantheaCon, the largest Pagan and magick conference in the United States.

I'd just finished a fun and informative workshop on Pan magick based on my *Book of the Horned One*. It had been wild and successful. It was almost midnight and the seventy or so participants were yawning, the energy in the room fading. However, I still had about thirty minutes left if I wanted to use them and I did. *Hm*, I pondered. Should I let them go or test drive something new, wild, and wolfish I'd been working on? Ha. My grin was wide and toothy. I waved the papers in my claws to get their attention and then shouted out, "Io Pan! Well, we have a bit of time left. So, y'all want to try something new, wild, and animalistic? Possibly insane? How about some werewolf magick?"

The participants all perked up and the volume of curious chatter rose. I gestured for them to stand up and they all sprang up and scurried over to form a circle around me.

"Werewolf magick? Hell yeah!" someone shouted.

Many added a variety of similar exclamations. These folks suddenly looked feral. *Perfect*, I thought. A few of the less adventurous participants scurried out the door. *Smart*, I thought.

"So, let me hear you howl. I'll start," I said, then growled.

They all gave it their best shot and it wasn't...terrible. But it was too human. Still, they were wide awake with eyes aglow. I realized they needed this. I now had the full attention of a bunch of reenergized Pagans and Witches. I could not have been happier. I had not expected this sparky reaction at midnight after a long day at the conference. I began to read quick bits from my *Werewolf Magick* rough draft about the Animalself, the need to tear away our repressive restrictive civilized programming, the importance of remembering our innate animal nature, and the importance of Gaia. They all nodded, hooted, and growled in response. One person in the back howled.

That seemed a very positive sign, so I continued.

I spoke about the revival of the ancient lineage of shapeshifting. More people began to utter animal sounds.

Ignoring my papers, I sermonized a bit on the Wildness, Wyrd, and Way, and how unleashed the werewolf magick of true Instinct, Intuition and Insight could be. I looked up. More heads were nodding, and the participants were crowding very closely around me.

"Yeah, yeah, so how do I become a werewolf!?" someone shouted.

The excited mob shouted in agreement. I felt myself slip into a light wolfish trance. The energy in the room was spinning and was triggering my inner beast.

*Well, this is interesting*, I thought.

I went with the energy of the moment and let loose a full-on, full-body, head-thrown-back howl from the depths of my soul. The *entire* group howled back and this time they nailed the feral part. The room was electric. *Oh, I* thought, *this is going to be fun.*

At that point, it was clear that no one wanted more words or explanations, including me. This once-sleepy crowd was now hopping, howling, and excited with very little effort on my part. A raw animalistic power rippled through the crowd.

I slipped further into a wolfish trance state and for a moment had an odd vision. The room faded and I saw us all in a stone cave covered with rough prehistoric wall paintings of beasts and bestial humans. We were a clan of Neanderthals, hunched over a dancing fire, covered in skins, bones, horns, and our faces daubed with red and black coloring. I saw us growling, swaying, and shifting into beasts. A thrill went through me as I realized how quickly this visionary trance state had come on. I suddenly realized that it was the influence of the revved-up crowd that was causing this reaction. I'd never done my werewolf magick with others before. It was a revelation.

I moved the group into beginner shifting work. Soon we were all hunched over, swaying and growling with increasing volume. I growled at them to settle down a bit as they started howling. Their heads went down and they all stepped back from me. Whoa! I realized that I was suddenly a pack alpha. At that point I simply forgot about my papers and rolled with it.

I began low growling words at them about the feral werewolf lingo used in werewolf magick, how it manifests the Animalself and halts human thinking. They all nodded, eyes gleaming. With examples and practice, I taught some basics to them and they quickly mastered growling, opening the chest, and putting their arms wide. After a bit of chaos, they all got it quickly, to my surprise.

They mastered the prowling, loping, swaying, and rocking in sync with growling, so we moved on to proper howling. I modeled full-body, make-'em-cringe howls, and soon full-body howls erupted from the deepest core of their beings and shook the room. I was shocked at how fast they excelled at all this and realized that the group dynamic *enhanced the intensity and proficiency of everything I modeled*. I made a mental note: Group work, like the cooperative learning I taught in my university classes, enhanced and sped up the acquisition of skills, even werewolf magick skills!

I moved the group to up howling and down howling and a variety of nuanced howls. When I asked if they wanted more, they all HOWLED back at me! The room was electric. All the hair on my body stood up. What was I unleashing? Not bad for thirty minutes! I grinned. I howled back and laughed wildly. I was in the groove now.

We moved on to up growling, down growling, yips, barks, and all kinds of wolfish actions and gestures. This was way more than I'd been planning, but they soaked it all up so quickly and I felt the group merging on an energetic level. It was fascinating, unexpected, and a bit scary, which made me grin even more. They soon learned how to combine all these sounds and actions and were swaying, rocking, and loping while growling, howling, and barking. They mastered everything in minutes like enthusiastic young wolves, soon helping each other. I wondered if I should take this further and lead a real werewolf magick group ritual. Hm. I could. I would! The group looked like they were game.

I raised my paws for quiet, and growled, "Y'all ready to try a simple were-wolf magick ritual?"

They all howled, waved their claws, and jumped about like a bunch of crazed punk rockers in a mosh pit. My heart swelled with joy. I howled along, of course. Once you are in the werewolf mode, howl-a-thons are irresistible.

I gruffly modeled the basic rite and communicated that human words were banned during the rite. I cued them on key visualizations and to follow me as the rite unfolded. I told them that, in the end, we would let go of the wer state and revert to human again. They honestly didn't seem to care.

Here is how the rite went, minus the prompts and cues:

- We formed a large circle and did the swaying low growl slip into trance.
- We sway-stomped and up growled nine times to banish our circle together.
- We prowled and down growled eleven times to cast the circle together.
- We howled the wolfish powers of the four quarters into being.
- As one, we joined in the center and long up howled our invocations to the werewolf gods and goddesses: Gaia, the Moon Mothers, and the Lord of the Forest.
- In our circle, we swayed with synchronized and deepening down growls and sank deeper into the werewolf magick trance state while letting our Animalselves arise.
- We began to shift to up growling with increased intensity and moved together into the center, becoming one furry, howling clan, claws reaching to the ceiling, howling as one, sharing the volcanic power of this feral unity in a wild and intense manner!
- At my signal, we brought everything down a notch with a series of low group down howls. We broke apart and slipped back into rocking and down growling while placing our paws on the floor to send grounding energy into the Earth.
- Then we quietly down growled and dismissed the powers of the four quarters. We did an up growl to banish the excess energies of the circle while loping counterclockwise.

- Finally, as our human selves reemerged, we all slowly up howled our thanks to the wolfish deities, raised our arms, and swayed until our human-selves were back in control.

Once we finished, we all shook ourselves back to full human focus (sigh) and came back together as awkward primates for a quick debrief and big group hug.

I hoarsely croaked a loving thanks and goodbye. However, the group didn't applaud. Instead, they broke into wild howls, and, while still howling, ran out into the mostly empty convention hall. I assume they scared lingering conference folk with their howling wildness. What a wonderful pack of crazed werewolves! I was happy and I felt my work here was done.

Shocked, laughing, and stupidly proud of my new neophyte werewolves, I loped to the bar for a much-needed beer with a remaining student who wanted to excitedly talk about what had happened. I listened and thought, *Wow,* that *worked.*

This is when I realized that I had to write *Werewolf Pack Magick*!

## The Takeaways

The synergy of the group at PantheaCon as it worked with werewolf magick was far more potent than I expected, that is for sure. I realized it offered people potent dynamics and it helped everyone bond and grow in wildness faster together and in sync. This realization gave me a lot of great werewolf pack magick ideas. I'd discovered several traditional group werewolf rites and festivals as I researched my first book *Werewolf Magick*; now, I would need to revive them and find people in my area who were drawn to this. I got busy.

After Pantheacon, *Werewolf Pack Magick* took on a life of its own. It was a different kind of beast, different from *Werewolf Magick* but building on that first book. I began to see it as a kind of wolfish Book of Shadows or werewolf grimoire specifically for groups. I'd been so focused on my solo werewolf magick work that I didn't initially realize that pack work—while it had entranced me and caused me to write some group rites—was something that people really responded to. Soon after I returned home to Seattle from PantheaCon, I began to get emails and Facebook messages from people all over who had been drawn to the wildness, shapeshifting, and the feral stirrings within themselves as I had been. Some were from other countries such as Brazil, Portugal, and New Zealand. They began to tell me about their own powerful werewolf magick experiences. Some always knew they were wer-like and had a great personal kinship to werewolves but had never seen a book like mine that confirmed it. Once they found the book, they jumped into the ritual work and had questions. Back in Seattle, people reached out to me about werewolf magick, and, of course, I invited them to visit me at my home. We got to know each other, spent a lot of time talking, and had a fun together. They wanted to do werewolf magick with me, especially when I showed them parts of *Werewolf Pack Magick*. These lovely folks soon became my nascent pack with which I continue to try out werewolf pack magick rites, rituals, and practices. Doing these rites with my pack changed everything in many positive ways. My pack members, their suggestions, and the natural changes to the work that occurs during our rites helped this book become better than it was.

The spark I'd seen at PantheaCon was suddenly a flame in my backyard. We were trying out many things on full moons (and sometimes dark moons for Hekate) but it is clear that the synergy and intensity I felt during the group werewolf magick ritual work at Pantheacon was no fluke. Werewolf magick practitioners are more vital and potent when working together in packs! Pack magick brings more energy, bonding, protection, and solidarity to the participants and enhances the solo werewolf magick experience. And, honestly, it is more fun with others, more of a howling party!

Every week, I still get more people contacting me about their own Animal-self experiences, their surprise at finding the practice of werewolf magick, and how much it means to them to find in it the special magick they had always been drawn to. These are my feral brothers and sisters, and I am so delighted that we have found each other and expect many more to follow.

I hope those folks from that first group at PantheaCon are all running amok in the forest somewhere. Since the publication of *Werewolf Magick*, I have done a ton of interviews, workshops, and presentations on werewolf magick to a growing group of folks. It continues to become wilder and bigger, even when done through distant cyber wer-work presentations due to the COVID-19 pandemic. This book is a gift to those who have written to me, my pack, and to all those feral Pagans, Witches, and wild ones who yearn for a wilder, freer Animalself consciousness and an end to the division between ourselves and nature. I tell my pack that my goal is to revive and revise the ancient werewolf cult so that after I die, there will be many thriving werewolf packs all over the world. Well, it is a full moon today, so I can dream! And howl, of course.

May you who are reading this discover the ecstatic Animalself you have always been and find wolfish brother and sister wers to romp and howl with. May you free yourselves from the restrictive chains of civilization, and, with your pack, return to your true home in the deep heart of Mother Nature, one with the ecosystem you abide in. May you be blessed by Gaia, by the Moon Mother, by the Lord of the Forest and be filled with the joy and freedom of the Great Wolf Spirit. Embrace the burning heart of your wildness, what you have always been.

May you howl and play with joy!

Denny Sargent
Full Moon, October 2021

# INTRODUCTION

——— )( ———

Why are we in love with werewolves, minotaurs, birdmen, and other half-human creatures? I believe it is because they are part of the oldest species memories we have from before *Homo sapiens* took the stage. Human-beast shapeshifters seem to have informed the oldest spiritual rituals and beliefs of prehistoric peoples as shown in the dream-like images and animal-human burials they left us. 40,000-year-old paleolithic cave paintings are full of wild ancient animals and shapeshifting animal-men and animal-women. It is generally agreed that these images reflect pervasive Animism, the honoring of all things as spiritual beings, especially the animals who fed, taught, and sometimes protected early man.

Archaeology continues to show that Animist magick and ritual practices existed from the dawn of time and seem to have similarities and connections with modern shamanic practices of indigenous cultures today. I have traveled widely and have visited and spoken at length with such shamans, and they agree that such practices are as ancient as their peoples. I know that Animistic shamans like the Ulch, Maya, and Huichol still practice such primal shapeshifting rituals with the help of the animal spirits and their own innate animal powers. They have told me so during my visits with these practitioners. Such primal Animistic magick makers use shapeshifting to call forth important visions, heal tribal members, seek out game to feed the community, and take journeys into the spirit world to aid or guide the deceased. These practices, and the lineage of ancient shapeshifting cults that have existed for thousands of years, influence the ideas, practices, and ethos of what has become the practice of werewolf magick.

Let me be clear: werewolf magick is informed by such practices but does not claim to be shamanism. It is not part of a complex culture or lineage. I honor the several shamans I have met, interviewed, and sat with in ritual. I learned much from them but do not claim any of their mysteries or practices in any way. However, they did greatly inspire me.

Werewolf magick is a unique and modern magickal process inspired and infused by a variety of primal traditions and historical information gathered from across the ancient world. Werewolf magick emerged as a recreation and revival of ancient Animistic and shapeshifting practices practiced by many ancient werewolf cults that came before it. This wild magick erupted through a spiritual, emotional and almost physical death and rebirth that was thrust upon me. When all in my life was lost, the Wolf Spirit found me, mentored me, and helped me unchain and free my innate Animalself. This very likely saved my life, as I shed my tired old self and let the wilder, freer, happier self emerge. I will forever be grateful to the three-eyed Wolf Spirit that has led me to this primal gnosis. Over a four-year period of self-renewal and rebirth, the Wolf Spirit helped me rediscover, study, and revive a series of ancient werewolf traditions and practices that were seemingly everywhere in the old world. It took three years to study, vet, understand, and craft the werewolf magick practices. This finally resulted in the book *Werewolf Magick: Authentic Practical Lycanthropy*. I know it is real and works because I did everything you can read in the book. Werewolf magick offers real keys for anyone willing to come to terms with and unlock their Animalself. Once this is done, once one fully and completely accepts his or her deep and powerful animal-being, then so much is possible.

*Werewolf Magick* lays out the historical roots and basic revived practices of shapeshifting magick and offers a series of pragmatic techniques for the motivated seeker to accomplish what the ancients were able to do. It takes time, energy, a deep primal love and connection with nature to challenge and free your inner beast or Animalself. Werewolf magick offers a complete course in werewolf spells, rites, rituals and clear ways to master pragmatic shapeshifting trance states and so become a werewolf or human wolf. It is not about growing fangs and fur, it is about freeing the primal animal you are but have forgotten and using the suppressed strength, instincts and powers thus unlocked. But werewolf magick is a kind of textbook, a way to attain that sought-after feral state of magickal consciousness for each individual. And all the work in it is solo work, as it needs to be. Yet people, like wolves, are not solitary creatures; we need each other.

*Werewolf Pack Magick* offers the next step in this process. It offers every wer a clan, a community, brothers and sisters in wildness. It is the werewolf magick Book of Shadows for those who have mastered or almost mastered werewolf magick who wish to speed up and strengthen the shapeshifting magickal process with others. Most every wolf needs a pack as does most every mage, witch, or sorcerer! Occultists and adepts of all kinds may learn and work alone, but as primates, our instinct is to come together in groups to work, play, mate, laugh, and celebrate. This book is for wers who have devoured and been transformed by werewolf magick and now seek others like them, of which there are many, trust me. The emerging and growing communities of furries and other kin show that the feral magicks and Neoanimism is erupting these days. These wonderful, often misunderstood folk, are expressing an intense identification with the Animalself. This yearning to transform into a human-animal, like in ancient cave paintings, reflects deep primal memories of animal-people and shapeshifters still existing in our deep, unconscious minds. This primal desire to let the Animalself emerge from its civilized cage seems to be growing in the world and we become more removed from nature.

The old shapeshifting stories, folklore, art and Animistic festivals are being revived within popular culture. It seems that we modern humans can suddenly see and feel the animal spirits walk among us again as the wild animals they embody are being exterminated. It is time for us who work magick to free ourselves from the false and self-destructive fetters of the modern world and to return to the truth we have forgotten, that we are animals, we are of Gaia, we embody eons of feral magicks and power, we just have to remember and own it.

It is time for the ancient werewolf (and other Animistic cults) to be revived again. It is time for the werewolf magick packs to emerge again as they did in ancient Greece, Rome, Scythia, Scotland, Ireland, Central Europe, Scandinavia and many other places. Shapeshifting Animistic sorcerers and packs and tribes have existed most everywhere in the world, and in some places, they still do.

But modern society is not kind to animals nor to the Earth itself and this must change if we are to survive. For this to happen, we need community, we need to create a new Animistic, feral-friendly culture. We need packs who are one with nature.

*Werewolf Pack Magick* is the second part of werewolf magick. It is the communal, clan-oriented grimoire for groups of wer shapeshifters. The primary goal of werewolf magick is to revive, recreate, and reintroduce modern 'werewolf cults' that are based on those that existed across the ancient world as described in *Werewolf Magick*. Werewolfery and shapeshifting has rarely been solitary and if the surviving shamanism I wrote about in the same book is any indication, such practices need to be expanded by our packs. I know that group werewolf magick speeds up magickal practices such as inducing trance states, spiritual shapeshifting, and the manifestation of the Wolf Spirit or Animalself within each person and aids many practical and spiritual practices. This book moves this magick into the social realm of Pack creation by following the historical examples of werewolf cults that worked and shapeshifted together. We can assume that such group members bonded on deep unconscious, intuitive, and instinctive levels as comrades within the natural world. I have experienced this in werewolf magick group work. It seems obvious that working together with a group of wild kin can be more powerful, fun and effective.

Unlike its predecessor, *Werewolf Pack Magick* is not exactly a training book, it is a sacred book of rites, rituals, spells, practices and festivals to be enjoyed by werewolf magick shapeshifters and maybe other magick makers in communal joy to increase their magickal effectiveness, relink with the ecosystem and have fun.

In *Werewolf Magick* I warned about doing shapeshifting work with others who are not prepared for this kind of primal power, yet I always envisioned groups of accomplished wers coming together to fulfill their true potential and experience innate animal joy in packs. I'd say that a whole pack is always greater than the sum of its parts and real wolf packs offer a perfect example of group coordination, solidarity, survival and prosperity.

Do all werewolf pack members need to be proficient in the practices and skills systematically explained in *Werewolf Magick*? One way or another, all members of a pack need to experience and become proficient at basic werewolf magick skills and techniques to be able to hold their own in such a pack. However, people are all different. Some will have done this work deeply and are more proficient and know more than others, but if decades in education have taught me anything, it is that cooperative learning and practice improves everyone in a group and speeds up any learning process as long as all do the work. Those who excel become mentors and the whole pack itself may help to mentor those with fewer skills and less wolfish experience. Just as beginners in any magickal order, coven, or circle need to learn the basics of that particular magick before working with others, so too do less experienced pack members. From there, proficiency at werewolf magick and shapeshifting can be acquired, enhanced, and reinforced in the communal setting of a pack, as long as everyone follows the basic protocols, practices, and ideals of our magick.

In this way, it is thus possible for a pack to evolve with the informed facilitation of just a couple of experienced "elder" shapeshifting wers. Their job would be to make the information and practices as laid out in the *Werewolf Magick* book comprehensible and usable, much like an elder in a training coven mentors new witches. However, the mastering of werewolf magick is done, *Werewolf Pack Magick* leans heavily on the mastering, expansion, and application of werewolf magick in a group setting. Guidelines are given in this book, but as is usual in such occult circles, each group will grow, practice, bond, and evolve in their own unique way, as will be reflected in their egregore or "group mind." To summarize, a pack may be effectively formed with just a few expert wers who have mastered werewolf magick and those new members who are still learning can learn much as they go from practicing with werewolf elders until they reach full proficiency in skills like shapeshifting. This interaction will help everyone bond, expand their learning, and enhance the pack.

Finally, *Werewolf Pack Magick* is about the deep, delicate dance of social interactions among any group of people. A crucial ingredient to the success of a pack are the rules and stated processes of that pack, because interactions of entranced wers are more primal, feral, and intense. Werewolf magick erupts from the deep unconscious mind as every wer's Animalself unleashed and magickally expanded. This means that pack rituals are, of course, quite wild, and intense as well as being vibrant and potent. Therefore, all members must be somewhat experienced in appropriate interactions in this new context and the pack container needs structure and coordination. This is true of any magickal group; all have rules, but wild is wild and when intellect shifts, new rules are called for. In Chapter 2, the structure, norms, gathering place and dynamics of a werewolf pack as well as the role of the alpha who mentors, protects and takes care of the whole pack.

A pack is a safe space and a tribe for those of us feral occult types who are often happier in wilderness and have often been misunderstood, neglected or even ostracized for being too wild or too different. A werewolf pack, like any arcane group, will function as a kind of family for some and bring out the very best of every member. A pack of well-organized, supporting, and focused wers can do amazing, mind-blowing things as the history and tales of such cults tell us, being more chaotic and edgy than many occult circles, but also much wilder, authentic and ecstatic! And most of all, we are fully and deeply part of nature and our ecosystem, more than most occult groups. All our gatherings are held there.

Well, my inner wolf is yawning at all these words, words, words! It is time to grab my little wolfish doggo and go out for a hike in the woods. If you want to know more about werewolf pack magick, go to a forest on a clear full-moon night and howl, asking all the lurking beasts and feral gods and goddesses, and especially the Great Wolf Spirit, what it is about! You'll be surprised at the answers that come out of the darkness. May we all become wilder and may the howls of our collective beast-selves awaken others to the authentic joys of life and bring us all back into the full embrace of nature. May the sheer joy, power, bliss and vitality of your awakening long-ignored Animalself fill you with a deep understanding that together, as part of nature, we are whole.

Come, you hidden werewolves! Shed your tired old skins and come dance together in fur and fangs with us in the primal forest! This is just the beginning of a feral magick revolution!

Denny Sargent
werewolfmagick.com

# CHAPTER 1

# WEREWOLF MAGICK
# REVIEW AND EXPANSION

————————— ☽☾ —————————

Werewolf pack magick is a very different animal from werewolf magick in many ways, though they share a common methodology and ethos. Doing the rites, rituals, and spells from werewolf magick solo in the woods will likely be ignored by humans. However, when you get a whole pack howling in a park, someone might call animal control or worse. This needs to be kept in mind. I was absurdly surprised at how loud the howling and growling was when I first did a ritual with my new nascent pack. Together, we are a surprisingly loud group of wolves!

The werewolf magick you are familiar with gets louder, wilder, and more boisterous with a pack, which has to be taken into account, though the benefits are huge. A pack offers a massive increase in power and emotional and magickal support. It offers a group of fellow wild wer friends you can hang out and be comfortable with and thus a lot more laughter and fun. Wolves, wers, and humans are social creatures and, to reframe a phrase, many paws make werewolf magick light work in terms of organizing and doing sometimes complex rituals. The synergy of a pack all calling up their Animalselves together is shockingly faster and wilder than solo work, as you'll discover. Keep this in mind as you read on, but remember your werewolf magick fundamentals. Things can also get more chaotic in a pack and becoming very familiar with the work and lore in *Werewolf Magick* is key to knowing how to keep all chaos minimal.

So, it is expected that you will have read and become familiar with the book *Werewolf Magick* before working with a pack. Knowing the core ideas, tools, principles as well as the rituals, rites and spells from that book is crucial for all pack members since this book builds on and extends all these things. This is especially important in terms of the instructions and practices for shapeshifting. If you have not read, digested, and practiced these rituals in *Werewolf Magick*, it is important that you do so before working with a pack and the more complex rituals and rites in this book.

**Note:** Werewolf magick adepts who have mastered the basics, especially shapeshifting, and are proficient in werewolf magick are referred to herein as a *wer* or *wers*.

## What Werewolf Pack Magick Is Not

There are some very disturbed people who identify as 'werewolves' out there and use fixated, dark personas to justify dark actions. Let me be clear, werewolf magick is not about harming or dominating others or about justifying dangerous delusions. It *is* about becoming more liberated, having fun, personally evolving, growing magickally, and reintegrating with and discovering the arcane secrets of nature. Our magick is *not* about 'horror movie werewolves' and other such tropes or werewolf media-saturated memes. *These people have nothing to do with werewolf magick.*

Our magicks are based on real history, Animistic and other practices to help us break free of the cultural programming that has led to the current ecological disaster. We do this ancient magick to help the Earth, ourselves, and all of humanity and to have some pack fun and support. We work to reintegrate with ourselves and our local ecosystem. This is done by looking at the ancient werewolf cults, opening to our own suppressed Animalselves and by adapting techniques used by the indigenous shamans I have spent time with. We prize free will, individualism, and unleashing the wildness within us as part of the wildness in nature, but we are never involved in malicious or harmful behavior. We reject racism, bigotry, sexism, and intolerance of any kind. To be clear: The stereotypical cursed, dominating, murderous werewolves are fantasies and fiction and are not of us in any way. Wolves in nature never do such things and the Great Wolf Spirit and our feral gods *will not allow this*.

**Please note:** This book is written for adults and contains language, blunt descriptions, and ritual actions which include the possible use of alcohol and other intoxicating substances where they are legal. Wild nighttime revels under the full moon are, of course, encouraged and explained along with other wild rites, spells, and so on. Ritual substances such as drops of blood, sexual fluids, and spittle are noted in rituals, *but no animals, including humans, are ever harmed*. All such choices are solely the responsibility of the reader and all instructions and advice can and should be changed as the reader will if they are uncomfortable with any instructions.

## Werewolf Magick During a Time of Pandemic

This book is being written during the COVID-19 pandemic which will hopefully have passed by the time you are reading this, but if not, it bears discussing. It has been proven that the COVID virus is spread easily, and pack work is very interpersonal with lots of hugging, howling, growling, and sharing of drinks in some rituals. Our wolfish ethos demands honesty and clear communication, the safety of pack members being paramount. The people I now do rituals with are vaccinated. Your pack must decide on what works for all of you, but there must be a clear pack consensus considering this issue and what is best for the wers of the pack and their loved ones. With that said, rituals can be altered as needed, of course, and adaptation and creative thinking is encouraged. Wolves are very clever critters!

## Review of Key Points and Practices of Werewolf Magick

What follows is a review of the basic ideas and practices presented in *Werewolf Magick* as you prepare for pack work. If you are proficient in the practices of werewolf magick and have a deep understanding of these practices, you may mentor those just learning how to do werewolf magick, newbies being werewolf "cubs" who are still learning this work and need practice. What follows is a good summation of most of the key ideas and practices you can refer to as you review and reinforce the exercises from *Werewolf Magick*.

## The Gods and Spirits of the Pack

The Great Wolf (or Werewolf) Spirit, often depicted with three eyes, is our tutelary spirit-deity and guide in our work. Easily called by wers and other shifters, the Wolf Spirit guides, empowers, and helps more directly in werewolf magick work. The Wolf Spirit is represented by the werewolf shrine or icon.

Gaia, the Earth Mother, nature, and ecosystem are all names of one entity, and the most important entity to our practice. We often say "To you, from you; All things." Gaia is our divine mother, the source of all we have, need, are. Doing what we can to stop the ongoing destruction of Gaia is our true will as wers. Unleashing the Animalself and shapeshifting helps us reintegrate with Her. The Earth Mother is symbolized by the sacred space and altar.

The Lord of the Forest is the guardian, protector, and embodied force of the Wildness and the complex and lovely wilderness of nature. Gaia is the Mother, the Lord of the Forest is the Father, though they are one and the same,;they have two masks. As She has many names throughout history, so does He. Often depicted as a horned god or one covered with leaves, in His primal form He *is* the forest and all wild places. The Lord of the Forest is represented in the stang.

The Moon Mothers or Moon Mother. The Moon, and the forces it embodies at different phases, is a primary deity for wolves and werewolves. It is She who calls forth the ebb and flow of all water around us and in us. When full, all wild animals are called forth to honor Her as are their energies, in Her darkness all wild ones dive deep within and work with darkness. In our work, we use the ancient goddess Artemis (new moon), Selene (full moon), and Hekate (dark moon), yet they are all seen as aspects of faces of the most primal lunar deity.[1] They are honored and invoked at different times and in different ways. They are represented by the three staves, white, red and black respectively.

## The Tools of the Pack

The magickal tools used in our ritual work are explained in full in *Werewolf Magick* so we will not explain them in depth here. But a couple have been

---

1. Sargent, *Werewolf Magick*, 54.

added, so here is the list of tools every werewolf magick pack should create or gather. These are the basic ones, but others can, of course, be added and some of the rituals in this book call for other items as well. All should be made of natural materials, the more originating from natural materials the better.

*The stang:* A natural forked branch representing the Lord of the Forest.

*A natural cup:* used for ritual work, associated with the Moon Mothers (Artemis, Selene, Hekate).

*A burning bowl, small cups or plates for offerings, candle holders:* All again should be as simple, natural and primal as possible, handmade is always best.

*The three staves:* short one- to two-foot-long sticks from trees with at least one point, all representing the Moon Mothers, taken with blessing from trees, oak preferred, and may be colored: (Artemis: white, Selene: red, Hekate: black).

*The sacred knife:* used for rituals and should be a natural as possible, every wer should have one.

New tools for pack magick:

*The pack drum:* best if it is a large, shallow drum often used by shamanic peoples like the Ulch. It should be decorated with werewolf symbols (see Appendix).

*The pack shrine:* the sacred heart of the pack, see Chapter 3.

*The werewolf magick oracle:* a set of images that can be on cards or other items used for magick and divination, see oracle in Chapter 3.

## The Use of Body Fluids in Werewolf Magick

The human body has been used in primal Pagan rituals from ancient times, including sexual fluids, drops of blood, and spittle. We mostly use such secretions to bless items or rites because of their power, but it is up to you. It is the body that is the primary tool of our magick, thus use of blood, spit, semen, hair, body oils, menstrual blood and so on was the norm in ancient Pagan religions and cults. We use only natural things in our work, *and this includes natural secretions from our animal bodies.* If blood and sexual fluids are beyond the pale for you, one substitute that still contains DNA is spit. *However, in this era of AIDS and STIs, it is imperative that blood work be safe, immaculate, and never shared.*

## The Use of Herbs, Gems, Minerals and Other Natural Items

In *Werewolf Magick* several herbs, stones, and other natural items are mentioned as being appropriate to use in our feral rituals, spells, and practices. Many of these are associated with wolves, werewolves, or other feral lore as is appropriate. All the ingredients we use must be natural; this is part of our ethos as is the idea that such sacred items not damage the environment or encourage overuse of such plants. It is best if herbs are grown by the werewolf adept or gathered at special times like the full moon. All such harvesting should include an offering and prayer or wer-lingo thanks to the spirit. In this book, you'll see sage and other herbs. Keep in mind that common cooking sage is just as good as over-harvested smudging sage. Harvesting bark like cedar should be done with great care so as to use older bark whose removal won't hurt the tree. This goes for all the other herbs and woods and leaves. If there is a question about how appropriate taking that item is, use a different, more common herb or flower. This is the same with stones, crystals, and so on. New age capitalism is causing havoc in places where crystals are mined madly with no thought to environmental damage. Far better to find such things yourself. Every stone of Gaia is sacred, and we are deep kin of Hers. Always keep your ecosystem in mind, harvest what is responsible to take, always show gratitude, and use items that feel right, regardless of the ritual instructions! As you go through this book, keep an eye on the herbs and consider growing them.

### Core Principles and Skills

The principles of Wildness, Wyrd, and Way manifest through each balanced wer through the blooming of the spiritual and practical skills of Instinct, Intuition, and Insight. These are necessary to practice werewolf magick in a pack and help all wers remain balanced and focused while romping and howling in the forest! It is up to every pack member who practices werewolf magick to come to a deep and sublime understanding of these powers and skills. With an understanding and adaptation of these concepts, our magick will flow properly and inform and manifest in all the pack does.

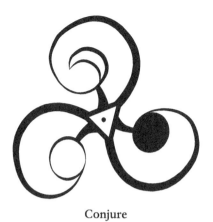

Conjure

## The Wildness

Before all things, the Wildness is sacred in werewolf magick. It flows within you every time you enter a forest or climb amid mountains with an open heart and consciousness. Wildness is the inherent spiritual living force that is both embodied in untouched nature and is the energetic source of all nature. Eons ago, most of the planet was awash in Wildness and all animals lived within the all-embracing planetary weave of a vast quilt of ecosystems that covered the planet. Today, the few existing areas that are really vital and green are powerful fountains of Wildness, but they are very few. Werewolf magick venerates nature and *the reality that we are animals* and are therefore part of our ecosystem. We deeply feel the loss of Wildness; it hurts. A key healing and empowering aspect of werewolf magick is the return and embrace of Wildness, the "elixir of life," and physical immersion in Wildness is the key to our magick. *As animals, we are free of all human blockages and restrictions* in Wildness and thus one with it. As the Wildness flows up from Mother Earth we become Wildness itself!

## The Wyrd

The Wyrd is the intricate weave and interconnections of energy and magick, the patterns, the tides and web of causality, fate, karma, energetic interconnections, and other forces which flow through our lives empowered. The Wyrd is the quantum web of timeless universal existence and thus interpenetrates and imbues all Wildness. It is best perceived in the astoundingly intricate web of any ecosystem which is beyond intellectual understanding. It is the Wyrd that is the interpenetrating matrix within which we work with and channel Wildness magick. Magick itself being a good synonym for Wyrd. It is only by being an integrated part of nature that we can comprehend the true reality that each ecosystem is a complex yet transcendent unfolding of Wyrd. Things arise and fall, ever flowing, flexible. Every animal and plant has its function and one feeds or is fed by another as seasons and landscapes shift. Older cultures lived within and drew most of their knowledge from observing the Wyrd and so adapted to it, and adjusted to the flows and shifts of nature and often worshipped it as a transcendent spirit. By interacting within its natural matrix with deep awareness as animals do we find the Wyrd becomes our ally, our teacher, and our truth and if will is aligned with the weave of the Wyrd around us, all falls into place and we see patterns that offer us direct connection with the divine spirit all about us.

## The Way

Taoists call it *Teh* or "the Way" and in Japan it is called *Wa*, a term that does not translate. Let me sniff about this bone and try to communicate the essence of this without leading you astray. 'The Way' isn't fate, or karma, it is simply the natural expression and unfolding of the totality of one's existence or being. Words and intellect fail here. The Japanese discuss *Wa* (Way) as "rightness" or a "feeling of sublime emptiness," a kind of pure non-ego awareness. Animals live within Wa all the time by simply doing what it is they do without thinking, something impossible for us except in liminal states of consciousness like deep trance or shapeshifting. Salmon spawn when it is time, birds do not 'know' when to migrate and wolves do not 'know' how to behave in a pack. It is simply their Way. Gnosis may be a good analogy, being direct knowledge or experience of the divine, of the essential unity without cognition. The Way is consciousness beyond categorization, yet ironically it is the ultimate goal of werewolf magick. It is through shifting into Animal-self consciousness that we can leap forth into the pure void of bliss-being. One only knows that one has reached this when we awaken to "What happened? Where was I?" The Way is not a noun, though to write it makes it so.

It is a verb, a beingness, and it underlies all real magick in the universe. In werewolf magick, the reality that there is no difference between any one thing and any other thing is the true secret of this state.

The core werewolf magick skills are Instinct, Intuition, and Insight. These are enhanced by our magick. They can be seen as arising from the deepest genetic 'group unconscious' or 'species unconscious' innate 'skills' that all animals are born with, including human beings. However, except for more conscious people, our culture and programming 'cage' tends to suppress these innate skills focusing more on upper cortex functions such as logic, empirical thinking and rejecting 'gut feelings' or instinctual reactions. werewolf magick revives and reveres the deeply wired 'skills' that are embedded in our very genes and body. Today, climate change is making us miserable, yet our empirical intellects cause us to mostly ignore this impending horror. Animals immediately react to such dangers.

## Instinct

Linked to the lower body center, Instinct is the expression of the deepest most primal animal or unconscious being. It is hardwired genetically, species wide. Instinct tells fish when to spawn, wolves when it is time to mate, birds when it is time to migrate. It is deep and not intellectual at all of course. In humans, Instinct sends warnings when we sense danger, though our intellectual mind may not. We fall in love and mate often urged by instinctual attraction. We know when our kids are in danger or upset; it is completely unconscious. In dangerous situations, we often react before thinking. We have muffled and chained our instinct, a powerful ally. Werewolf magick, and especially unleashing your Animalself in shapeshifting, unleashes the power and intensity of your instincts in remarkable and often important ways, not the least of which is trusting that inner voice of your Animalself to react without thinking. In my life, this has saved me from serious accidents. Instincts become increasingly important in your life and in magick.

## Intuition

Linked to the heart center, Intuition is knowing something is real and true without knowing why or how is the guiding hand of intuition. As humans, we often relax and step back from furious thinking when we want our unconscious mind to give us advice or finding a place we don't remember or feeling out a stranger or a place. Intuition is more heart centered in that it is a feeling more than an idea or an aha moment. The "voice" of Intuition comes when the Animalself is allowed to whisper "You can trust that person," or "Don't go to that party," or "This looks good but it is not right for you." Often Intuition trumps logic and experiential proof and is deep-feeling based. "That person doesn't feel right," or "That path doesn't seem ok," are examples of Intuition. Animals are deeply cued by Intuition, often their survival depends on it. Knowing when to run, what rivers to avoid and when humans can or cannot be trusted is Intuition based on very sensitive sensory input. Werewolf magick practices sharpen the senses and the unconscious skills and Intuition suddenly becomes an important and potency ally.

## Insight

Linked to the upper body center, Insight is the tip of the Animalself consciousness, emerging into but not subsumed by the human reality. As Instinct triggers immediate knowing, Insights arise in consciousness fully realized as clear knowledge or truths. Insights are not logical nor are they based on reasoning and intellect. They are perfectly formed 'aha' moments that arise from the unconscious mind where lives the Animalself amid archetypal alchemies and are recognized as *true and right* immediately, even though they may seem at times illogical. Geniuses enter fugue states intentionally when faced with huge problems or quandaries and allow Insights to arise and thus solve difficult problems or offer a new way of seeing reality. The work of werewolf magick and the enhancement of the Animalself allows more access to such experiences and in a shift state of being, Insights come fast and furious, especially in nature. After returning to normal after shapeshifting, insights often arise from the experience and should be noted down as they are often seen as originating from the spirits of nature.

Werewolf magick sees these three feral modalities as a continuum uniting the deepest roots in animal and genetic consciousness through the guidance of our Animalself.

Accessing and balancing these three states of internal awareness is the key to staying rational while at the same time being utterly subsumed in the sensory tsunami of shapeshifting to wer. Mythology is filled with utterly bestial, cannibalistic werewolves but also conscious and balanced werewolves. By being aware of these three states of consciousness while working werewolf magick, through deep meditation and the balancing energetic support of nature and consciously focusing on the Wildness, Wyrd, and Way, you can adjust your consciousness along the experiential continuum of being you are in.

## The Animalself and Shapeshifting

The Animalself is the animal you actually are. It is the primal deep mind or 'primitive self' deep within your lower cortex and in your genes. Begin with this: We are animals, primates to be exact. Remember, we are 98% the same genetically as chimpanzees.[2] In tribal cultures I have visited with, it is accepted that humans are simply other animals living interdependently in the ecosystem. Wild animals are venerated as primal teachers and kin and offer powerful magick as well. Our modern cultures and dominant religions and beliefs deny this basic truth and leave all "civilized" people disliking, denying, and rejecting their primitive Animalself and kinship with other animals. This separation from nature is the source of so much of our misery and our suicidal destruction of our world. Unleashing and coming to terms with our Animalself offers freedom, happiness, and a way to reintegrate with nature and open up an amazing amount of power.

Such powers were once the norm in the ancient world as the stories of the werewolf cults show. Myths, history, and folklore of werewolf cults and practices are wonderful and fascinating, but werewolf magick offers real results if you are willing to invest your energy by utilizing strong will and a desire to free your Animalself from the psychological and emotional prison of civilized restrictions.

---

2. Lovgren, "Chimps, Humans 96 Percent the Same, Gene Study Finds."

Once the Animalself is contacted we can move into shapeshifting. The practices leading to shapeshifting are:

- We invoke or call on the Wolf Spirit for help in the task of becoming free of your civilized "cage" and programming. This is done in wilderness work, in ritual, in dreaming, and so on as described in *Werewolf Magick* as we grow in skill with the Animalself.

- We become proficient at calling forth our Animalself consciousness at will to subsume our conscious mind and thus shift into primarily Animalself consciousness. This is done through increasingly more complex practices and rites like the Praxis Rite that is found in the Appendix.

As our skills grow, we then move into shapeshifting as we deepen our relationship with the Wolf Spirit in wilderness and form a bond which helps us progress. There are many techniques that deepen and facilitate shifting. They include:

- Using wer-lingo, or non-verbal animalistic sounds and actions like howling.

- Practicing entering liminal states and trance states through swaying, prowling, leaping and other physical movements and gestures.

- Spending time in real wilderness while *living as the Animalself* within a truly wild ecosystem. The energies and spirits will then acknowledge and help you practice deeper shapeshifting werewolf magick rituals.

- Later returning to wildness and doing advanced shapeshifting, utilizing the gut 'fire center,' visualization and primal invocations, gestures and intense imagination to more fully shapeshift. At this point, the feral gods and spirits will acknowledge and welcome you and the gnosis or direct knowledge of the Wildness, Wyrd, and Way will be open to you and some astounding skills and understandings will erupt within you.

Going deeper, getting better, this is what this book is about. Solo werewolf magick is important for getting the basic skills, but experience has shown me that a pack of wers can evoke their Animalselves more intensely and shapeshift faster, easier and deeper, and together. They enter a werewolf trance state more intensely and better as well. Wolves do best in packs, like the ancient werewolf cults who were so powerful that even today we know of their histories and exploits. While the core lessons of shapeshifting must be sought and learned from werewolf magick, expanding shapeshifting skills follow.

## Using the Double or Etheric Body

In many ancient cultures—including Greek, Roman, Egyptian and Norse—the soul of a person had several distinct parts. One is the eternal soul, but another, often used in magick, is the energetic body of a person called the Double. In current occultism, this Double is referred to as the astral, etheric, or energetic body and it is a separate spiritual entity, yet it can independently travel out of the body through the will of the adept.[3] It can, with much practice, travel in the physical, astral, and spiritual worlds carrying with it our consciousness *in whatever form we wish* through focus and magick, including that of a wolf or werewolf. Doing the work in *Werewolf Magick*, the Double was strengthened and energized, it being a key to shapeshifting into werewolves. Now, it is time to take this further. The Double can also be projected outward, not just expanded within to shift ourselves. It can be used as a vehicle for astral travel or work as will be explored in this book. Your Double can thus function as a vehicle for our consciousness since our work with the wolf-power has strengthened our Double, which we shaped into a wolf or werewolf form previous practices in *Werewolf Magick*. It is this energetic wolfish Double form we evoke and then "wear" or project outward so we can work with it internally or externally.

To make things clearer when discussing this entity, we will call this external Double by one simple term: Fetch. Your Double is very flexible. Projected and working with it as a separate part of you will not interfere with your internal shapeshifting work, but you will likely need to focus on one or the other at any given time, for shapeshifting is internal and Fetch work is external.

The projected and manifested Double or Fetch can be used in these ways:

- To "Astral Travel',"that is, to project your consciousness into the etheric form of a wolf or werewolf and go forth in this world or on astral worlds and in dreams. Often, it is said that witches "rode a wolf to the sabbat" while their body lay comatose.

---

3. Lecouteux, *Witches, Werewolves and Fairies*, xiii.

• To fully, with great effort and practice, manifest and project your full consciousness into the wolf or werewolf Double and actually roam this world. This is likely the origin or "real" werewolf encounters. This requires years of practice and is dangerous and is referenced but not explained in *Werewolf Magick* due to the problems.

The Double, with much work, can be fashioned as a wolf or werewolf and gain independence of a sort. Then it becomes a Fetch or Familiar, a separate magickal entity that can be projected and used in several ways after being conjured as the etheric energetic Animalself to be "worn" (to "wear the wolf skin" as it is said), ridden, or sent with your consciousness as a separate "familiar" to do spellcraft or observations.

While the core lessons of Fetch work are explained in *Werewolf Magick*, information on expanding Fetch skills is presented later in this chapter.

## Pack Shapeshifting

The following cites and expands werewolf magick practices from the book werewolf magick.

Shifting practices and proficiency should be done as is explained in *Werewolf Magick*. Key rituals should also be done as a pack for bonding and increased skill. Everything done in a pack is going to be more intense, faster, and deeper than your solo work. Pack work will bring you together and intensify and increase your power and magick. What follows are ideas for doing the key shapeshifting rites and rituals as a pack to expand the potency of each. The Praxis Rite (see Appendix) is a great simple pack initial shifting rite, and practicing it in a pack is much stronger, and more intense. Another useful shapeshifting intensifying tool is the Shapeshifting Trigger explained in Chapter 2.

### Rituals, Practices, and Spells Expanded for a Pack

The Praxis Rite is done before almost every major ritual or event.

Here are suggestions for expanding and deepening its power:

Begin by opening up to the wilderness around you by standing barefoot and as devoid of clothing as you feel comfortable. Breathe. Take your time, expand your consciousness and aura into the ecosystem about you. Breathe deeply, slowly, let your Animalself awaken and rise up without rushing it. Silently honor, give and receive energy from nature with every breath. Begin rumbling (deep chest growling, mouth closed) and begin to rock back and forth with every rumble, let your Animalself open and unfold. This will slide into a trance state that can then be deepened in the Praxis Rite.

Slow it down. Lengthen the swaying and growling. Open it up by making changes to the various parts of it that the pack feels is natural. Go deep with each chanting and extend each part.

The Praxis Rite (in Appendix) can and should be changed, altered and adapted creatively by the pack, for the pack. It was originally created for solo work but can be so much more.

The Wilderness Shapeshifting Ritual should be done as a pack campout for bonding and increased intensity in shifting.[4]

Finding a campsite where your antics won't terrify the other campers (too much) and doing this rite as a pack is important for bonding, empowerment, and learning shapeshifting. Some will be more experienced than others, this is what a pack is for. Mentoring, sharing experiences and adding or changing parts of the ritual are crucial for it to work as a pack experience. This is also a time to really get to know each other, and build trust and communication on verbal and non-verbal levels. The pack must be of one mind eventually and exist to be better as a whole than the individuals. Doing the following is a good start:

- The pack should plan to have pack meetings before and after the ritual work.
- Make a plan to discuss expectations, goals, and feelings.
- The alpha should have all gone over the ritual carefully, step by step, the more experienced wers adding their comments, experiences and ideas as they like.
- The ritual can be done more than one time. It may be best to do it with the most experienced wer (likely the alpha) observing and facilitating the

---

4. Sargent, *Werewolf Magick*, 109.

ritual for all the members. A post ritual discussion can then improve all doing the rite again the next day.

- All members should keep diaries and then share their entries around the fire during that evening's discussion.

The Advanced Wildness Shapeshifting Ritual, done as a pack, is a kind of advanced werewolf magick graduation for the pack and will solidify the egregore or spiritual entity of the pack.[5] The pack should have bonded, become fast friends and pack mates, and learned to work well together in a ritual space before this is planned.

The expanding suggestions follow those stated above, but with a few differences:

- A pre-campout meeting should be held at a home to discuss the intensity and complexity of this ritual and how it will be organized and done. This is also a time for making changes and making it a real pack ritual as opposed to a solo one.
- This ritual is more complex and more potent and therefore requires more skill and communication. The alpha will thus have more responsibility for setting it up, facilitating it all and adjusting on-the-fly as needed.
- At this point, pack members should be at a similar skill-level and be able to go over, adjust, and do the ritual as a pack and this should all be discussed at the campsite as again the alpha has all go through the various stages of the ritual and have everyone agree to cues, changes, and so on.
- Play and fun activities must be part of every ritual campout experience! Exploring, werewolf games, skinny dipping in a lake, fishing, day hikes, and so on should all be part of the experience! Think of this as wild werewolf pack scouting! Such energetic outdoor activities build energy and strength that will help empower the shifting!

## Shapeshifting Trigger Talismans

A new expansion and intensification of the shapeshifting trance states for all who practice Werewolf Magick is the shapeshifting trigger talisman. Such a tal-

---

5. Sargent, *Werewolf Magick*, 117.

isman can, through intensive magick and self-programming, activate that singular trance state more quickly than usual. In many of the ancient werewolf legends, werewolves had certain items that triggered their transformation, often it was a wolf skin, a belt made of wolf pelt or another magickal item that would empower the werewolf sorcerer into shifting quickly. Such a talismanic item that could quicken and expand shapeshifting has been contemplated since the publication of *Werewolf Magick* and the results follow.

## Shapeshifting Trigger Talisman Rite

### SET UP

Shapeshifting takes time and much energy, focus and will. Yet there are times when you face a problem or trial that calls for all your wer abilities and strength quickly. Such quick wer shifting is possible for those who have assiduously learned and practiced the shapeshifting practices laid forth in the book *Werewolf Magick*. The reason is that until you have visited a place or state of consciousness, how can you remember it and conjure it in your mind and body? Once you have achieved the goals of shapeshifting in the wild and have been through the shapeshifting initiation rites as per the descriptions in *Werewolf Magick*, you can develop some shortcuts. This will likely not get you to the advanced shapeshifting without great skill and practice, but if you have really achieved success with the Wilderness Shapeshifting Ritual, it is likely to shift you quickly and deeply into the wer state of being.

### NEEDED

A Shapeshifting Trigger Talisman that has been prepared will be needed for this rite. The most practical physical trigger items are pendants, rings, necklaces, and other jewelry. However, a special stone or shell, an earring or other items can be imprinted and used. The most potent and traditional trigger talismans can be formed using a tuft of wolf hair, a wolf's tooth or bone, and a wolf skin belt or pelt. Keep in mind *that any animal items must have been found, not murdered, or must be very old. No canid should ever be intentionally killed for these items in our work.* The trigger should be consecrated on the full moon and can be done alone, but it is best with the whole pack, maybe during an esbat or other ritual gathering. In this way, every wer in the pack could bring their own trigger talisman to charge and further empower it with the group energy. That being said, here are some wolfish examples of shapeshifting triggers to prepare and use:

- A belt, bracelet, cord or another item fashioned of wolf or coyote skin or fur. It can also be from another feral beast you are akin to. Similarly, a tooth, claw, or bone from one of these animals is a potent charm.
- A small copper knife that has been stuck into the stump or branch of a mountain Ash tree on the full moon when you were in full shifting state. (This is from an old Russian werewolf spell.)[6]
- A werewolf magick charm of another sort made of red jasper, onyx, obsidian, a moonstone or a "holy stone" (stone with a natural hole in it) you found.
- A small totem carving you created while in wer form from oak, mountain ash, cedar or another sacred tree. Magickally useful stones, scents and plants are listed in *Werewolf Magick*.[7]

### The Quick Shift Trigger Blessing Rite

There are two options for fashioning your shift trigger. You can do it solo, alone in the woods or do it with the pack, where all pack members can charge their triggers together at the same time. Both of these options have pluses and minuses, as you'll see.

## Individual Empowering of the Shift Trigger

It may be that a wer wishes to bless and charge the trigger solo, which is fine and maybe more personal. The procedure is the same for the most part. If you are the wer doing this work, you will do it on a full moon and may also repeat the the Pack Blessing Rite for Talismans and Tools several nights after as you wish to increase the potency of the talisman. Keep in mind, traditionally there are three nights of a full moon.

The wer should go to a place of Wildness—the wilder the better—where they can be undisturbed and as unclothed as possible. Have a copy or a copy on

---

6. Thayer, "Russian Werewolf Spell."

7. Sargent, *Werewolf Magick*, 53.

your cell phone of The Pack Blessing Rite for Talismans and Tools to use. It's found in the Appendix.

### NEEDED

A nearby safe wild place and a calm centered focused attitude, a crosspath is
   best of course.

The shift trigger item that you are wearing

Deep familiarity with the Growl Banishing practice and the Praxis Rite

A simple liquid offering to the werewolf gods such as lunar holy water[8] or any
   sacred blessed water or wine

Some nuts, seeds, or berries to leave for the spirits and animals of the woods.

### YOU WILL DO THE FOLLOWING

Start with the Up Growl Banishing Rite (see Appendix), then move to the Praxis
Rite (see Appendix) slowly and carefully and enter the deepest shift state pos-
sible: Take your time. Next, move to the Pack Blessing Rite for Talismans and
Tools (see Appendix). End with the Up Growl Banishing Rite.

When you are done, continue rocking and growling as the Animalself takes
over. Vigorously rub your shift trigger with your sexual organs, your chest,
and your hair, wherever hair is on your body, marking the item with your feral
scent. Make offerings as you will to the Great Wolf Spirit, the Lord of the Forest, the Moon Mothers, and Gaia. Potential offerings include pure water or
wine at the center of the area you are at, the middle of a crosspath if possible.
Then, hold the item in both paws and walk to the north perimeter edge of
your space and slowly rock and stomp a clockwise spiral while down growling
and focusing all the powers swirling about you into the shift trigger until you
reach the center of the spot you're at.

Do the the Pack Blessing Rite for Talismans and Tools as a solo rite. As darkness falls, shift your sight and see the item now glowing and writing with strange
wilderness energies. Then low up howl invoking the Great Wolf Spirit to descend
into you and your item and complete the blessing. Let your Animalself guide you

---

8. Sargent, *Werewolf Magick*, 176.

to do what is instinctive and powerful in charging the item as you enhance and seal the wild feral power into this talisman.

When done, place your hands on the earth and down growl MA MA MA to seal the powers invoked into the talisman while visualizing the shining wolfish shapeshifting power locked into the talisman.

Stand and up howl three times, thanking the Wildness, the Wyrd, and the Way and all the gods and spirits. Pour out the last of the water or wine, sprinkling some onto the shift trigger.

Up growl nine times while up growling from the center outward in a counterclockwise spiral and you release all the excess energies not locked into the Shift Trigger.

Shake your whole body and do the finishing part of the Praxis Rite to ground yourself back into human.

Finally, at the end, speak from the heart and thank all the powers invoked and all the wild creatures and scatter the food offering you brought, then go with a final howl!

### If Done with the Pack

Do the same steps from the individual empowering listed previously, but all together. This can easily be done by the whole pack together, within a larger ritual like the esbat or sabbat if desired. In this situation, once the triggers have been charged with the Pack Blessing Rite for Talismans and Tools together, each wer's trigger could then be passed around the circle from wer to wer while each wer adds his or her howl, power and blessing to it before passing it to the next wer until all are blessed by the pack and it is then being worn by the owner.

### Final Notes

However the trigger is empowered, it should be worn by the wer daily until the next full moon. During the whole lunar cycle that you are making it yours, the trigger should be "fed" with all your sexual energy with a constant focus of love, will and visualization on making it a potent shift trigger. The shift talisman as a magickal tool that can grow in power and potency, it is up to each wer. You may wish to repeat the Pack Blessing Rite for Talismans and Tools several times along with any other werewolf magick rites toward making your trigger talisman an increasingly powerful and potent tool. As is common in this wolfish work, the Great Wolf Spirit and your Animalself will "advise" changes to this rite as you repeat it. Go with what works for you, remembering that visualization and repetition are key. Continue to empower and honor and "feed" your shift trigger. And never lose it or give it to another.

There are times when you will want to shift into a wer state quickly. Maybe you are tired or out of sorts or maybe you or a packmate is in danger. I've been in sketchy urban situations where I needed my wer "form" quickly and in such situations I couldn't stand around rocking and howling! This is why I wear my wolf tooth shifting talisman trigger. When needed, I can quickly focus on it with some growling and get all wolfish as needed.

To do so, while wearing the shift trigger, grab it and up growl several times as you unleash your Animalself and quickly visualize what you've learned, then shift!

To return to "normal," take it off and down growl several times, letting the Animalself slide back down inside you and then shake yourself, letting the fur, fangs, claws etc. "fly off" you and fade away.

## Expanding Fetch Work

Most Fetch work is individual and if you have done all the work that is in the Fetch chapter in *Werewolf Magick*, you may already have a personal Fetch shrine.[9] However, once the pack is fully in sync, creating and using the pack egregore or spirit as a pack Fetch is very possible. First the pack shrine separate from individual shrines) will be created as explained in Chapter 3 and this will be the home of the pack Great Wolf Spirit as well as, if you choose, the collective spirit Fetch of the pack. Once this has been set up and the power degenerated, then work can be with a collective fetch. Here are some suggestions for doing this as a pack based on some practices in werewolf magick, all of these should be preceded by pack discussions:

- At another gathering, a discussion should be led by the alpha about a pack Fetch. All must be of one mind about this. If so, then all should take some time to create a sigil, with input from the whole pack, representing the collective pack egregore or spirit to be used as a Fetch. One member

9. Sargent, *Werewolf Magick*, 127.

should then create a final drawing all agree to and all should then name that pack spirit and the image should be kept in the pack shrine until it is potent.

- Once the pack shrine has been set up, blessed and tended for long enough time to build a potent charge, the pack shrine ritual should be done again with a different focus: to pour Animalself energy into the shrine as a united pack with the Fetch sigil displayed.

- At the appropriate time in the ritual, the sigil is passed around to every member of the pack and it is charged, maybe with drop of blood from each. Then it is installed within the shrine with the special name given to the pack Fetch growled eleven times followed by a howl while everyone visualizes the sigil at the heart of the Great Wolf Spirit.

- The shrine ritual is ended and from then on the Fetch of the pack can be activated and utilized for Fetch spellcraft. It is recommended that all pack members reread Chapter 6 in *Werewolf Magick* beforehand. Here is a general procedure for using the pack Fetch:

- Fetch work can be done amid any esbat, sabbat, or other group ritual as desired. The sigil has been drawn on a piece of bark or nice paper and is now passed around paw to paw to be empowered as all growl-chant HA and intently call on the pack Fetch.

- The alpha holds the sigil as the growl chant gets louder and louder and as he or she holds it up high, all howl the name of the Fetch three times, all visualizing the goal of the Fetch work and it is then placed in the center of the pack circle as all sit down and shift deeper into fugue state.

- All then sit in silence, eyes closed and rumbling while entering the Fetch and, releasing your Animalself consciousness, travel with it and do the pack work already assigned to the Fetch.

- After a time, the alpha slowly, softly up howls to call the pack back and all re-enter their bodies. After a time, the alpha begins a slow MA MA MA growl and everyone joins in and to release the Fetch. Slowly come back, stretch, and, as the alpha burns the sigil, all howl.

- Then all sit and discuss what they experienced, how they felt and what could improve the Fetch spellcraft.

- Creativity, Instinct, Intuition, and Insights should always be used in any werewolf magick. Adapt, change, and innovate as the pack desires. I'm sure the pack will think of many possible spellcraft uses!

## Adapting These Werewolf Magick Practices for Your Pack

Look at the many practices and spells in *Werewolf Magick* and, as a pack, decide which ones are most suitable for your pack. Such work done with a pack is explosive! Some suggestions for adapting spells from *Werewolf Magick*:

- When the pack is first forming, going out into the woods and doing the Calling the Wolf Spirit Exercise together is a potent pack exercise and will bestow the blessing of the Wolf Spirit on all, a great way to start off.[10]
- Having the pack individually do the Werewolf Dream Spell to Meet Your Inner Wolf and then meeting and comparing everyone's results is great in a lot of ways.[11] Members of the pack will begin to visualize themselves as the werewolf they really are and may also wish to take werewolf pack names influenced by this spell. Remember: will, connection with the Animalself, mastery of your etheric double, and visualization are all keys to shifting work.
- The Wolf Power Exercise can be used in the pack to build confidence, energy and potency in the work.
- These spells work well in pack mode: Werewolf Lunar Holy Water Spell, and the Lunar Eclipse Purification Spell.

Here are some great rituals to do as pack magick workings: Hekate Lunar Wolf Spirit Ritual, Solar Werewolf Empowerment Ritual, The Divine Wolf Star Ritual, and, for a pack member or friend of the pack, the Ritual for Honoring and Guiding the Dead with Anpu and others.[12]

## Pack Werewolf Lingo Expansion

Reconnecting with the long-neglected internal power of Instinct is one of the core pillars of werewolf magick. Especially in a pack, a powerful way to do this

---

10. Sargent, *Werewolf Magick*, 80.
11. Sargent, *Werewolf Magick*, 83.
12. Sargent, *Werewolf Magick*, xiii.

is to use animalistic sounds and actions and few or no words in that it activates the animal mind. In werewolf magick, we mostly use emotionally charged howls, growls and barks rather than words. We call this collection of non-verbals *werewolf lingo*. The following sounds are some of the most useful and common nonverbal communicative tools of werewolf lingo that are referenced in many spells and rituals. Learning to vocalize such werewolf sounds takes time and may stretch your vocal cords. Look online for videos of real wolves vocalizing to get more examples.

## Werewolf Lingo Review

All werewolf lingo can have an up shift up or a down shift. An example would be an up howl (aaaarooOOOO!) or a down howl (AAAARrrooo!) These mean and conjure different things:

Often in ritual work, down howls, growls, and so on bring energy down. This means invoking or calling power or letting energy flow into the pack or into the earth, depending on the rite.

However, in ritual work, up howls, growls, and so on bring energy up. This means evoking or directing energy up or outward in many ways.

For example, bringing lunar power into yourself or a talisman would be a down howl. Banishing negative energy or sending a prayer to the lunar goddess Artemis uses an up howl.

The most versatile werewolf lingo is growling and howling. Use your instincts! This is less about learning and more about being. Growling can be used for trance shapeshifting work, to warn others, to show deep contentment, to show focus, and so on. Most common modes include:

- *Loud/Low growling:* Fairly obvious, think of raising your voice or whispering.
- *Rumble growl:* This low, deep, in the chest inaudible growl with lips closed is akin to wer purring or a meditation mantra, great for centering, focusing, calming, and enhancing the Animalself consciousness and so on.
- *Howling:* This is essentially the same in many ways but more like a song or invocation. Howls are beyond a doubt the most iconic werewolf sound and practicing with a pack you'll discover amazing harmonics that are as potent as any spoken invocation.

## Other Forms of Werewolf Lingo

All of these types can be immensely expressive depending on the tone, loudness, emphasis, up or down expression and so on

- *Yip or Bark:* short, staccato, cut-off barks expressing joy, amusement and playfulness or for getting attention. Yips or barks can also be used as friendly warnings. ("Watch it!")
- *Whines:* These deep, guttural whining sounds communicate wanting something or attention, or to communicate empathy with someone who's down or hurt.
- *Chuffing:* This sound, a kind of guttural-closed mouth-cough, is like canine laughing or "Huh!" A kind of wolfish eye-roll or "Whatever!"

## Pack Magick Werewolf Lingo

As a group, werewolf lingo is more feral and powerful than words and helps a pack communicate instantly and instinctively and accomplish pack objectives, thus it is more communal.

Every wer will take time finding his or her voice with this. Some are baritones, some more alto, and some are soprano growlers and howlers! Finding your true wer voice requires non-thinking instinct. Remember: your vocal cords are not wolfish. You have to practice to make them work that way and expand your voice box and deepen your growly side! A big part of pack work is finding that perfect place where all pack members can howl, growl, and so on in harmony and this takes time, just like singing in a choir. Watch some videos of wolf packs howling together to see what I mean. Getting a group to howl as one is a sublime and beautiful experience.

## Pack Magick Werewolf Lingo Uses

Spiritual Banishing or Attacking: Pack in a circle faces outward, side by side or linked arms. Joint banishing howl or growl is used to blast away all extraneous energies, malignant forces or entities. The pack utilizes the fiery gut center of energy and will. The real power of this use comes as the mind goes completely blank as the sheer animal force and power erupts through and can be done any time the pack feels threatened or needs to clean up after some magick.

**Note:** Growling RAaaa! is perfect for this.

Manifesting and Centering: A harmonious pack howl or growl or calming rumble helps focus and empower any magickal work for any pack rituals or spells. It both pulls all the pack power together and projects it in a unified and focused way. The pack faces inward toward the focus of the magick in a circle, arms linked or thrust forward or even in a group hug, arms about each other facing center when howling or growling. The pack often begins low and rises high for sending power or begins high and brings the combined tone down to focus on empowering in the center of the circle like a song of unity and love, depending on the spell or rite.

**Note:** Rumble growling is perfect for this.

### New Expanded Werewolf Lingo

Since *Werewolf Magick* was published, the following important growl forms have become commonly used in our rituals to invoke the key powers of werewolf magic. You will see them used often later in this book. Briefly, they are growled with slight inflections as notes to call on the following powers. For example, MA would be growled with a very slight mouth-closes slight "mmm" sound with mouth opening into Ahhhh. Like: MmmAaaaaaaa. HA and AH begin mouth open, RA begins as deep intense growl then opens to a "rrrr" sound, AH-HA a growl with a dip between. Use your instincts:

- The Earth Mother (Gaia): MA
- The Lord of the Forest: HA
- The Moon Mothers (Artemis, Selene, Hekate): AH
- Great Wolf Spirit: RA
- The werewolf Gnosis (So may it be!): AH-HA

The most repeated practices and useful information are all in the Appendix for easy and quick reference. Review, practice, and memorize them if possible; they will be referenced often in this book.

# CHAPTER 2
# STRUCTURE AND DYNAMICS
# OF THE WEREWOLF MAGICK PACK

W erewolf magick, like the Craft and most other occult traditions, can be a solo experience or a powerful synergistic group experience. A group of wers is, of course, called a pack. Werewolf magick rituals and play are more powerful, exciting and wilder if done in a pack, but all pack rituals can be adapted to solo work if you wish but are more vital with a pack. What follows are key aspects of pack work, but each pack is autonomous and will determine specific procedures for their pack.

There are no fixed rules beyond those of a real werewolf pack: nurturing, loyalty, helpfulness, strength, intensity, tolerance, autonomy within the pack, truth, constant communication, honesty, love and real respect. Consent and honoring autonomy hold all these together.

If you are a racist, using the pretense of magickal or group work to control others, are a homophobe or bigoted in any way, you are *not* practicing werewolf magick, nor are you honoring wolves who don't attack other wolves due to the color of their fur.

## Ethos of the Pack

The werewolf pack is a magickal group based on the ancient and prolific werewolf cults of the past, historically existing from prehistoric times through the Renaissance now being revived and reclaimed. We derive our practices and ideas from archaic Greece, Roman, Norse, Celtic cultures as well as the persecuted medieval surviving Pagan witch cults of Europe. (See *Werewolf Magick* for a more detailed history of these cults.)

Pack magick is incorporating and reviving the core of these cults and the gnosis of the Great Wolf Spirit to regain the powers, magick and other gifts that were lost when our culture rejected Mother Nature and the Animalself.

While we are not wolves, we can look to wolf packs for inspiration as the ancient werewolf cults may have done. Wolves seem to generally have more consistent ethics than many humans. In packs, wolves care for each other as individuals. They form friendships and nurture their own sick and injured. Pack structure enables communication, the education of the young, and the transfer of knowledge across generations. Also, wolves play together into old age, they raise their young as a group, and they care for injured companions. When they lose a pack mate, there is evidence that they suffer and mourn that loss.[13] They truly live cooperatively—a good model for our packs and maybe our current human culture as well.

The core of the werewolf pack reflects the practices and ethos of the past werewolf cults and the model of wild wolves as well. To this end, we seek:

- The freedom and wildness of the Great Wolf Spirit.
- A restriction and taboo-free life that is more open, primal and loving.
- To reunite with our Animalselves and rediscover the deep connection we had with all nature beings and Gaia.
- To have fun, play, and laugh as the animals we are and bond with others of like mind!
- To offer the blessings of werewolf magick to others who wish to partake of it.
- To tap into and utilize the bountiful magick and sorcery available to us as wers, keeping one paw in the animal world and the other in the "real" world.
- To embody the ecological gnosis and spiritual work of helping, protecting and healing nature and our local ecosystem as well as our beautiful planet.
- To create a new community of Wildness, Wyrd, and Way, foster healing, nurturing, creative expression and support each other's feral evolution.

---

13. Living with Wolves, "The Social Wolf."

## Pack Creation

A werewolf magick pack can be created by as few as two wers who have read and mastered the practices of werewolf magick explained by the book of the same name. New members join the nascent pack in three stages.

First, the pack gets to know that person informally and discussions are had. Newbies should have a curiosity, a deep interest in our magick and also intuitively feel right. Instinct is the best guide here. If this is a person of interest, they should be encouraged to read the book and practice werewolf magick on their own for a time.

Second, after a time of mentoring, hanging out and getting to know the new cub and confirming that the cub has made progress in doing werewolf magick, the pack then votes to induct the new cub. If the cub accepts, then the Inducting Ritual, found in Chapter 5, is done in a tavern or pub to which the cub is invited!

From this time on, the cub is a probationary pack member. The pack, and especially the alpha, mentor and guide the new cub in mastering werewolf magick and specifically the spells and rituals of bonding with the Wolf Power, shapeshifting and so on. The cub is encouraged to go into the wilderness and do the shapeshifting rituals or the pack can go as a group and guide the cub through the shapeshifting process.

When the pack agrees that the cub would be a great wer addition to the pack, then the pack initiation is performed at a large pond or small lake. This ritual can also be found in Chapter 5. From that time on, no longer a cub, the wer is a full pack member.

## The Need for a Pack, the Alpha, and Pack Order

Wolves, males and females alike, may go through periods alone, but they're not interested in lives of solitude. A lone wolf is a wolf that is searching, and what it seeks is another wolf. Everything in a wolf's nature tells it to belong to something greater than itself: a pack. Like us, wolves form friendships and maintain lifelong bonds. They succeed by cooperating, and they struggle when they're alone. Like us, wolves need one another.[14] The truth about wolves and wolf packs has evolved as has the research done by naturalists. The common wisdom is that the hierarchy of a wolf pack is inflexible but this simply isn't true.

What keeps a wolf pack functioning as a loving, organized, and cooperative unit is the same thing that keeps a werewolf pack together and working well together: a dedication to each other and to a balanced, flexible but clear formation. This is embodied in the facilitating of the alpha. The alpha is the organizing principle and caring center of both wolf and wer packs.

Wolves do not have an innate sense of rank; they are not born leaders or born followers. The alphas are simply what we would call, in any other social group, parents.[15]

The alpha of the pack simply is the most responsible and committed wer of the pack and all wers of the pack acknowledge this. He or she is the one who coordinates, mentors, helps packmates, leads discussions, keeps records, often leads rituals and organizes things. The alpha is the wolf that is best suited to keeping the pack together, safe and nurtured. It can be a male or female wer, and roles shift change due to situations. A wer takes on the role of alpha if the whole pack agrees, but things can also change if all agree that another should be alpha. This is all a natural process. The alpha is usually the one who does the most work and who is fair, open, a good referee, and is trusted by the whole pack. The role of alpha can and likely should change periodically. A werewolf magick alpha can be any sex or gender or genderfluid and loves who they will. Such things do not matter and sexuality and gender are fluid in werewolf magick and in wolf packs as well. All wers have equal say in the pack, but the alpha is held in highest respect and obeyed and listened to when all are in wer form by consensus.

The alpha keeps track of "admin" work, organizes and communicates gatherings, keeps the pack's sacred tools and items, and organizes all things necessary for events with help from pack members. This entails managing the pack and including the items used, costs, and so on. In the wild, the real alpha wolf

---

14. Living with Wolves, "The Social Wolf."

15. Davis, "Why Everything You Know About Wolf Packs Is Wrong,"

is always the last wolf when the pack travels, making sure that all are safe and all is well. This sums up the role of an alpha perfectly!

In a small pack, a permanent beta (second-in-command) may not be needed. Different wers can volunteer to be beta for larger rituals as needed. In larger packs of over six wers, there should be a consistent beta as an alpha "back up" or aide. Such a beta is like vice president in a sense and is aware of all the responsibilities of being an alpha because the beta assists the alpha often and is always ready to step in as alpha when needed. The alpha chooses the beta, but the pack confirms this while generally honoring the alpha's wish. If the alpha is absent for a time, it is the beta who takes over. If the alpha leaves the pack, the pack can confirm the beta as alpha position or open the discussion to choose another alpha.

## Organization and Enforcement of Customs

As primates, we are similar in social organization to wolves in many ways, though more aggressive. Like any pack, interpersonal relationships will organically sort themselves out through discussions, bonding, play and a variety of interactions, most pleasant, some maybe not. The alpha watches and subtly guides this wolfish alchemy. Each wer brings gifts and powers to the pack but everyone must pull their weight physically, emotionally, and magickally. Truth and honesty are key to everything in the pack and all is transparent and resentments are now allowed to fester, thus open discussions are held often, usually when the rituals are done. The alpha has the toughest job, facilitating and enforcing the basic guidelines and norms and offering gentle or stern non-verbal or verbal reminders as well as counseling, to solve interpersonal conflicts and whatever issues come up.

Ethics and guidelines as stated here can always be changed or added to as the pack decides through discussion and vote, except those concerning tolerance, respect, and acceptance. New rules must be unanimous in pack votes and all abide by them. If any germane issue comes up, the alpha opens the discussion and the whole pack discusses and votes.

Anyone who cannot follow the basic norms as agreed upon gets two warnings and private chats and then a vote is held to expel that wer. Such a vote must be unanimous except for the wer in question.

If one or more pack wer wishes to leave the pack and find a new pack, they should discuss it with the alpha privately, and then announce it to all in a group discussion. There is complete freedom to leave of course, but to leave with support and love and consensual agreements helps to maintain pack to pack bonds that may be useful. New pack creation is not uncommon in the wolf world. Territory and meeting places, tools, even the pack shrine could even be shared between sister packs with mutual communication if done in a respectful way.

## Respect, Consensus, and Wer Interactions

Honorable pack interactions are crucial when all are shifting. These should be discussed and agreed upon. The key is empathy, compassion and a fierce loyalty to each pack member that encompasses caring, and respect.

- A wer respects the personal integrity and the will of every pack member. The norms of consensual agreement must be discussed and agreed upon.
- A wer is loyal to every pack member.
- A wer remains wholly conscious to supporting, aiding, and helping the Wildness and will of every pack member.
- A wer respects the personality and state of being of each pack member.
- As the Wildness is unleashed and made real and physical, autonomy and respect never fade.
- A wer accepts the stated norms of the pack and can begin any conversation around these things.
- The alpha may warn about or stop a situation that breaks any of the aack norms.
- A wer may simply need space. Shifting and Wildness is overwhelming at times and many things arise when we tear away our programming. A pack member may withdraw at any time in any place from the wer work if needed—crossed paws are the signal of needing space—the rest of the pack supports such withdrawals and provides a chill place for this.

## Sexuality and Pack Relationships

In groups like a pack, sexual issues will arise. Many people today are opening up to a wider variety of sexual expressions, fluidity, and kinds of relationships, thankfully breaking from former rigid sexual and gender taboos. We are becoming more natural sexual animals, a good thing. Real wolf pack relationships are long-lasting, intense, and communal and far more sexually varied than you might think, including wolf same sex relationships. A good example of a documented gay wolf is Koani, the wolf whose life is documented in the film *True Wolf*.[16] Of course, we are not actual wolves, but like wolves and other animals, we see open sexuality as natural and accept ourselves as animals with a variety of mating instincts and desires. Evoking your Animalself helps remove false, puritanical, anti-sex programming and calls you to own and be with your whole sexuality without judgment or guilt. In our wild rituals, desires and feelings will emerge. This is fine, this is natural, but they also manifest appropriately amid the whole pack. As relationships form, the key is to keep the human egos out of the picture when in wer state. Instinct, love and caring come first, human ego trips, no. All these kinds of appropriacy topics will generate many conversations that must be open and caring, and the alpha will referee discussions regarding sexuality that become an issue. Each pack has to work out these issues and tensions with love and true will, and all will be well as long these cardinal rules are kept:

> *The emotional and physical wellbeing of the pack and all its wers comes first.*
> *Consent is always important in any state of consciousness. Abuse, violence, coercion and shaming of any sort are never ever acceptable or tolerated in the pack.*

## Customary Pack Items

The pack should discuss and agree upon specifics about all such things. However, wearing natural, comfortable, black clothing is recommended, as are leather and fur items that are not from endangered beasts. Acquiring used or neglected fur items is acceptable and, in fact, honors the long-deceased animal.

---

16. Anderson-Minshall, "Riveting Wolf Documentary Worth a Gay Gander."

In ritual, much clothing is often discarded and, as wers, we are not ashamed of our bodies but, in fact, revel in this expression our animal selves. All nudity must be agreed upon by the whole pack and be consensual while having fun in wild wer revels. However, make sure to dress in a way to avoid hypothermia! Wearing werewolf magick talismans and jewelry is encouraged. It is recommended that at least one piece of werewolf magick jewelry should be a shape-shifting trigger as described later in this chapter. The pack is a shapeshifting primitive wer tribe and should look like one!

### Ritual Tools and Items

The pack as a whole should create or procure all ritual items needed for the pack rituals including all items necessary for group rituals. These include but are not limited to the stang, the three staves, a ritual bowl, a ritual cup, a platter for incense, and natural cloth for altars or other work (red, black, white recommended, green is also useful). Ritual implements or items used in group work include: a ritual cup, a ritual knife, and the pack shrine.

For spell work and divination, a set of werewolf magick icons (see Appendix) can be painted or carved on natural materials. All pack members should share costs, procurements, and ritual fashionings for all these and any other items the pack adds to this list. All of this is being coordinated by the alpha who is charged with storing and bringing the pack items to events.

Each member should also have their own tools and items they wish, including a werewolf talisman or amulet, a special knife used for werewolf magick work, their own cup and clothing for this work, and any other items they feel appropriate. Each may wish their own stave as well for private werewolfery.

## Pack Socialization and Customs

There is no shapeshifting without feral gestures, actions, and general Wildness. When wers lope, run, stalk, and howl in woods alone, they can be as they wish. However, when we unleash the inner wolf in the pack and revert to a more nonverbal, instinctive level, we need to remain aware of how the increased intensity affects us and our packmates while still having wild fun. Once all have shifted into their feral wolfish states of being, in general werewolf lingo and feral actions replace conversations and human body language. Interactions become, well, animalistic. While most of these interactions are instinctual, the following section listing gestures and actions are some common ones all should abide by. As the pack bonds and relationships form, wers will become more empathic and such interactions more natural and intuitive.

## Appropriate Pack Interactive Gestures and Actions

*Baring Teeth:* Depending on stance and situation, could be a wolfy grin, a precursor to a chuff, an agreement or, if connected to a low growl and frown, a playful back off.

*Snapping fangs:* Rapid snapping of teeth. Means playful, fun challenge, excited.

*Clawing:* Clawing things is a magickal gesture used in wer magick, especially for empowering, banishing, or cursing. Casual claw swiping of pack members is attention getting, loving, playful, hyper fun, teasing, or can mean "Hurry up!" Growling and clawing that is aggressive is generally not ever acceptable and biting is completely forbidden.

*Bumping and Rubbing:* Wolves and wers are very physically affectionate. Hugs, gentle bumps, and casual brushes are all acceptable while in wer form. Unlike many cultures, we have become isolated in terms of touching as a way of bonding common to all primates. Returning to a feral state helps us return to a norm we have forgotten. Nudging, bumps, side hugs, and whatever the pack agrees is acceptable. Such wolfish scenting marks friends and loved ones as well as pack members and bonds the pack.

*Rocking:* Growling, rumbling, howling, and especially rocking indicate a trance state and can also be a kind of wer meditative practice. When the pack is just hanging out, groups of wers can rock and rumble or growl together for a number of social reasons: bonding, sympathy, impromptu wild spell work, sharing feelings, or just group expressions of togetherness without a reason. Think of instinctive actions and chants at rock concerts; it is what packs do.

*Loping, Leaping & Lunging:* When the pack is lit, playing, roughhousing, dancing and such are common. When Wildness takes hold, movement and playing erupts. As we shift into deep wer form, we let go of intellectual worries and anxieties and let instinct and intuition guide our behaviors, not artificial civilized taboos. Respect and love of our fellow wers and nature are the only rules. Letting the body do what it wills to do, such as loping, leaping lunging and other intuitive animal reactions and actions is important and healthy in the pack.

There are many other possible animalistic actions and they will emerge by instinct and intuition from your body and deep instinct, not your thoughts. This is a deeply healthy and expansive part of werewolf magick. Once you are comfortable in your wolf skin, such escapes from the human world often become deeply healing and helpful.

## Performing Rituals Rites and Spell with a Pack

As I moved from solo werewolf magick ritual work to working with a pack, I found it was somewhat more complex than I'd expected, thus this hands-on explanation. The central issue is how to do rituals like those that follow while in a shapeshifting trance state where the Animalself is in charge. Keep in mind that, in a pack, it is always an evolving conversation over ritual procedures and your pack will likely find new creative and practical solutions to make sure each ritual pushes and enhances the experience and doesn't hinder it, especially when shifted into wer form where things can get very free-form. Here are some basic suggestions and practices that I have found worked in a pack setting.

First and foremost, the shapeshifting trance states and magickal unfolding of the ritual is paramount to anything else. It is expected (trust me) that invocations may shift and mistakes will be made, these are not important if the power, feral intensity, and the focused experience glows! Unlike grimoire magick where exact pronunciation and formulas are crucial, werewolf magick cares much more for the experience than perfection.

Throughout the book, you will see comments like "Be creative," "The pack will decide," or "Change the ritual as the pack wills it." It is *expected* that rituals, rites, and spells in this book will be changed, at times simplified, added to, edited, and so on as pack members, together, decide what does or does not work for *your* pack. Just like the nascent pack I'm working with, we shifted the order of the Praxis Rite intuitively and it worked better for us. Everything in this book can be and should be adapted or tweaked to fit the pack using it through experience and cooperation.

The alpha is always the key to organizing, preparing, and having the pack know and practice the rituals, especially the more complex ones.

The pack needs to read carefully each ritual that will be done and remember at least the key elements and flow as much as possible. It is ideal to have regular pack gatherings for fun but also to block-out and run through upcoming rituals a few times.

Right before the ritual is done, before the jump into the Wildness, the ritual or rite should be reviewed and rehearsed one last time. This helps with flow and focus and is a great way to focus on the upcoming adventure.

Repetition helps. The esbat and sabbat rituals might be a bit awkward the first few times but as they are done more often, they will become easier and more like second nature.

There are three basic approaches to dealing with invocations and other power words in these rituals, rites, and spells:

1. The alpha reads the key words and the rest of the pack repeats them as a call and response. This puts the burden on the alpha to be a bit less entranced but allows the rest of the pack to go deeper into their trance.

2. All the pack members read the key phrases or words in the ritual, but the alpha keeps it on track with prompts as needed. This means a lot of candles or, and this works, the ritual can be shared to everyone's cell phones and even in darkness, it can be read on the cell by all. This works well and allows the cells to be turned on and off and the lettering can be switched to white on black background.

3. The ritual is memorized by all the pack. This is recommended for the longer festival rituals. Keep in mind that absolute accuracy in most of these phrases is not required and words of power can be put on a cheat sheet or done as a call and response. The more often used practices will become ingrained as they are done often.

In general, the goal is to be in full wer trance in the grip of the Animalself, little time and focus should be on distractions or unnecessary perfection. If all flows well and a wild, fun successful magickal event happens, errors simply won't matter to wers.

Most of these rituals have been done "en masse" and we changed things as we went, sometimes in different ways at different times! The coming together of pack members opens every ritual up to ad hoc changes and shifts in the ritual. Substituting incense or words, hanging gestures, even moving parts of the ritual around or just simplifying the whole ritual are all on the table before the ritual starts. Once the ritual has begun, it must be done that way all agreed beforehand to avoid chaos and magickal issues. Always finish what you begin.

Everyone should always growl the words uttered in these rituals: deep, low, guttural, from the core of your inner beast, not spoken or acted out. This takes some getting used to! It is unimportant if the actual pronunciation gets garbled as long as each wer intone the words it hears in wer growl. All the words in werewolf magick rituals can be seen as "barbarous tongues!"

Relax! Let errors go by, the goal is to have fun and conjure what the ritual calls for from the hear with feral love and will! Never get fixated on errors or things that slip, as cognitive intellectuality is our enemy in our work; the goal is think little and *be* more.

The alpha may gently prod a pack member with gestures to move the ritual along or light the candles or carry the stang, whatever is called for. In general, the alpha is the facilitator and director of the ritual. Later on, pack members can take over this alpha role as they like.

Remember the goals of every ritual, rite and spell: to do magick of a powerful and important kind, to create a sacred space for the Animalself to arise and act with a feral autonomy, to come together for enhanced magick, power, healing, growth and the joy of being in a pack that supports and nurtures each other. To reintegrate with nature, with our ecosystem, through the innate powers of the Wildness, Wyrd, and Way.

The goal is also to have fun. Not a little fun—a whole lot of howling, dancing, laughing, wild, and ecstatic fun. Werewolf cults were often cults of ecstasy; this is the foundation of werewolf magick.

Stang and stave on werewolf pack altar in the woods.

## The Rally Grove Wilderness Lair of the Pack

Every pack needs a territory, a wild home and sanctuary to retreat to, a place
to do rituals, recharge, and connect with the deities and powers of Wildness,
Wyrd, and Way. A gathering of wolves is called a rally and the rally grove for
your pack is the lair and home of the pack. The more often it is used, the more
potent it will become. Pack members may visit as often as they wish, alone or
together.

### Preparing and Consecrating a Pack Rally Grove

The pack's rally grove is the wild home. When seeking a place to do work or
rest, the pack should seek the wildest, most vital place where the energies are

conducive to the feral powers and are accessible for all pack members. This rally grove should ideally have several things.

It should be very wild and full of trees and plants, of course, but also needs to have a clearing or open area to do ritual work in. It should be secret and as undamaged by humans as possible with a powerful wild Earth power to it. If possible, it should contain a crosspath, a place where trails meet, animal trails being better, three paths meeting best. It also has to allow fairly easy access on full moon nights and far enough away from humans so that howls and such will not attract outsiders. Working alone, this is all easier to work out, but once you have a pack you can't keep the volume down! This is why the pack should find and consecrate a main rally grove which will be a lair for the pack to constantly return to, thus it will build in power. However, events and situations may change things, so it is good for the pack to consider consecrating several sacred areas as rally groves as needed. For example, one in the mountains or another by the ocean, for camp-out rituals and so on.

The ritual process of preparing and consecrating a pack rally grove consists of two separate sequential rites: Preparing the Rally Grove Rite and Consecrating the Rally Grove Rite.

## Preparing the Rally Grove Rite
### Set Up
The pack should discuss what kind of sacred wild place they would like, keeping in mind all that has been discussed but also what each wer desires. Once it has become clearer in everyone's mind, then physical and online maps and images of the area and what areas of wilderness there are nearby can be looked at and discussed. The alpha and pack members can do initial scouting for possible rally groves or the whole pack can get involved and make it a quest. No matter what, when one or more suitable rally groves are found, the whole pack should check them out and discuss the merits of each one. Google Maps or a similar app should be used to verify how close numbers of humans are to this space as well. If any pack member is adamant that it is not right, then the search moves on. Chances are you may have to get creative and maybe go further out from your personal lairs to find a truly vital wild place that fits the

bill. The pack can certainly gather and do an appropriate rite from this book to petition the gods and Wolf Spirit for help in this! Once one that is liked by the whole pack is found, it must be prepared ritually. This begins the magick of weaving the Wildness, Wyrd, and Way since to prepare the area to become a sacred place, these things must be done as you will see. Once the pack has found the right rally grove, the pack is set to begin the process.

## ITEMS NEEDED
Hand held pruning shears

Three copper coins

Flask of water

A sharp magickal knife

A piece of green cloth the size of a bandanna

A little skill in weaving small boughs

## THE EXERCISE
The pack gathers about one week before the full moon and go to the potential grove. All enter in silence and stand in the center of the area that was chosen still in absolute silence, open and feeling the place. All breathe deeply and feel the earth beneath, the Wildness about and the sky above and expand their awareness.

Then, with arms raised, the whole pack rumbles for a time deeply feeling the powers of this place externally and internally.

Then, paws out to the side, all *silently* call upon the Lord of the Forest, *silently* being still and open.

Let the presence of this place, the genus loci, and the touch of the Lord of the Forest come to you all. Close your eyes, breathe even deeper and slower, feel the earth below and trees around and sky above. Listen. Is this absolutely right? Are you welcomed?

All silently ask for a sign to indicate you have the blessing of the Lord of the Forest.

All open their eyes in silence and wait for an omen.

It may be any number of things: a bird call, a gust of wind, a sudden moment of clarity and love, a powerful scent, a clear rune or image appearing in tree patterns. You will all know.

When one is perceived, and the most psychic pack member may be the one to note it, he or she raises his or her paws and begins a slow, low up howl of thanks and greeting and all join in. If the omen is good and all feels right, you have found the right grove!

Now, all must locate the center point of the grove. This should be the center of the clearing where the ritual work will be done, where the crosspath is. When this is found, all touch the earth here and thank Gaia with one long MA and place the green cloth on the earth.

Then the alpha takes up the stang and all walk outward counterclockwise, and softly rumble as they prowl in a line, feeling the power of this land with every step.

As the pack treads the spiral, all carefully note the many kinds of trees and, after three turns of the spiral, all stop and form a circle and up growl together and then discuss and identify the three dominant kinds of trees in this grove. For example, in my grove, they are cedar, fir and rowan. All then up howl three times, silently asking the Lord of the Forest and the tree spirits for permission to work with them.

The alpha takes up the coins, the container of water, and small clippers and with the whole pack, seeks out *three healthy trees of three different kinds* as noted. If all three trees are equidistant from the center of the crosspaths, this is best. These trees will help protect, hide, and empower your groove and the wild work done here.

When the pack reaches each chosen tree, all place a paw on the tree and commune with it, asking for its blessing and willingness to give the pack some small branches, all in silence. When all feel it has agreed, the pack vibrates HAaaaa and the alpha takes the pruning shears and cuts three thin, foot-long branches, buries a coin and pours some water for the tree while the pack continues to growl long HAs to thank that tree's spirit. Do this with two other trees of different species in the same way.

When done, go back to the center of the area and lay out the three bundles of thin branches from the three master trees on the green cloth. Use the knife to cut off any leaves or small nubs, keeping some of these small leaves aside for later use.

One bundle will be dedicated to each of the werewolf magick powers of Wildness, Wyrd, and Way and the pack can decide which species of tree embodies which of these powers. It is up to you all. Think on the nature and presence of each tree. Discuss and decide.

When ready, the pack together all hold up each bundle in turn and blesses it by which quality each tree's bundle represents like so:

*Io Evoe* [17] *HA! By this tree's power we call the Wildness! - (all up howl)*
*Io Evoe HA! By this tree's power we call the Wyrd! - (all up howl)*
*Io Evoe HA! By this tree's power we call the Way! - (all up howl)*

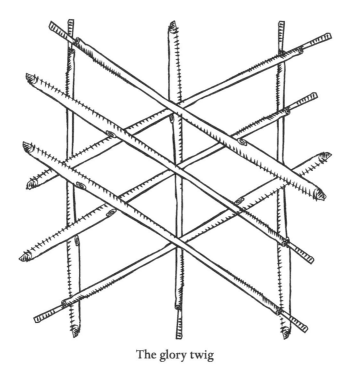

The glory twig

---

17. Io Evoe = an ecstatic cry meaning *Honor! Hail Hurrah!* (Greek) Used often in this ritual.

Now, the most talented weaver wer of the pack sits and weaves the twigs from the three separate bundles together as per the illustration above. The three different long twigs are first laid out like so:

*The upright three* are from the tree representing the Way

*The three branches slanted to the right* represent the Wildness

*The last three long twigs slanted to the left*, represent the Wyrd.

While this goes on, all begin rumbling and going into a light trance, especially the weaver.

The weaver thus interweaves them as per the image. He or she will be crafting an ancient amulet called a glory twig used for protection and blessing as per the image above.

As the weaver works, the pack stands about the weaver in a circle.

The pack can face outward and do the up growl banishing if the area feels like it may need it, but if it is clear of other human energies, it need not be done.

All then face inward and link arms or hold hands and sway altogether and rumble, filling the amulet and area with positive energy and protection vibes.

As it is finished the whole pack opens their mouths a bit and the rumble becomes a low Haaaa Haaaa Haaa until the glory twig is done and lays on the green cloth.

Then all lean forward and low growl the following:

*Lord Of The Forest, We Call Thee*

*By Sacred Earth And Sacred Tree*

*Faunus Lycan Guard And Empower*

*By Wer And Wolf this Sacred Hour*

*Strong and Safe be our Lair! So May it Be!*

*HA! HA! HAaaa! I0 Evoe!*

All up howl. Stand in a circle about the glory twig and do the Praxis Rite to shapeshift, empower the now-glowing charm and mark your territory!

When done, sit and meditate on this sacred symbol for a time and rock back and forth and rumble in trance, eyes half closed, and "see" the new expanding web of power and protection you have created. Let the Lord of the Forest silently teach you its mystery and the deep story of this place which is now part of the pack. Later, write down what was revealed.

Stay as long as you like, have some food and drink, discuss the new grove, as you like.

When done, all place hands on the earth and offer a final silent prayer of thanksgiving that also gives thanks to Gaia. Finish with a deep pack vibration of MA.

The weaver slowly folds the cloth over the glory twig, keeping it intact and covering it with leaves, stones, or whatever else so that the amulet will remain hidden in the grove's center.

All stand and end the Praxis Rite, thus returning to human form and, after a final up howl, all go loping forth after making sure all has been gathered and the place is as it was.

The alpha brings the collected leaves that were taken off the glory twig, later, if none are toxic (check!) They will be put into red wine to infuse it for the rally grove blessing ritual.

## Consecrating the Rally Grove Ritual

### Set Up

Beforehand, the alpha will have placed the few leaves (from the three sacred trees that were chosen) into a bottle of red wine to steep for a few days. Then the pack gathers at twilight on or near the full moon. The pack will return to the now claimed and blessed pack rally grove to do the rite of full consecration. This is done in order to make this grove sacred for werewolf magick and a place of sanctuary, healing, and growth for the pack. All should arrive at sunset with all the items needed.

### Items Needed

A bottle of red wine within which leaves gathered from trees in the grove are
  steeping

A small burning bowl and dried rosemary mixed with dried leaves taken from
the grove

Containers of pure water

A large natural sacred cup or bowl, silver if possible

A green or natural color beeswax candle and holder

The stang

The staves

Some natural food for the pack and animals, berries, nuts and so on

The rite

### THE EXERCISE

The pack enters the area in the gloaming of twilight, rumbling all together in
happiness and the powers welcome all home!

All find the center, uncover the glory twig, shake off the cloth, and then lay
it down again and place the items in the center with the other items. The stang
is stuck in the ground in the absolute center, to the north of the cloth. Some
wine is poured into the cup, which is to the west. Rosemary and dried leaves
is then lit in the burning bowl to the east so it smolders. The candle is set in
holder and lit, placed to the south. The three staves are placed in a downward
triangle formation about the cloth. The pack stands in a circle facing this altar,
linking arms, and up howling three times, thus announcing their habitation of
their new lair. All do the Praxis Rite together.

Then, all raise paws to the now full moon (hopefully in the sky now) and
down growl AH AH AH. This calls to the moon powers to descend and consecrate this place and the pack.

All reach their paws out to the forest, down growling HA HA HA to the
Lord of the Forest to descend and consecrate this place and the pack.

All then place paws on the glory twig and focus all this energy on it while
calling up the power of the Earth Mother with an up growl of MA MA MA
to arise and consecrate this place and the pack. Finally, all stand and up grow
loudly:

*Io Evoe Wildness! AH-HA!*
*Io Evoe Wyrd! AH-HA!*
**Io Evoe Way! AH-HA!**


All howl. The alpha then pours out some of the wine in a clockwise circle around the whole area

And finally sprinkles some on the glory twig and then all growl the following:

*Lord Of the Forest we call thee*
*By sacred Earth and sacred tree*
*By moon, wer and wolf so mote this be*
*That here we are forever free!*
*Io Evoe! Io Evoe! Io Evoe!*


Howl!

Three pack members take up the three staves and walk in different directions to the edge of the rally grove space, equidistant from each other and the center and stick them into the ground, marking the perimeter of the sacred space as the pack howls three times!

The rally grove is safe, secure, and now marked by this pack. By now, it is getting dark.

All stand about the altar and hold hands or lock arms and sway side to side rumbling. Slowly, the rumble changes to RA…RA…RA, rumble growling as all deeply manifest their wer form and feel the unity of the pack and this new pack home. The chants rise in intensity and end with a huge round of howling and all walk or lope or prowl about the area in wolfish glee!

All then sit about the altar and party, passing the cup of wine about the circle to drink, sharing food, laughing, howling as they like and sharing what omens and visions they have had. This is the new pack home.

It is traditional to mark the territory by peeing in the woods around the edge of the official grove! This can be done as people choose or all can lope off together in different directions and go pee and howl!

When it is time to go, someone goes and gathers the staves and brings them to the altar cloth. Another pours the last of the wine and some water into the ritual cup and all pause. The alpha then gently takes up the glory twig. The rest of the pack takes up the tools and moves the cloth and then digs with paws a hole, large enough for the whole glory twig to fit. The alpha places it in the hole, then all cover it up, leaving the cup of the last of the wine with some water in. The cloth is shaken out and the other items stowed and all is made as it was, then all stand up and up growl:

*By moon and tree and Mother Earth*
*By Great Wolf Spirit let there be mirth!*
*Io Evoe Wildness! Wyrd! Way!*
*This be our rally grove, so may it stay!*

All howl!

Then all take up the cup and chant AH-HA AH-HA AH-HA and pour out the wine/water on the center, where the glory twig will forever lie!

All howl a lot of howls, tons of howls, stomping dancing howls!

Then all stand and shake off the trance, and finish the end of the Praxis Rite. In a clockwise manner, all spiral outwards in a line, alpha in the rear, until all reach the edge of the sacred space, the path in and out of the grove. No banishing is necessary. This is your home now.

When leaving, all up howl slowly and softly one more time and then, rumbling with happiness, all go.

# CHAPTER 3
# PACK BONDING PRACTICES AND RITES

—————————— ❩ ❨ ——————————

Repetitive vibrating of sounds (like mantras) are a powerful tool in many different spiritual and occult practices. Meditation and chanting in general are potent. Vibrating animalistic non-intellectual sounds is a feral technique that really works intensely on many levels to bring out the animal in you.

To enter the deep trance state involved in shapeshifting as described in *Werewolf Magick*, you have to master deep growling, howling, yipping and other forms of wer-lingo that is, non-language communication forms that are purely animal and therefore evocative of the Animalself. After much practice with these unfamiliar verbalizations, the chest opens up, the voice box becomes more flexible and the body "remembers" the primal animal-voice of deep growling and so on.

## Werewolf Pack Rumbling

### SET UP

Once you have reached a point where you can deep growl low in your diaphragm, you can begin to create a rumble with every deep out breath *with your mouth closed*. This will vibrate deep inside you, vibrating your whole torso. It is like a big-cat purr or a low dog growl. I have been working with others on expanding techniques like growling and howling and introduced rumbling, or deep, quiet, guttural low diaphragm-growling with every out breath with the mouth closed. This can be accomplished with relaxation, practice and invoking the Animalself in a calm, meditative state, in nature if possible, of course. Once you have the rumble going, you can deepen and widen it. Sitting and calmly rumbling for long periods of time is immensely meditative and elicits a light trance state. It is great for calming and centering when upset. It is a very potent practice with a whole pack of wers. It can be used when there is a pause or meditative space in our rituals, as you'll see, and it can be of use when entering a sacred space, deepening a shapeshift or when coming out of an intense ritual experience. To use rumbling to slip into a light shifting trance or deepen a shapeshift state, do the following:

ITEMS NEEDED

A calm, relaxed space, in nature if at all possible

A time you can be relaxed and undisturbed

Comfortable clothing

Some practice

A natural cloth or pillow to sit upon if needed, sitting upon the earth is best

THE EXERCISE

Find a comfortable place in nature where you won't be disturbed if possible. Quietly, do the growl banishing to clear the area of unwanted energies. Place your paws on the earth and vibrate MA as deeply as you can to honor Gaia. Points if you can rumble it! Sit as you like, relax and close your eyes, and begin to breathe deeply.

When you are relaxed, eyes still closed, reach out to the Wildness about you and call to the Lord of the Forest with a rumble-grow sound of HA. Inhale deeply three times and feel the power of the Wildness fill, sustain, and empower you.

Now, begin to rumble-growl, first with your mouth a bit open. Then as you deepen it and relax into a slow in/out rhythm, rumble with your mouth closed. As you do so, let the Animalself arise gently into your body and consciousness. Let it slowly take over the rumbling and be open to the silent shifts and guidance as you sink into it and the Animalself takes over.

At a certain point, you will be on autopilot and thinking will fade as you simply become a wolf at rest just being in animal consciousness.

When you feel your human self begin to arise without effort, let the Animalself slide back into the dark cave within you as this consciousness emerges. Let the rumbling shift to long, slow, deep relaxed rumbling. Open your arms to the Wildness and the Lord of the Forest and growl HA three times in thanks. Place your hands on the earth and exhale MA three times. Stand, stretch, and go.

This is a simple and powerful exercise that can be used to address anxiety, over-thinking, worrying, and other negative stresses. Using this technique to drop out of "human" mind-babble into the here-now aware animal state is remarkably refreshing and helpful! I have found it good for self-healing as well. Try it.

## Werewolf Magick God Chants

### Set Up

Syllable vibrations are called *mantras*, meaning a repetitive syllabic vibration that manifests a certain deity or power. Such mantras are used in rituals to focus and connect with the divine. Just as the vibration-sound of OM invokes the power of the divine in yoga, Tantra and Hinduism, our magick has a set of key vibration-syllables to invoke and manifest werewolf magick spiritual deity forms and powers. That being said, I consider what I call "rumble vibrations" a kind of mantra system because they take the deep rumble and expand it simply with a slight inflection and opening of the mouth. For the sake of clarity, I'll be calling this practice rumble vibrating though you can see this as werewolf mantra work. Here are the key rumble vibrations for the key werewolf powers. Take time to remember them. You'll see them referenced a lot:

- The Lord of the Forest: HA
- The Earth Mother (Gaia): MA
- The Moon Mothers (Artemis, Selene, Hekate): AH
- The Great Wolf Spirit: RA
- Werewolf Magick Gnosis: AH-HA
- The Animalself: pure rumble, mouth closed

These are useful and common for calling upon deity forms ritually as you'll see and once you are familiar with them and the powers they conjure, you can use any of them any time it feels right in your work.

The final simple werewolf rumble which we use a lot for relaxing and meditating is for calling upon the key gnosis of werewolf magick, the Animalself, the spiritual core of our work. When ending a rite, it can be seen as a final centering, like OM. This reifies that all the Wildness, Wyrd and Way are *One*. What follows are similar simple exercises to use to become fluid and fluent with these various rumble mantras.

## Items Needed

A relaxed body! It takes a little time, like any exercise, so go slow and know
   you will expand both your physical ability as your voice box and lungs open
   up more and strengthen.

Attention to your mouth, voice box and diaphragm. Note that HA and MA
   and RA are not exclamations or cheers. They begin with a rumble and the
   mouth is slowly opened just a bit and the sound vibrated slowly. Not HA
   but Haaaaaaaaaaa with a very deep growly tone.

Ability to blend your rumble vibrations with other pack wers in a pack. Once
   you have taken the time to practice this alone, then it needs to be practiced
   in a pack. This takes listening skills so you may blend in sync with the other
   wers, like a choir. These are used often in many werewolf magick rituals,
   rites, and spells and they may be used in creative ways not specifically noted
   as well.

## The Exercise

Focus! The intensity of doing the rumble mantras in a pack is amazing and deep and the practice can be used as a warm up practice any time a pack meets. If the pack is feeling down or things are "off" for one reason or another, ten minutes of rumble mantra work will get the pack centered and back on the same page to become one, in sync, unified pack.

Listen! Often it will be the alpha's job to read the pack and recommend a particular rumble chat or several sequential chants for specific situations. Rumble vibrating practice is a great pack warm up to do at any time. Simply, all sit and rumble then together, with a cue from the alpha, spend time vibrating the following rumble mantras three or more times each, cued by the alpha.

- The Earth Mother (Gaia): MA
- The Lord of the Forest: HA
- The Moon Mothers (Artemis, Selene, Hekate): AH
- The Great Wolf Spirit: RA
- Wildness/Wyrd/Way Gnosis (So be it!): AH-HA
- The Animalself: pure rumble, mouth closed

Gestures can then be added:

- MA: touch the Earth with paws,
- HA: Reach out to the forest on either side with extended open paws to the woods,
- AH: reach paws up to the moon,
- RA: Paws and claws up and thrown forward
- AH-HA: paws on heart or in group hug. All of these can be changed as the pack decides, creativity is all.

A simple rumbling can begin when using any of these tones and is also a good way to end a session or ritual, along with a final exclamatory long group up howl to bring the pack together, of course.

## Werewolf Pack Games

Once the pack has shapeshifted into a wild feral mode, the energy in the circle will rev-up during a ritual, but play and fun is what wolves do a lot of the time, so set aside time for wild play, or why bother, right?! However, games should follow ritual work since once wild play begins, rituals may be forgotten. Aside from sheer enjoyment, such play bonds the pack, hones survival skills, expands senses, is great exercise, and enhances each wer's Animalself. It also blows off steam and with a bunch of wers, this is a good idea! Here are a few werewolf games that are a blast at night in the woods, and your pack can change these or continue to create others as they like.

Note: Overly aggressive actions during play are called out and rowdy wolves have to sit the game out. Though a certain amount of wolfish roughhousing is normal, some clear guidelines need to be agreed upon and accepted beforehand. The alpha is the referee, and warns about overly rowdy behavior with a loud **growl** as a clear signal to bring it down a notch and chill a bit or get a time out. All of these werewolf recreational activities are done in the woods or other natural places where all can wolf-out without being disturbed. The rally grove of the pack is a perfect place to unwind this way. All of these can be done before, after, or as a break in the middle of other werewolf ritual work as well, like at a sabbat or esbat.

## Night Stalking

### Set Up

The goal of this exercise is to become truly quiet, stealthy, focused on your animal senses and thus gain enhanced sensory and other skills within the living night forest about you. And honestly, it is really fun.

This is a werewolf Zen-like stalking meditation in the form of a kind of werewolf exploration through a forest at night. The area should be scouted out by the alpha ahead of time since brambles, ravines and other issues are to be avoided. A route that offers many interesting diversions before returning to the ritual site can be planned as little or as much as seems wise. Wild game trails, natural paths, and so on are ideal. The job of the alpha is to bring up the rear and keep an eye on things but not interfere with the fun.

### Items Needed

An adventurous attitude

As little clothing as you wish

Sandals or shoes for sure

The alpha should carry a flashlight, just in case.

Silence except for rumbling.

### The Exercise

At first, once out of the candle or fire light, all should enhance their Animalself with some rumbling and let their wer sight expand until all is clear, then all keep rumbling deeply together, sink deeper into trance, and then open their eyes to amazing night vision. The rumbling may continue through the whole stalking fun as each wishes.

There should be significant space between wers as each stalks slowly, careful and quietly into the dark woods. Remember, stalking! Slow careful steps, making as little sound as possible. In this way, night roaming animals may be seen and surprised.

Each wer's human mind should become more silenced with each careful step as the Animalself takes over. With each careful step, the senses should be focused on and expanded as the nuances of feeling bark, the smell of the earth, the sounds of night animals, and the feeling of a breeze becomes intense and meaningful. Time is suspended as the slow, stalking, expanded senses, trance state and visions quietly fill each wer. Encountering a night creature, a creek, a mossy tree all take on deep and potent symbolic meaning. Soon, the auras of all living things will be seen and scents and sounds never noticed before will take on meaning.

By the time all the wers return to the ritual place, all will be in a deeper feral trance caused by the Lord of the Forest having filled and opened each wer to the joy of this wooded world.

Upon return wers should remain silent for a time together and let the mystical experience of being a wolf in the woods settle in. Maybe all can take time to note their experiences in their journals or just meditate on the spirit of the Lord of the Forest. Later, all should share their experiences and what the forest showed or whispered to them.

This is a powerful werewolf meditation that can be done alone as well, but take precautions.

## Werewolf Tag
### Set Up

This activity will help you release Wildness energy after shifting, hone speed, agility and instincts and intuition and to have fun. A wer's instincts need exercising while also strengthening the bond with the Animalself. Letting the Animalself express itself physically heightens all your reflexes. It should be done in a fairly open area in the woods or another wild place. The rally grove is perfect.

### Items Needed

A set boundary of the area being used

The area should be carefully cleared of obstacles

Knowledge of the basic rules of tag, but with werewolves

No use of words; wer lingo is used and much barking, yipping and
      growling is encouraged

When a wer makes a paw tag, he or she should howl

Depending on the rules set, the winning team or wer is toasted!

All wers should have done the Praxis Rite and be playing as entranced wers

### The Exercise

There are a variety of ways to tag and no one right way, so the pack should
decide. Some choices:

- The wer who is "it" is chosen randomly by some method (eeny, meeny,
  miny, moe…) and whoever they tag becomes it, easiest way and can go
  on for a while.
- Each person tagged is out until one person left is the winner (short game).
- Two teams are chosen. When one team member touches another team
  member, they join that team. Needs a bunch of players.

Wers lope about barking and yipping, claws and paws out. Any touch with
even one claw is a tag.

## Get the Bone!

### Set Up

Essentially this is a keep away game that every canine plays, and it is quite simple. The pack is divided into two groups and a large bone placed in the center
of the space. Alpha barks and they compete to get the bone and keep it from
the opposing group. Bone may be tossed to team members and snatched from
opposing members, but no excessive grabbing or pushing.

Everyone with a dog knows that keep away with a bone or stick or toy is
a favorite canine game and can go on for a long time. Wolves in packs do this

exact same play behavior. It is free-form and a great way to burn off energy and have fun. A wer's instincts need exercising and this heightens all reflexes. It should be done in a fairly open area in the woods or another wild place. The rally grove is perfect.

### ITEMS NEEDED

A reasonably sized clean and dry bone

A set boundary of the area being used

The area should be carefully cleared of obstacles

### THE EXERCISE

Knowledge of the basics of "keep away" and "catch the bone" are called for, but with werewolves.

No use of words, wer lingo is used and much barking, yipping and growling is encouraged.

Some tussling is involved of course, and doing so with the bone is okay but no grabbing arms, legs, fur, and so on.

Game continues until alpha howls or a timer goes off.

Winner gets to keep that bone and can make it what he or she wills.

## Hunt the Prey Hide and Seek

### SET UP

A short discussion should be had about this game.

This is pretty much hide and seek but with the idea that those being sought are wolf-hunted prey. Think deer. The parameters should be clearly described and shown. It is important to have some woods around the clearing. Be specific on how deep into the woods the hiding wer can go, maybe ten to twenty feet? Parameters of the area are decided on and, again, made safe from tripping obstacles.

### ITEMS NEEDED

Nothing but a good night sight and keen ears and nose.

Shoes or sandals should be used

THE EXERCISE

All stand in the circle and the alpha chooses the prey as he or she wills, (eeny, meeny, miny, moe ...?) The remaining pack closes its eyes and rocks and growls slowly getting louder while the "prey" scampers off to hide. When the alpha howls, they all scatter and find the prey! When found, the prey can scream and squeal as hilariously as they like and then the successful hunter becomes the new prey and it continues like that as long as the pack wishes.

## All Play is Magick

Many more wolfish games or variations should be created by the pack. Allowing your Animalself to emerge and play increases the potency and power of your shapeshifting and other ritual work while opening you up more fully to the Wildness, Wyrd, and Way of the beast. Fun and play are evolutionary imperatives and, for us wild ones, they are a crucial part of integrating with nature.

# The Werewolf Magick Oracle Rite

Over the years, a number of icons have been created and reimagined from ancient magickal sources and werewolf lore. Many others were channeled by the author through trance experiences. The more traditional symbols are shown and explained in *Werewolf Magick*.[18] This resulting Werewolf Magick Oracle is thus a combination of traditional esoteric symbols and newly crafted pack symbols or Icons. As a set oracle, they are referred to as werewolf magick icons and they are used together as an oracle set or can be used individually for werewolf magick spellcraft.

SET UP

Prepare beforehand a set of small werewolf magick oracle icon pieces no more than 2 x 2 inches each as pictured in the werewolf symbols in the Appendix. They can be drawn, painted, carved, burned onto thick paper or on small pieces of wood, bone, stones or another natural material. It is up to the pack and there may be more than one set, but one set should be designated the pack

---

18. Sargent, *Werewolf Magick*, 58.

oracle. This oracle creation is best done in ritual on the full moon, up to the pack or artist fashioning the oracle. The pack oracle is then kept in a small leather or cloth bag for future oracle readings.

Werewolf Magick Oracle

A wolf's eye symbol should be inscribed on the bag and this oracle pouch will be kept in the shrine (though any pack member may use it when they need to). Oracle work is often most potent as a pack activity, though it can be used by individuals as well during any chill pack time or solo.

The oracle rite is envisioned as being done as part of a large ritual. Some examples are the esbat, the sabbat, an initiation, and so on. Most every werewolf magick ritual has a time for chilling out, eating, partying and so on. This is a perfect time to do this oracle rite. If the pack is gathering to only do the Werewolf Oracle Rite, then it is understood that the following will be done like so: Up Growl Banishing, the Praxis Rite, (both in the Appendix), the Oracle Rite (which follows), then, when done with the oracle, the last part of the Praxis Rite and the Up Growl Banishing should be done.

## Items Needed

A wild place to do this rite, the full moon being best

The completed oracle

The stang

The three staves (optional)

Some dried mullein to burn and a dish to burn it in

## The Rite

The stang, upright with the oracle bag hanging on it, is in the center with the mullein and the staves are laid out around it on the ground in a triangle: black, red, white, if they are being used.

All stand in a circle facing the oracle and stang.

The mullein herb, if used, is lit and the scent fills the area.

If the Praxis Rite has not been done already, do it. If it has been done, then all stand up and rumble and center themselves. Then, all rock back and forth in sync while down growling with each forward motion, diving deeper into the trance and shift state calling upon the power of the Wyrd, which interconnects and binds all things, being the source of mystery and knowing.

After a time, the alpha raises paws and low up howls softly and then all somberly invoke the deities like so: All grow-vibrate MAaaaaaa to call Gaia. All open paws wide extending, reaching out and growl vibrate HAaaaaa to the Forest Lord. All raise paws up to the moon and growl vibrate AHaaaa to call on the Moon Mothers. Finally, all extend paws toward the oracle and grow-vibrate RAaaaaaaaa to call upon the Great Wolf Spirit.

The oracle is then taken up by the alpha, shaken or shuffled, and then handed to the first wer to the left who pulls one icon, memorizes it, replaces it in the bag, and passes it to the next wer and so on.

The alpha is last to get the oracle and he or she pulls an icon out. The oracle is then passed around and each wer pulls the oracle he or she originally chose. More than one wer may have pulled the same oracle remember!

Then each wer announces the oracle they pulled and growls aloud the omen and meaning from the Werewolf Magick Symbols Oracle found in the Appendix. He or she then interprets that oracle as they feel it fits them, with growly tones, of course. This reading and personal interpretation is then repeated by each wer going around the circle, the alpha going last.

When all are finished, the alpha can then pull one more icon as an omen for the whole pack which can be discussed.

**Note:** wers can later also use the oracle to do other more personal reading for themselves or other pack members at any free time in any pack ritual. As with any divination system, there are many possible ways to use the oracle icons and new divination techniques and formats can be creatively used. Using three (past, present, future) works well, for example. Finally, any of the images from the Werewolf Magick Symbols Oracle can be used by pack members as decorations, talismans, tattoos, and so, if their wer self wishes to do so.

## Werewolf Pack Astral Icon Spell

SET UP

The werewolf magick symbols can be used for more than oracle work. They can be used as icons for spells and magick like most potent magickal glyphs. Using a werewolf magick symbol or other glyph as a focus while entering a visionary trance state is a way to unlock and receive specific hidden wisdom you are seeking. This can be done as a pack or alone. Using the Eye of the Wolf glyph to open my consciousness as I was seeking to earth more gnosis in this way resulted in some of the ritual work in this book! Being in a shapeshifting trance state perfectly prepares wers to enter the astral plane and receive visionary gnosis from the deep unconscious realm of the Animalself through the Wyrd. Doing so as a pack adds depth, power, and meaning to this work. I have been a great fan of sigil work for forty years and using such a glyph to reify and trigger the deep mind is very potent, as you'll see.

Each astral visionary session should focus on only one icon; all icons are in the Appendix. Each icon used evokes the deep gnosis and wisdom teachings of *that* primal power. The wolf eye icon should be the focus of the first astral pack work, it being the key icon of the Wolf Spirit and thus of werewolf magick. Working as such, the pack discovers more about the gnosis of werewolf magick. *Participants should keep notes of the working and outcomes.*

## Items Needed

A "portal." This can be any medium size round mirror or, better, a black mirror.

A black mirror can be easily made by carefully painting the back of a piece of glass or a large, watch glass black. This is best done on the dark moon. In a pinch, a black plate with some water in it can be used. The Eye of the Wolf icon should be painted on the back of this portal as well.

A beautiful natural place where the pack will not be disturbed.

The three werewolf pack staves.

Some mullein and a burning bowl.

Journal and a pen for each pack member.

A black candle.

The stang.

A chosen icon to focus on and learn from. It should be drawn before the rite on a round piece of thick white paper in black. This is placed on the portal.

Some simple food and drink like chocolate or energy bars and water or sweet tea.

## The Spell

The "portal" is set in the center of the ritual space with the paper copy of the icon on it. The three pack staves, in order of black, red, white, are laid flat on the ground around the portal forming a triangle. All stand, face out, and do the Up Growl Banishing.

The mullein herb is lit and the alpha walks it around the circle, letting each wer breathe in a bit of the smoke thus opening up the psychic senses. The black candle is lit to the north by the stang.

All then turn toward the portal and do the Praxis Rite.

They all sit about the portal and rock back and forth and rumble.

At this time, a sacrament may be passed about to partake of.

All continue to rumble. After a time, the alpha begins to low growl AHhhh and the pack follows, meditating on the moon, and thus letting the Animalself arise completely while opening their third eye.

All continue rocking and low growling AHhhh while sinking deeper into the trance and shift state, silently calling upon the source of oracles, the Wyrd, which interconnects and binds all things, the source of mystery and knowing.

After a time, the alpha raises paws and up howls softly and then all somberly invoke the Great Wolf Spirit with a long, low up howl and a long intoned RAaaa.

With that, the image of the icon is passed around the circle counterclockwise and all intently look at it and imprint it in their memory. When it returns, the alpha places it under the portal and all begin to rumble.

As all rumble, the alpha makes the sign of the wolf mudra over the portal and low growls these words to open the portal. This mudra is made with either hand, index, and pinky fingers raised and little fingers and thumb touching, thus forming a wolf head.

*LYKOS, LUPUS, LUPERKAI!*
*Anoíxte kai deíxte!*[19]

All repeat each of the words after the alpha and then continue to rock forward and back in sync, softly rumbling while intently projecting their consciousness into the darkness of the portal - down and deeper with every rumble, while holding the icon image firmly in their mind. When all are deeply into the astral, the alpha growls and all join the growl and let go of the icon image into the darkness, then all fade to silence.

Almost immediately a fountain of visions will erupt from the depths of the portal.

Each wer must remain passive and open to all these visions without thinking at all, simply letting them arise and mentally remembering them or noting them down in a journal.

---

19. *Great Wolf* (Greek), *Wolf God* (Latin), *Werewolf God* (Latin)! *Open and reveal* (Greek)!

After a time, the alpha signals the end of the astral session with three long, low up howls and the pack carefully returns back into their bodies and their wer consciousness. This is signaled by rumbling. When all are rumbling, all open their eyes and take up their journals and note down their visions as they rumble. When all is done, the alpha raises both paws and then sharing begins.

Each wer then explains about their visions, the alpha being the last one.

What follows is an intense discussion about shared visions or images, meanings of what was seen and any deep wisdom they reveal about the icon. This sharing helps everyone understand their visions, the powers of werewolf magick and the wild gods, especially ones pertaining to the pack.

When it is done, the alpha picks up the image of the icon from under the portal, stands and begins to growl RAaaa over and over as all join in. Then he burns it, letting the ashes drift down onto the portal and all stand and howl! Each wer takes some of the ashes and rubs it on the third eye.

When done, the pack up howls three times and all shake intensely for a time to end the shifting and let the visions, trance state, and the astral planee go, then all touch the earth and growls MAaaa three times to earth it.

All items are packed away, some food and drink are shared to help earth each wer, and then all gather in the center and do the up growl banishing:

*LYKOS, LUPUS, LUPERKAI!*
*Anoíxte kai deíxte!*[20]

## Pack Senses and Skills Enhancement

This section contains two sets of werewolf magick practices to enhance, expand and more fully activate wer senses and also to expand wer skills. These practices can be done as exercises within a larger ritual such as the esbat or sabbat or may be done as separate wer get-togethers.

The practices of werewolf magick are never static. The goal is to build upon what works and take everything further! Solo work is vastly different from pack

---

20. *Great Wolf* (Greek), *Wolf God* (Latin), *Werewolf God* (Latin)! *Open and reveal* (Greek)!

work in many ways and pack work makes all the werewolf magick evolve faster and helps in expanding all the practices, skills and powers of werewolf magick.

Once we have entered the werewolf trance state and shifted into our more bestial Animalself, we are subsuming the upper cortex cognitive functions and turning over much of our processing to the lower cortex animal consciousness. Riding that thin line between human and non-human the werewolf is one historical example. This and the enhanced senses one gets from such a shapeshift is key to our magick.

When in full shapeshift mode, my hearing becomes enhanced when roaming at night. I can hear the slightest sound: small creatures moving about, the rustling of raccoons, and snorts of sleeping deer. My sense of smell becomes far more intense and I can smell the musk and spoor of animals, the different smells of trees and plants, and I smell water long before I hear a stream. I can also smell the traces of people before I hit a trail. My sense of taste expands. Tasting different waters or herbs is intense when I am shifted and everything tastes over done or too spicy or sweet and at times I even experience synesthesia. My sense of touch also becomes over sensitive, almost painful at times, and most all clothing is too uncomfortable, which pushes me to roam about naked whenever in a shifted state. Brushing through the leaves, walking in a stream, feeling the twilight breeze, bathing in a stream are intense and almost erotic sensations that light up my whole nervous system. My sense of sight becomes amazingly clear and my night vision almost supernaturally so. I have snuck up on a raccoon and startled it and I often walk through the forest with minimal natural light. All sex is always much more intense and ecstatic in wer form, which is obvious when you consider all the sense expansions when shifted. Also, being in a wer state, enthusiasm and fearlessness abound.

Are these shapeshifting sensory experiences verifiable and provable? Well, that raccoon I scared likely thought so as did the deer I hung out with. Are these experiences real or subjective? Remember that people do amazing superhuman feats under intense primal instinctive reactions, like a mother lifting an auto off a child or wounded soldiers carrying several wounded people off a battlefield. Such stories are numerous and most parents, including myself, have experienced instinctive "animal like" reactions when tracking or protecting our kids from dangers. Animals don't cognate when reacting instinctively and thus do so decisively and quickly without a thought using somatic memory, instinct and reflexes. Most of our senses and actions are wired through our brain and get filtered through all our upper cortex intelligence, in other words, we need to think about most everything before acting. Animals and shapeshifters can instinctively experience nature through their senses directly. We work on accepting and reacting, not indecisive pondering. We seek to just *be*. This state we call the Way.

## Werewolf Magick Pack Senses Enhancement

This practice can be done as a part of any esbat or sabbat, and if so the Praxis Rite would not be necessary to repeat. It is recommended that each of the senses focused on should be focused on and expanded in wer trance states one at a time, maybe over a series of five gatherings. It is a powerful practice and will both bond the pack and extend their abilities and experiences.

### Set Up

Below is a chart that shows the sensory skills that werewolf magick enhances. It includes symbolic and magickal correspondences with the traditional elements, werewolf magick tools, and the rumbling wer vibration tone for activating each sense as well as practical ways to focus on each sense. This chart is for personal reference as you seek to hone each enhanced skill when you are in wer form. You may, for example, desire to increase your night sight. Carrying your knife, focusing on your internal expanding fire center filling you while rumbling RA over and over as you walk through the woods at night, helps you focus on that skill and expand it. It is to be used creatively as you will and those who have other occult training and practices will likely find it useful in the future:

| Senses | Touch | Smell | Sight | Taste | Sound |
|--------|-------|-------|-------|-------|-------|
| Element | Earth | Air | Fire | Water | Spirit |
| Tool | Stone | Stang | Knife | Cup/shell | Small drum |
| Vibration | MA | HA | RA | AH | AH-HA |
| Trigger | Touch the earth | Smell woods | See trees | Taste water | Listen to the forest |

*Elemental Attributes:* Earth/Touch, Air/Smell, Fire/Sight, Water/Taste, Spirit/Sound.

**Note:** This rite is far more effective with a pack, but can be done solo with some changes.

## ITEMS NEEDED

A wild place to do this work, as far away from humans as possible with enough area to prowl around to experience the heightened sense. The rally grove is perfect.

## BASIC ALTAR SET UP

Tool of sense being used (see chart) (ex: fire = knife) If one of the tools in use is the tool focused on, then nothing.

## A SMALL ALTAR IS CREATED TO THE NORTH WITH

The stang

Cup of pure water

The pack drum or another small drum

The herb lavender and a burning bowl

A small beeswax candle

A one foot wide or so flat stone or blessed cloth of black

There is a flat place in the center of the circle of grass or dirt to place the flat stone or cloth or cloth there

Containers of fresh water for all to sip as they need, especially if taste is the focus.

**Note:** All items used in the rite help trigger senses; stone (touch), smoldering lavender (smell) a candle (sight), pure water (taste) a small drum (hear).

## THE EXERCISE

All stand while the alpha takes up the smoldering lavender and circles the pack clockwise while all deep down growl HA HA HA. Then the same is done with the candle as all deep down growl RA RA RA. The same is done with the cup of pure water as all deep down growl AH AH AH. The same is done with the stone as all deep down growl MA MA MA. Finally, the stang is honored by all the wers while very deep up growling, going inward evoking their animal self. All up growl together AH-HA!

Then all do the Praxis Rite together, swaying in sync. When all have attained shift, all lock arms and howl then separate and sit in a circle at the alpha's cue.

The alpha uses any words that they wish to identify the specific sense being enhanced, while leading a short, guided meditation practice focusing on expanding that sense in the woods for each wer. All take a few minutes to deeply meditate on what this would be like. Meanwhile, the alpha takes up and places the right tool for that sense in the center. (see chart on page 72.)

For example, if water/taste is being focused on, then the cup of water. Then all begin a low, deep rumble up growl while visualizing and activating the water element and sense. Since taste and water are the focus, all would then begin vibrating AH AH AH and all would focus on that sense (the sip of water) and let go of the human mind and open that sense completely through the manifesting Animalself with intense focus. Once all are in deep focus and open to expanded Animalself experience, the alpha passes around something again to focus on that sense, like a cup of wine or lemon water.

A very similar process is done, the particulars chosen for which sense is being expanded.

Once all have finished going deep inside their experience, focusing on that one sense, all then slide into rumbling, closing their eyes and going deeper into trance while extending that sense as far as possible. After a time, the alpha will know when to bring the pack back to their bodies and will slowly down howl three times, all joining in on the third down howl as they come back to their bodies with newly expanded senses.

Now the pack may sit in silence, using the now-expanded sense just practiced as a wer. For example, if taste is expanded, then pass around other things to taste like wine, chocolate, and so on to fully enjoy the enhanced perceptions. After such inner exploration, the alpha taps the drum to bring all back from the sensory obsession and then all finish the Praxis Rite. All touch the earth with both paws, rumbling AH-HA to come back to a lighter wer trance.

All sit, relax, smoke, drink and snack as they wish and, if they will, each in turn speaks of their experiences.

When finished, the Up Growl Banishing is done and then all may go or finish the larger rite one is being done.

## Werewolf Magick Pack Skills and Powers Expansion

Once you have learned the shapeshifting techniques presented in *Werewolf Magick*, you have entered the zone of werewolf magick and the many feral qualities of your Animalself-infused human self will likely emerge in many aspects of your life. You may grow more "fur" or become a bit wilder around the edges, depending more on Instinct, Intuition, and unexpected Insights than over-thinking or obeying others. It is expected that, as a wer, you will become more a comfortable animal in life and especially in the wilderness or with animals and maybe a bit less comfortable among humans. A more open, forthright, gregarious and confident persona may emerge. Wolves aren't spooky and gloomy; they are wild, playful, and generally friendly, unless you are a rabbit. You will also likely take much less crap in life and speak your mind. In short, you will likely become freer of negative cultural programming and our oppressive anti-life, anti-nature modern world. You will hopefully become wilder and, I hope, more fun! There are always downsides though. Watch out for impatience and maybe a shorter temper, especially about things that trigger your wolf-self like rudeness, aggression, large crowds, mistreatment of nature and animals and so on.

Opening up to and releasing your Animalself out in nature will always recharge you if you deeply open to it in the woods or in the mountains or on the beach, You will intuit ways to positively guide your growing feral wolfishness while focusing specifically on qualities you want to enhance and expand with the aid of skill and power enhancement practices.

### Set Up

This practice uses meditations to expand and enhance the feral skills you wish to embody and evoke in your human and wer forms. This exercise focuses on all three powers, but could be broken into three separate sessions as well.

It is based on a body-energy system which offers three simple feral power zones on the wer body that aligned and focus the three skills and powers of werewolf magick:

| Body Energy Centers | Feral Skills | Feral Powers |
|---|---|---|
| Upper body center: (Neck, head, crown) | Insight | Way |
| Core body center: (Heart—chest) | Intuition | Wyrd |
| Lower body center: (Gut, sex, base) | Instinct | Wildness |

The werewolf magick powers or skills were reviewed in Chapter 1 and are explained in depth in *Werewolf Magick*.

Each feral skill flows from the body center power from nature as noted above and its skill or wer gift is best activated and accessed through each wer's body centers after shifting.

What is the benefit? The intense focus and unleashing of these feral skills engendered by the feral powers that drive them using the power centers on the body to expand and unleash them more fully deeply connects the were to the ecosystem and the feral powers of the Animalself. In this wa,y it expands, familiarizes, and connects both internally and externally.

With practice and focus, your Animalself heightens all internal experiences and brings an enhanced power of natural Instinct, Intuition, and Insight that most humans have forgotten. Unleashing and expanding your Instinct, Intuition and Insight offers a tremendous boost in becoming a more aware wer and thus more conscious and open to the intense power of the Wildness, Wyrd, and Way and more able to channel and use these feral powers in any of your spiritual work. These exercises can be done alone but are much more synergistically powerful when done in a pack. This meditation rite can be done anywhere in nature where you will not be disturbed; the more in wilderness the better. As with the previous exercise, this exercise can be done within a larger ritual, adjust accordingly.

## Items Needed

Wers must be familiar with the body energy centers and their attributes (see chart)

The small werewolf-magick drum

Some sage or cedar bark and a burning bowl (sage could be homegrown regular sage)

A low fire or candle is in the center of the circle as a focus

Pack members should wear their werewolf magick amulets (or trigger talismans) for increased focus and effectiveness

## The Exercise

Pack all does the Up Growl Banishing (unless it has already been done).

All do the Praxis rite and shift together (unless it has already been done).

Then, all stand in a circle and the alpha, by modeling, has everyone place their paws on each body center. All the wers deeply rumble for a time, and with eyes closed, focus and feel the reality of each power center and its skill:

1. *Lower center: Belly, sex, root - Wildness -> Skill: Instinct*
2. *Core center: Heart/torso - Wyrd -> Skill: Intuition*
3. *Upper center: Neck, head, crown - Way -> Skill: Insight*

The pack then reaches out and touches paws with each other, palms extended to either side, hands pointing up, and all rumble growl loudly in unison. Everyone sways side to side in sync while visualizing the energy of the earth—the forest, moon, and more—flowing on circles around the group clockwise until the alpha feels a Wildness circle has been cast and raises paws and up howls. All join in.

Now the alpha lights the cedar bark or sage and walks around the inside of the circle clockwise and lets each wer wave the smoke to head, heart and loins, blessing the three body centers. As they do so, each wer utters a low quiet up howl as they focus intensely on cleansing and empowering the three centers.

All sit with eyes closed for a few minutes to focus on these things, breathing deeply in and out while meditating on expanding and enhancing their feral skills and powers via the three body centers that anchor and channel them. Each of the body centers is visualized as a vortex of energy that interconnects with the nature that surrounds the pack. After a time, the alpha vibrates MA then HA then AH and the pack repeats these rumble chants and opens their eyes and all rumble as the exercise begins.

The alpha stands and sticks the stang into the center of the circle and cues the pack to up growl three times, each time sinking deeper into the deep mind primal as the Animalself takes more control and the shift deepens. The alpha then growls:

*to zóo anadẏetai, to zóo anadẏetai, to zóo anadẏetai!*
*Animalself arise! Animalself arise! Animalself arise!*

All howl, lit up with their very enhanced Animalself and werewolf power and surge of energy! The pack closes its eyes again and continues to grumble. Now, the pack will focus on, empower and expand each of the specific skill and power and body center as follows.

First begins the focus on Wildness without, Instinct within.

The alpha begins to rumble chant MA, a cue to focus on and power up the lower body center, all follow the alpha's lead and do this as well as the alpha growls:

*Enstikto lẏkou, sikotheíte!*[21]
*Wolfish Instinct, arise!*

All continue low, quiet growling MA MA MA. Each wer goes deeper into the base (lower body) body center and lets the energy of their etheric body reach down into the earth with every MA.

All then begin to rock forward and back, deep inhalation when rocking forward, deep breath out when going back, eyes remaining closed.

With every inhalation each wer feels Gaia's power rise and fill the lower center with primal power and with every exhalation and rock forward, all focus on their internal, expanding instinct skill.

---

21. All Greek phrases followed by English translations, both spoken.

When all have seemed to accomplish this expansion, the alpha slowly up howls and all cease rocking and join the alpha in up howling. All then visualize the power raised from Gaia as a green ball of vibrant energy glowing in the lower body center as and the interwoven skill and power that was invoked expand.

There is a silent pause to let all wers center.

After a short time, the alpha begins to low growl chant HA HA HA and then, eyes still closed, all the wers focus their attention on their heart body center and the power and skill associated with it. All join and then the alpha low growls:

*Diaísthisi lýkou, sikotheíte*
*Wolf Intuition, arise!*

Now begins the focus on Wyrd without, Intuition within.

All continue low, quiet growling HA HA HA … and each wer goes deeper into the heart body center and let the energy of their etheric body reach out into the forest all about them focusing on and "seeing" the vast iridescent webs of life, causality, matter, and energy that interconnects all of nature and themselves.

All keep low grumble chanting and begin to rock forward and back, deep inhalation when rocking forward, deep breath when going back, eyes remaining closed. With every inhalation, each wer becomes the web of Wyrd, the vast interconnectedness of the ecosystem of which they are a part and which fills their hearts with primal power. With every exhalation and rock forward, each wer focuses on their heart-centered expanding intuition skill as it grows from the connection with the Wyrd.

When the alpha feels all have connected, he or she slowly up howls and all will cease rocking and join the alpha in up howling. All then visualize the power filling their body center via the web of Wyrd all about them as a blue ball of energy glowing in their heart center as the interwoven skill and power expand.

After a short time, the alpha begins to low growl chant AH AH AH and then all focus their attention on their head body center and the power and skill associated with it. All join in, eyes still closed, and then the alpha low growls:

*Enstikto lýkou, sikotheíte!*
*Wolfish Insight, arise!*

Now begins the focus on Way outside, Insight within.

All continue low, quiet rumble growling AH AH AH. Each wer now goes deeper into the upper body center and lets the energy of their etheric body reach up into the heavens that arches above them, focusing on and seeing the vast stillness, openness and ungraspable mystery of space and the great Moon Mother that is the lens of all mystery and magick. The moon is merely a portal to the great mystery of life which pervades all of nature and the universe of which we are a part.

All keep low grumble chanting and begin to rock forward and back, deep inhalation when rocking forward, deep breath when going back, eyes remaining closed. With every inhalation, each wer becomes the full moon which reflects the great mystery of the cosmos. The essence of all life and being—this satori moment of enlightenment—fills each mind and opens each wer's third eye. With every exhalation and rock forward, each wer focuses on this illumination, being open to a receptiveness of this gnosis and the cosmos. This illumination is visualized as a softly luminous pearl-like radiance that pervades all things with pure spirit.

When the alpha feels all have connected to this great mystery, he or she slowly up howls and all then cease rocking and join the alpha in up howling as they celebrate the experience of pure consciousness filling them from the universe with no thoughts.

After a time, the alpha will know that it is time to emerge from this practice and that the inner exploration, understanding, and expansion/absorption of the three centers is complete. The alpha slowly begins to quietly up growl and all join in. As all do so, they slowly pull back to wer consciousness by swaying slowly sway side to side and visualize all the energies conjured and absorbed by the three centers of the body until the whole body is "seen" as glowing. This glow is then absorbed by the body and as all sway and growl, the Animalself begins to slide back down into its deep unconscious lair. Then all place their hands flat on the earth before them and the alpha will growl-chant the following and all will repeat as all growl and slowly release their werewolf form and return to (somewhat) normal:

*To zóo epistréfei ston ýpno!*
*To zóo epistréfei ston ýpno!*
*To zóo epistréfei ston ýpno!*
*Animalself, descend to sleep!*
*Animalself, descend to sleep!*
*Animalself, descend to sleep!*

All are then encouraged to stand and shake themselves back into a shallower shifting consciousness. Then, all place their paws on the earth grumble chanting MA MA MA and let all the excess energies sink into Her. Then all howl, sit, relax, have something to eat and drink, and share their experiences. All insights, visions, or received visions should be noted in their journals as well as shared. Finally, the last part of the Praxis Rite can be done unless this is part of a larger ritual. This meditation-practice should be done a number of times to sharpen those powers. Awooo!

## Pack Bonding Rites and Rituals

All the rites, rituals, spells, and practices in this book seek to unite the pack and increase familiarity and bonding. Here are several which are extremely important in accomplishing these goals. From reinforcing the free, arising Animalself to bonding with the moon goddesses who in many ways empower our work to forging the crucial and evolving egregore of the pack in the form of the pack shrine, these rites all emotionally, magickally and intuitively interconnect the pack members and, more importantly, their Animalselves, as a united pack.

### *Werewolves Release Rite*

#### SET UP

While originally written as a solo ritual in *Werewolf Magick*, doing this updated rite with a pack is far more wild and powerful in different ways as the pack releases their Animalselves as one great dance. Part of preparing to work seriously with werewolf magick in a pack is letting go of restrictions and fetters that stifle you. Your feral Animalself is caged by these conscious and unconscious fetters. To free your primal self, you need to break out of your civilized "cage" and shred all that stops you from being your true self. This simple rite will help remove blockages and open the way for more feral, freeing energy. It is great to do as a pack but it works well solo too and can be done multiple times. It is a wild rite with some running, so a bunch of space is called for. All should read the rite before doing it, of course. The rite should be done at night or at twilight on a full moon. It is really best if everyone is naked. Participants should scout about and decide before the rite and where all will run wildly at the end to avoid colliding wers!

> **Note:** If you are doing this solo and are in a "bad way" or feel trapped like a wolf in a cage, put a few drops of blood into the container of wine or some sexual fluid *beforehand*. As you do so, focus on what is caging you and what needs to be released! Follow the directions below but adjust for being solo.

#### ITEMS NEEDED

An open and safe place in the woods like a large clearing or a field, with cross paths if possible.

A bottle of rich red wine and large cup

Some food for animals such as nuts, seeds, and berries

Your small, sharp ritual knives

A full moon

The stang

Candle as desired

Burning bowl and dried oak leaves

Sandals or light shoes unless the area is grassy without rocks, brambles etc.

## THE RITE

Go to the wilderness place chosen.

All clothing but footwear is shed and placed in a safe place.

All then turn around and, still in a circle, do the Up Growl Banishing.

The pack stands in a circle and centers themselves and rumbles and sways side to side in sync for a time, thinking deeply on all the crap and restrictions, programming and negative cages they still want to break out of and banish, then all howl intensely, howling all those feelings and needs as a petition to the Great Wolf Spirit! Then the ritual items brought are placed in the center of the area, and the stang stuck into the ground with all helping to do so.

All the ritual items are set up around the stang and the candle and herb are lit.

Each then takes some of the animal food that was brought and all walk clockwise and scatter the food for the animals and wild woods spirits with rumbling to thus honor the Lord of the Forest, the Earth and the wild animal spirits and beseech them for aid in this rite. Thus, the circle is cast.

When all have trod the circle, all face each other and do the Praxis Rite.

Then the alpha takes up the chalice of wine and spills some out to each quarter, growling the following with the pack repeating what was intoned:

East:

*We exist in the howl we sing*
*The breath of winter, the winds of spring*

South:

*We exist in the heat of fire*
*By scarlet eyes and blood-boiling higher*

West:

*We exist in embrace of moon daughter*
*Leaping streams and tide pull of water*

North:

*We exist with paws claws in earth*
*Dive deep in animal, primal rebirth*

The bottle is passed around clockwise and each wer drinks some wine or offers some to the earth. Then, when the bottle returns to the alpha, what's left is offered to the Earth, Lord of the Forest, Moon, and Wolf Spirit while all rumble chant for each with: MA, HA, AH, RA. Finally, all come close together and low rumble AH-HA. Then all separate and pull back. Then the alpha deep growls the following line by line as the pack repeats this personal vow in a growled.

*By dance and howl and full moon power*
*By prowl and stalk and midnight wild hour*
*All anger, all hate, all blood madness all fate*
*We release to the sky, we release to the moon*
*We caress mother earth, by unknown rune*
*Of claw and fang and dreamtime will*
*We pass through red rain without a kill*
*Faunus Lycan, forest lord, We invoke thee!*
*Of all restricting-curses, may We be free!!!*

Then, making space, all explode into action, performing a wild howling dance as they like, the wilder the better. As the pack dances, leaps howls, shakes, growls and completely lets loose, they visualize releasing all their culturally inflicted emotional, psychic, mental, and spiritual restrictions and offering them to the full moon goddess who shines from above with many howls and AHh-hhhh growls! Then, each wer completely unleashes their Animalself until all collapse on the ground and lets go and offers everything being released to Gaia with an open heart and many deep rumble down growls. All these energies and all their pent-up intensity thus sink into the earth. All then lie on the grass and stare at the moon in silence and just...be. Open, unencumbered, free. Breathing deeply, all gently feel the Earth Mother filling them with calm and life energy and they utterly relax, in silence.

After a time, the alpha low up howls and all slowly stand in a circle. The alpha takes the knife and cuts some of his or her hair and lets the wind take it and howls! All join in and each in turn takes the knife and does the same, letting go!

When done, all raise their paws in the air and embrace all of the Wildness about and the full moon above as the alpha growls the following and all growl hack line by line:

*By howl by blood, moon tides and wood*
*By spirits of wildness, both feral and good*
*By the fury and power erupting within*
*We release all our chains, all restrictions and sin*
*We are as open as nature, we lope as a beast*
*We honor all life, the greatest and least*
*In our heart the wild god now grows as a Tree*
*From poison, traps and cages, we now **run free!***

Then, howling a long, loud up howl, alpha leading, all spiral out counterclockwise and keep running out from the center to the trees, howling, yipping, laughing, until tired. Then calm, all stop and become one with the dark forest and begin to sway and rumble growl MA over and over and release the Animalself and the shifting energy into woods, seeing it pervade everything, as a mist that then gently drifts toward the full moon. All shake intensely, and then touches the earth or a tree and release the shifting energy. All visualize losing the fur, claws and so on, shaking as needed, until all are soon ready to return to the "real" world. They return to the ritual space, gather up clothes and tools, group hug and quietly return to the mundane world, for now.

## Bonding with the Moon Mothers Rite
### Set Up
We tend to focus much on the Earth Mother, the Lord of the Forest, and our tutelary deity, the Great Werewolf Spirit, but what connects them all is the moon and the lunar powers that weave the web and Wyrd of astral forces and magick as well as the tides of the oceans, the weather and the waters that flow within all living things. Without the Moon Mothers, the goddesses that

embody the powerful lunar forces of life and death and the gateway to the astral worlds where our magick manifests, we would not have potent were-wolf magick.

This rite puts the pack in-sync with these lunar powers, within and without. This rite is best done by the ocean on a deserted beach or by a lake, pond or river as long as it is as natural and free of interference as possible. This ritual is best run by a female wer officiant, if that is not possible and the alpha is male, then the alpha may be the officiant. This decision is why this rather formal term is used for this ritual.

## ITEMS NEEDED

An iron cauldron and the makings of a fire with a bunch of twigs gathered
  from these trees: willow, cedar and yew (or cypress), all dried. Leave an
  offering of one silver dime at each tree.

A burning bowl and some dried willow leaves for it.

A white candle.

A full moon or near full moon and clear sky. Time the rite so the moon will be
  above you.

Three small bottles, one with spring water, another with river or lake water,
  the other with salty ocean water.

A bottle of white wine.

Three small glass jars.

A small bowl.

The three staves of the pack.

A wand of willow harvested and blessed by the officiant for this rite.

## THE EXERCISE

All gather at the place and set up a natural found altar to the west or in the direction of the water, a stone or piece of wood that has been in or near the water is perfect. The stang is set upright behind it and the tools noted and other items are arranged on it. In the center, a fire pit is created with gathered twigs and it is arranged so that the small cauldron can be placed on or upon it, but not yet.

The pack stands in a circle about the small fire pit and cauldron to the side, rumbling and swaying in unison. Then the Up Growl Banishing is done.

The officiant lights some of the dried willow leaves in the bowl and censes the area walking counter clockwise, growling the following three times, growling with the pack repeating each time:

*Apo Pantos Kakadaimanos! Luna Dea Sit!*
*Begone all negative spirits and energies! The moon is here now!* [22]

The rest of the smoking leaves are tossed into the body of nearby water. All then do the Praxis Rite together.

Afterward the pack remains about the cauldron growling Ah Ah Ahhh and swaying forward and backward, emphasizing Ha with every forward motion and so intently bringing down the moon energy as the officiant takes up the three bottles of different water and pours some of the spring water, the river or lake water and the salt water into the cauldron.

As the pack continues their rumbling Ah Ah Ahhh, the officiant then takes up the willow wand, touches it to the water and holds it up to the moon to channel the lunar vibes flowing down saying three times:

*Férno to fengári káto*
*We call down the moon!*

Then the officiant stirs the waters clockwise with the wand three times and then uses it to draw a large triangle in the sand (or earth) about the cauldron and fire pit. One point of the triangle should point toward the ocean or body of water nearby. The officiant then growls the following line by line with the pack growling along, call-and-response:

*Artemis, Selene, Hekate*
*Three are One, One is three*
*As we will, so mote it be.*

---

22. All Greek phrases followed by English translations, both spoken.

*Luna Dea Sit!*
*The moon power is here!*

The small fire is then lit and the officiant places the cauldron on the stones over the now burning twigs, with help if necessary, and then places three leaves, one each from the three kinds of wood being used, into the cauldron and stirs the leaves and waters clockwise with the willow wand. Growling the following, the pack continues vibrating Ha Ha Ha, and growls the last English line after the officiant does so.

*Férno to fengári káto*
*ópos i Ártemis*
*We call down the moon! As Artemis!*

The officiant then takes up the wand and the wine and chants *Io Artemis* while the pack repeats and then goes to the top left corner of the triangle that was traced and draws a crescent through the corner and pours out some wine as offering on it, growling *Io Artemis!* as all repeat, with paws in the air toward the moon.

The officiant then takes up the wand and the bottle of wine and chants *Io Selene* while the pack repeats and then goes next corner of the triangle that was drawn and draws another crescent through that corner saying:

*Férno to fengári káto*
*os Selene*
*We call down the moon! As Selene!*

The officiant pours out a bit of wine on that corner as an offering. Then pours a bit of the wine into the cauldron growling *Io Selene!* which the pack loudly repeats.

The officiant then takes the wine and wand to the last triangle point, draws a third crescent and growls:

*Férno to fengári káto*
*os Hekate*
*We call down the moon! As Hekate!*

Triple Moon

All repeat that phrase, now in deeper luna-inspired trances.

The officiant pours out a bit of wine as an offering on the crescent that was drawn, then pours a bit more wine into the cauldron growling *Io Hekate!* which the pack growls back.

The officiant, with the help of other wers, fans the fire and feeds it while the pack wers rumble Ah ah ah. All take turns stirring the liquid in the pot with the willow moon wand as it warms. The officiant raises both arms to the moon as calling down the power while growling the following. The pack loudly repeats the last English line with growls:

*Férno to fengári káto*
*ópos i Ártemis, Os Selene, os Hekate! Io Evoe!*
*We call down the moon as Artemis, Selene and Hekate. So may it be!*

The whole pack then loudly growls, paws up: *Io Artemis! Io Selene! Io Hekate!*

When the water is steaming but not too hot, all the wers take off their clothes (if they have them on) and stand over the cauldron so that they can breathe the steam and view the reflection of the full moon in the cauldron. All focus and mentally flow into the reflected moon growling *Ah ah ah* over and over until it naturally fades and all become entranced by the lunar reflection and her power suddenly flows up from the reflection into everyone's werewolf bodies. As one, all do a long, slow, quiet down-howls, absorbing Her blessings and remaining entranced with the reflection of the moon. All continue down howling melodiously, now swaying side to side in sync, deepening the trance while focusing on the moon and being filled with Her power.

The officiant slowly begins three long and powerful up howls. Everyone joins in, expressing love and gratitude for this blessing and communion, this merging with the Moon Mothers.

After a time, the officiant growls and all growl-repeat line by line:

*Artemis, Selene, Hekate*
*Three are one, one is three*
*I call as werewolf, now bless me*
*As we will, so mote it be*
*Io Evoe! Io Evoe! Io Evoe!* [23]

Now, in silence, all scry into the cauldron and receive lunar visions in silence for a time.

As the small fire dies down, the officiant tests the water to make sure it isn't too hot. If it is, more water from the nearby body of water can be added.

When all are ready, the officiant takes up the small bowl and uses it to scoop up the blessed cauldron liquid and pours it over his or her head and body, loudly growling AH!

Then the bowl is passed clockwise to the next pack member who does the same and so on until all have been blessed by the sacred waters.

As each pack member does this, they see themselves filled with the moon power's silvery essence and as this power fills their werewolf being, each loudly growls AH!

---

23. *Joyful praise* (Greek).

All stand, dance, sway, and rumble AH as they absorb the blessing and dry in the breeze.

When all is done, the officiant raised the willow wand as all howl and the officiant growls the following with the pack repeating line by line:

*Artemis, Selene, Hekate*
*Three are one, one is three*
*Beast and moon, one are we*
*As we are. So mote it be!*

The magick is complete! Now is a time to share visions, party, drink the rest of the wine, dance naked, jump in the water, and have some fun as all desire. Let the wild lunar rumpus start! Of course, if it is chilly, clothes should be put on.

When all are ready to go, the officiant uses the small bowl to scoop up the liquid that is left in the cauldron and fills the empty bottles with this sacred elixir which can and will be used ritually in other werewolf magick rituals to bless places and items, anoint wers, humans needing blessings, and so on.

Pack members clean the area, scatter the fire ashes into the body of water, wash out the cauldron, make sure nothing remains, and pack up leaving no trace. Leftover pure food or wind should be offered to the body of water with a big Ahhhhhh!

Then the pack walks counterclockwise about the area, earthing the rite and stomping away the triangle while the officiant growls three times, and pack repeats:

*Blessings and honor to you Moon Mothers three*
*Artemis, Selene and Hekate*
*Io Evoe! Io Evoe!*

Werewolf Pack Shrine

## Creation and Ritual of the Pack Shrine

When a pack begins to join, establishing relationships, doing induction and initiation rites and getting to know each other, the practices and rites take time as well as a whole bunch of full moons. Once the rally grove or home base is found and empowered, the pack will have begun becoming its own entity with its own spirit. Once all this happens, once there are three or more proficient werewolf magick wers, then a true pack has formed.

This means it is time for a pack shrine to be created and empowered (see Werewolf Pack Shrine image). This will hold the heart, the unity, and the evolving egregore of the pack. As the pack and its energies begin to coalesce and take magickal shape, the shrine will grow as a nexus or center of power for the werewolf pack cult and the place where the pack interfaces with the Great Wolf Spirit and all the werewolf magick gods. As such it needs to be created, empowered and maintained by the pack once the pack has formed and is committed to the work. The core of the shrine will be a container of natural material, such as wood, that can be transported to rituals. Many sacred items will be kept with the sacred icon of the Wolf Spirit in or with this container, including tools, herbs, the oracle and other items the pack deems appropriate. All of this together is referred to as the shrine.

The following items are always kept with the shrine, though not necessarily kept within the shrine container if size is an issue. Other magickal items will naturally be added to the shrine as the pack evolves and grows. Intuition, inspiration, insight, and creativity will guide the pack in all this, each pack being a unique and organically growing work of art.

The following items are kept in or with the shrine when not being used:

- The most potent key sacred icon of the shrine will be a wolf or coyote skull that has been appropriately gotten and ritually blessed. This is the center of the shrine. In *Werewolf Magick*, the ritual dealing with such remains is made clear and rules for treating them with utmost respect are detailed. It is extremely rare to be able to get an actual wolf skull, *especially one that has been found and not killed by hunters*. Antique wolf or coyote skulls are acceptable. Coyotes are not endangered and an appropriate found skull that has not been the result of hunting can be found fairly easily. Once received, the shrine skull is blessed as a talisman (see Appendix) and dyed or painted red with a natural colorant and werewolf glyphs should be inscribed or painted on as the pack desires (see Pack Blessing Rite for Talismans and Tools in the Appendix).

- A protective container made of natural materials to hold and protect the magickal items, especially the sacred skull. This, along with larger items like the stang, comprise the complete shrine. It should be portable and decorative and fairly easy to carry and transport. The skull can be packed with oak leaves, stones, tools along with what is mentioned in this list and other items as the pack desires. The skull or bones should be cradled with natural cloth or dried leaves and herbs for safety.

- The pack stang always lives in or with the shrine container, depending on size, and in general should be displayed upright if possible. It embodies the Lord of the Forest.

- The staves of the three Moon Mothers also live in or near the shrine container. If they don't fit within the shrine, they can be arranged to form a triangle on or about the shrine container

- A found or handmade paten or small, flat slab of stone, wood, or ceramics is found or crafted and is to be inscribed or painted with the Eye of the Wolf icon symbol or another appropriate werewolf magick sigil or even a new symbol chosen or created by the pack. This is the "pantacle" upon which the skull rests within the container. A simple covering for the skull should also be made or crafted out of natural cloth, leather or another material and laid over it for protection.

- Three small natural bowls for offerings; ceramic would work best. One for burning herbs, another for pure water, the third for "food" for the god. These can be set upon the shrine when the container is closed for offerings.

- The pouch of oracle icons, if used, as described in the Appendix.

- The pack icon: Eventually, after the pack has worked together and discussed this, a pack wolf spirit or egregore spirit sigil or symbol can be crafted by the whole pack in an appropriate werewolf magick ritual of the pack's choosing and then embedded in a small stone or wood amulet. This is kept in the mouth of the skull or surrounded by the canid bones. As the skull is the home to the Great Wolf Spirit, the icon is the empowered holy egregore-werewolf deity for that pack. Many discussions and a lot of pack work may be necessary to channel the right icon for the pack via the Great Wolf Spirit.

Other possible sacred items kept in or around the shrine:

- A sharp, appropriate sacred pack knife, best with a natural (bone?) handle and hand forged steel or iron.

- Special candle holders and beeswax candles.

- A larger, natural, sacred vessel used for pack rituals. Ideally an appropriate symbol or symbols should be on it. Again, that is up to the pack. See icons in the Appendix for ideas.

- Bundles or pouches of sacred herbs, stones, vials of holy oil and other such items.

- Other idols and images of the werewolf god or other deities such as horned woodland gods representing the Lord of the Forest, images of Artemis, Selene, Hekate and images or symbols of the Earth Mother Gaia. Such items should be natural and handmade is always best.

The shrine is the collective holy place center of the pack, though it is kept and tended by the alpha. Pack members may rightfully ask the alpha for access to the shrine at appropriate and agreed upon times. Nothing is allowed in or around the shrine container without the complete agreement of all pack members.

The shrine should be consecrated and empowered and completed on a full moon, during an esbat, using the ritual that follows. The creation and empowerment of the shrine should be serious and focused but also, as with much of werewolf magick, should be creative, communal, playful, wild, and festive.

## Maintaining the Shrine

As mentioned, the shrine is kept and cared for at the home of the alpha who weekly feeds the indwelling Wolf Spirit / God with simple offerings such as natural water, simple food as has been described in this book and burned dried rosemary or another herb or leaf. Local flowers can be kept before the shrine container with beeswax candles in appropriate holders or a lamp with natural oil case well.

The altar where the shrine is kept can and should have other items as well, of course. I keep my werewolf mask I use at All Hallows, antlers, amulets, werewolf images, herbs and so on my werewolf magick altar with the shrine container. This is all up to the pack and the alpha and pack members would do well to have their own werewolf magick altars set up in their abodes too. As usual, creativity is encouraged.

The werewolf pack shrine is usually only brought to significant rituals like esbats, sabbats, and whatever is deemed important to the pack. Spells and minor rites or very specific rituals like the preceding one are not appropriate for hauling the shrine too, but werewolf festivals, initiations and special events may call for the shrine to be there. The pack decides!

Werewolf Magick Altar with Shrine

When present during werewolf magick rituals, the shrine can be used as or part of the central altar or, if more appropriate, be set up to the north. In such a setting, it can be decorated as is appropriate to the ritual. When present, the shrine is acknowledged as the nexus of the pack as well as of the powers of Wildness, Wyrd, and Way as well as of our feral gods and goddesses and, especially, of the Great Wolf Spirit. It is the center of our circle.

Whenever the shrine is present, the stang should be set upright behind it and all should face it and honor it, feeling the power ever growing within it. Once it is present, offerings should be placed before it on three small plates or bowls. Pure water, pure natural food, burning herbs as appropriate. When in doubt, use rosemary or crushed oak leaves.

The up growl banishing (and other banishing practices) are done around the shrine and initial ritual practices such the Praxis Rite should be done *before* the shrine. If another separate altar is being used for whatever ritual is being done, items can be moved from the shrine as needed for whatever the ritual requires or the shrine itself may become part of the central altar, as the pack wills.

## Ritual of the Werewolf Pack Shrine

### SET UP

This ritual is used to initially consecrate the shrine.

However, it also can and should be repeated to awaken and reinforce its powers and honor the deities it embodies. For example, this rite should be done for every sabbat where it should be present, but also at any other ritual where it is deemed proper to bring and install it.

Each step of this ritual must be intensely visualized by the wers of the pack every time it is done, especially when it is consecrated. This rite can be added to, altered, and changed as the pack decides over time. As the pack evolves and grows, so will the shrine and the pack egregore or unified spirit. As always, creativity, intuition, and creativity rule!

### ITEMS NEEDED

The full shrine with tools (stang, staves, etc. as mentioned).

Each of the pack wers should be dressed in full werewolf magick regalia as they will. Each should be wearing a wolfish talisman or their shapeshifting trigger if possible.

Each wer brings a red flower, that has been empowered by them as they will.

A red beeswax candle and holder.

**Note:** *The following three items can utilize the three vessels that are part of the shrine.*

The pack cup or vessel filled with deep red wine in which a bay leaf has been soaking.

Three small natural bowls for offerings of natural food, pure water, burning herbs.

Herbs for burning: For the consecration, crushed oak leaves and rosemary are used. For other events where the shrine is present, whatever herbs are appropriate.

### The Ritual

When initial consecration is being done the shrine is set up to the north, the Up Growl Banishing is done.

All raise paws and up howl three times to awaken the gods and Wolf Spirit and create a glowing sphere of power around themselves and the shrine.

All raise paws up to the sky to bring down the powers of the Moon Mothers with an up growl chant:

AH! AH! AH!

Then all thrust paws toward the shrine visualizing that energy pouring into it.

All stretched out paws to either side toward the surrounding woods and awaken the powers of the Lord of the Forest with an up growl chant:

HA! HA! HA!

Then all thrust paws toward the shrine visualizing that energy pouring into it.

All stretched out and touch shrine with paws and awaken the Great Wolf Spirit With an up growl chanting of:

RA! RA! RA!

Then all visualize wolfish energy pouring into it and "see" the spirit awaken.

Finally, all place paws on the earth and up growl chant:

MA! MA! MA!

Visualizing the power of the Earth Mother rising up and embracing and earthing the power of the shrine and collected powers gathered.

All then stand and gently rock forward and back together and up growl chant AH-HA!, AH-HA!, AH-HA!, focusing on the egregore or collective spirit of the pack as it manifests within them all and glows within the shrine. Paws are then placed over each wer's heart, filling it with a light that connects to the shrine, like spokes of a wheel and then all reach out and hold hands in a circle of energized silence. What follows is core ritual whether it is the initial shrine consecration or an installation:

The alpha lights the candle and also the crushed leaves in the burning bowl. Then the alpha growls the following with great drama, which all growl repeat line-by-line:

*Bones And Ashes Deep In Earth*
*What Never Dies Will Have Rebirth*
*From Darkest Shadow To Brightest Light*
*Arise Wolf God Whose Eyes Burn Bright*
*By Great Moon Mothers, Black, White And Red*
*Trikona Flow Down With The Honored Dead*
*Come Lord Of The Forest And Every Tree*
*Arise With Gaia, Lykos-Theos: Be Free*
*As We Thrice Howl, So May It Be!*
*Io Evoe Lykos Theos!*
*o Evoe Lykos Theos!* [24]
*Io Evoe Lykos Theos!*

The whole pack unleashes three intense and long up howls, paws out to the shrine, while visualizing the Great Wolf Spirit manifesting and arising from the center of the shrine.

All then do the Praxis Rite as deeply and intensely as possible while continuing to visualize the manifestation of the Great Wolf Spirit as it fills and settles into its shrine.

All now hold hands in a circle about the shrine and begin to sway side to side and rhythmically rumble in sync for a time, intensifying the visualization.

Then, at the alpha's cue, all slightly open their mouth and change the rumble to growling low and long vibrations of RAaaaa RAaaaa RAaaaa ... all still in sync and still swaying and solidifying their vision of Lykos Theos being here now manifest with all that has been invoked flowing through every wer into this manifestation. After a time, with a cue from the alpha, all raise their still held paws and increase the volume and intensity of the RA growl-chant until it reaches such a wild frenzy that all erupt into howling and then all reach for-

---

24. *Hail and honor the Wolf God!*

ward and touch the shrine and with a final, activating, group howl, letting go of all the power raised into the being of the Wolf Spirit now present and awake and aware! All then bow in silence to the deity now manifested.

Then, a time of calm and deep breathing as things settle.

The alpha then relights and adds to the burning herbs and walks it three circles about the shrine, replacing the burning bowl before the shrine while taking up the candle and doing the same. The same is then done with the pack cup while sprinkling a bit of the wine about and on the shrine and on the silent wers.

Then, after taking a minute to regroup and breathe in the energy, each wer, one at a time, places his or her red flower on the skull in the inner shrine and growls RAaaaa offering a silent prayer from the heart to Lykos Theos, the Great Werewolf Spirit, and bows and step back for the next wer to do the same. The alpha does this last.

Then all come to the shrine and gently place all the paws together (all for one!) gently on the skull and stand in silence allowing all the power conjured to center and settle as a fiery force that has filled them now flowing into the shrine which now glows.

At a cure from the alpha, all together down-howl, long, low and intensely, then fling their paws in the air and howl a lot! The shrine is now consecrated and empowered.

Other ritual work or a party may then ensure about the shrine. When all is done and everyone is ready to go, the shrine should be closed or quieted.

All stand in a circle about the shrine as before and raise paws and down howl slowly three times to quiet and let sleep the gods and Wolf Spirit.

All raise paws up to the Moon Mothers and release them with a down growl chant:

AH! AH! AH! while visualizing that energy arising and dispersing.

Then all stretched out paws to either side toward the surrounding woods and release the Lord of the Forest with a down growl chant:

HA! HA! HA! while visualizing that wild energy flowing out and dispersing.

All then touch shrine with paws and visualize the Great Wolf Spirit circle the shrine and prowl out of the circle and into the aether with low, calming down growl chant of:

RA! RA! RA! and all raise their paws and honor the leaving.

Finally, all place paws on the earth and down growl chant:

MA! MA! MA! While visualizing all the Earth Mother rising up and embracing all the powers that were gathered.

Finally, all stand and lock arms and down grown AH-HA!, AH-HA!, AH-HA! While leaning into each other and focusing and absorbing the spirit of the pack which is here-now.

A moment of silence then all up howl together as one.

The shrine ritual is finished. The shrine container can now be closed and put away with a final howl. It is then taken back to the alpha's home.

## About the Egregore of the Pack and the Pack Fetch

As the pack grows and evolves and becomes more proficient in shapeshifting and ritual work, the bond grows between members and, as with other packs of feral beings, a "group mind" or spirit forms. This is a potent collective power that integrates the forces and gods of werewolf magick through the unity of the wers in the pack and can be conjured to work with as a fetch. As the pack evolves and grows, so does the spirit of the pack. At a certain point, that pack wolfish spirit will be "seen" by the more psychic wers and it can be useful as a separate, conscious group Fetch if the pack so desires it.

This decision and discussion will happen once the shrine has been completed and after the pack has become more experienced, closer, and more focused. The extensive section of Fetch magick in *Werewolf Magick* should be read if this is of interest to the pack. So may it be!

# CHAPTER 4

# RECURRING PACK RITES AND RITUALS

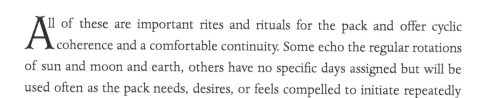

All of these are important rites and rituals for the pack and offer cyclic coherence and a comfortable continuity. Some echo the regular rotations of sun and moon and earth, others have no specific days assigned but will be used often as the pack needs, desires, or feels compelled to initiate repeatedly when the time feels right.

Lit stang

## Werewolf Pack Full Moon Esbat Ritual

*"The word **esbat** comes from the Old French s'esbattre, "to amuse oneself." Yet the primary purpose of the meeting is to worship the old gods ..."* [25]

SET UP

On or near the full moon, the pack should regularly go to its hallowed rally grove for a full werewolf magick esbat, much akin to the esbats of Witches,

---

25. The Free Dictionary, "Esbat."

many of whom identified as werewolves in the middle ages. This monthly celebration of werewolfery is a chance to catch up, party, do magick, honor the werewolf gods, excel at shapeshifting and whatever else the pack desires. Aside from partying, some training or mentoring is encouraged as is spellcraft. The esbat ritual is a great ritual to drop a variety of practices, spells and meditative activities into. *Werewolf Magick* offered a variety of such activities and many of the spells, games and practices in this book can be inserted within an esbat as well, as the pack desires. It is expected that the alpha and pack will communicate beforehand in deciding what will occur and the pack members can suggest such things as oracle or spell work or sensory expansion as a drop-in. In short, esbats are an open "container" where other things can and should be done. One of those can be a serious woodland, another is making music and dancing, always it is up to the pack but of course doing magick and having fun are critical. Weather will likely influence the date chosen, clothing and length of the esbat! Having access to a dense grove of trees or even a covered shelter or campsite open at night or even a natural backyard may be useful at times.

The pack can go to the ritual site at twilight to make set up easier.

All pack members should be wearing their werewolf magick charms, especially well-crafted trigger talismans, and be decked out in wolfish attire.

If it is warm, wear clothes there but bring a bag to put them in and shed as much as you will.

If you go naked or near naked, bring sandals to protect the feet.

If it isn't warm, wear loose black clothing and cloaks or coats and blankets: be prepared.

Also: All pack members should bring talismans, magickal tools, flowers, or other items to be placed on the stang to be charged. Also offerings, such as small wreaths of ivy or flowers, are appropriate.

## Items Needed

A full moon, hopefully overhead

Access to the rally grove or a similar wild and safe place

Several bottles of red wine seeped since new moon with pomegranate seeds

Pomegranate juice for non-drinkers.

Pure water to drink

"Holy" water gathered from a spring, lake or river with appropriate honoring

A dried crumbled herb mixture of: oak leaves, rosemary and willow leaves (or mullein)

Smoking herbs as desired

Several containers of spring water with three grains of sea salt in them

Some food or a feast: Fresh cooked or dried meat and a lot of other great food, as natural and healthy as possible.

The pack ceremonial cup or bowl

The three staves (black, red, white)

The stang

The pack drum

A beeswax candle to be lit and solidly inserted in the cleft of the stang.

Other candles and holders or lamps to illuminate the space

**Note:** Be aware of fire restrictions and what the fire danger rating is. Only the stang candle is necessary, battery lamps are acceptable.

Primitive rattles, rhythm sticks, and other musical instruments as desired

Dried willow leaves, mullein and rosemary to be burned and a burning bowl

Other appropriate items for a werewolf magick ritual as each determines

*Optional*: The shrine (This would entail adding the shrine activation)

## THE RITUAL

The esbat begins with the ritual stalking. As the pack approaches the pack grove or wherever the esbat is being held, all become silent and enter the woods in a single file. The alpha carries the stang first, then the beta or another carries the drum lightly tapping on it, and three different pack members each carry one of the three staves and others carry all the other items. Together, at the cue of the alpha, all enter the path leading to the grove, and begin to rumble and think intently of the image of the Moon tarot card: A watery path leading to the full moon with a wolf and menhirs (tall stones) on either side.

As all enter the path rumbling, all visualize smiling, guardian wolf spirits on either side, welcoming you back to your home.

The alpha stops and all bow to these guardians and silently ask permission to enter and be embraced by the wolf guardians, the goddesses of lunar powers and the Lord of the Forest with a long low musical up howl.

All wait, listening for a response from the forest. It may be the cry of an animal, a sudden gust of wind or something more ephemeral. When it comes (wait for it!), the beta slowly and lightly taps a solemn beat on the drum and all proceed deeper into woods, to the sacred space.

As all enter the grove, the alpha then parts the veil with the stang by opening arms wide and all intensely howl and relax, y'all are home. The beta does a soft roll on the drum and then strikes it three times loudly and. All walk about joyfully and yip and bark greetings to the spirits of the forest, the Great Wolf Spirit, the Moon Mothers and the Lord of the Forest and the spirit of this place (genus loci) who knows and welcomes you.

From now on, it is all wer lingo and pointing claws, there is no talking until the feasting and partying except when growled invocations. Lots of expressive and humorous growls, yips, howls, whines and so on are all fine, but no extraneous words.

As the drumming becomes a regular heartbeat, the pack walks about the rally grove clockwise a few times and all begin low continuous rumbling at first that after a few circles shifts to up growling of RA with each step. All grab their shapeshifting trigger talisman or other talisman and the chanting grows and wers begin to sway back and forth as the circling continues. All slip into trance state deeper, deeper, until everyone's conscious mind is subsumed by the wolf Animalself. All inhale the scents of the night forest, feel the breeze and moisture in the air, all slide into the shadow moon-lit wild world of Wildness, Wyrd, and Way. As the pack continues to sway and trod the circle, all shiver and shake and shift, casting off the detritus of civilization! As all slowly tighten the circle being tread, all are shifting and visualizing growing fur, claws and fangs as each wer opens the dark flower deep mind and lets the chattering ego sink into shadow. The Animalself now rises to the fore as everyone's growls get deeper and more feral. Then the alpha raises the stang and howl and all join in and all stop, in a tight circle about the center of the grove.

The alpha raises the stang and sets it in the center and all add a paw and it is set into the earth with a down howl.

All place hands on the stand and honor the Mother with deep MA MA MA vibrations.

If the pack shrine is present, this takes the place of the altar and all items are arranged around it. If not, another altar is created using a flat stone, a piece of wood or a simple green cloth.

All begin to set up the altar while the beta taps a simple rhythm. Those not setting things up should stand about the action rock and rumble to the light drumming to help conjure the feral energies. The altar or shrine is behind it with the candle inset into the crook of the stang in a way that is stable. All other items, including the staves and personal tools, musical items and amulets, are laid out as the pack desires. Last, food, drink, and so on are arranged to either side of the altar or shrine. flowers, greenery and so on are all encouraged, this is a big ritual.

Then the herb mixture is lit as is the candle and all raise their paws and up howl loudly three times. All turn and face outward do the Up Growl Banishing while the beta strikes the drum once for each of the nine growls and also up growls into the back of the drum each time, thus vibrating it.

The beta will continue to lightly tap the drum as it feels right, during the next process, letting the spirits flow through the sounds of the drum as all do a quicker version of the Praxis Rite in sync with the drum. When done, all begin to rumble and sway side to side in sync.

**Note:** If the shrine is present, the shrine activation rite is done in place of the Praxis Rite.

The alpha then takes up the burning bowl and the "holy water."

Then the alpha walks around the inside of the pack circle counterclockwise and begins growling AH AH AH as all pick up the chant while the alpha sprinkles all the wers and the altar (or shrine) as the growling and swaying continues. All wers visualize this holy moon water washing away everything negative that has gathered on their fur over the last month.

The alpha then puts the water down and takes up the burning bowl and walks around the inside of the circle counterclockwise, and censes each wer while low up growling HA HA HA as the pack picks up the HA chant as well, all, still swaying in sync. All visualize inhaling the breath of the forest filling them, removing all stale air, thoughts and feelings from their wolfish forms.

Then all touch the earth and together rumble MA MA MA... to honor the Earth Mother and let go of anything else that needs to go so that all can be pure wer, one with the nature that embraces them.

Now, all stand in silence for a time, deeply breathing and then all reach out expanding their energy fields, first reaching out with paws to the forest, then down to the earth and finally up to the moon while rumbling and deepening their shapeshifting as they have learned. Now the beta again begins to softly tap the drum in a very slow beat as the pack again sways together and the shifting takes a deeper hold. The beat gets louder and faster and finally, with three loud strikes being the signal, all howl and let their beasts fully arise!

The drum is then silent for a time and may be placed by the shrine or altar.

The alpha takes up the large ritual cup filled with the blessed red wine and holds it in a way so that the moon is reflected in it if possible. If the moon cannot be actually seen, it's power is invoked with will and is intensely visualized by all.

All wers gather closer so they can see this and all "see" the moon power as a brilliant ray of silvery light beaming down and filling the cup illuminating their wolfish bodies, increasing their feral powers while all rock forward and back deeply down growling over and over:

*IO, IO, IO! (as: eee-rock back, ohhh-rock forward)*

All visualize the moon power being drawn down into the wine and into their bodies.

Then, the now-glowing cup is raised up by the alpha and is touched by all. All then down howl three times as the beaming light flows into the circle and washes over everything.

As the moon power fills all with brilliant silvery light, it empowers the pack and all present begin to see each other's true werewolf forms.

The cup is then passed counter clockwise from wer to wer, each drinking some and blessing themselves with a drop or two and a couple on the earth, then an up howl of thanks!

Each wer does this and is filled with the lunar power. Finally, the alpha takes the cup, takes a sip, and offers a few drops of wine and howls as well. Then the alpha pours the last bit of wine on the stang and sprinkles the altar or shrine finally on the earth.

All then stand in a circle with paws up praising the Moon Goddess and all vibrate AHhhhhhh, now having been possessed, blessed and transformed!

Then the alpha loudly growls the following lines and all wers repeat:

*Io Evoe* [26] *Artemis! - all place paws of glowing light on their sex organs*
*Io Evoe Selene! - all place paws of glowing light on their hearts*
*Io Evoe Hekate! - all place paws of glowing light on their head*

Then all wildly howl as the moon power completely fills each wer's werewolf form completely and so all are completely enveloped by full werewolf consciousness!

A bit more wild yipping, howling and so on may occur until all settles down.

All reform in a circle and begin just rumbling and swaying in sync for a time, reveling in their wolfishness. The alpha then takes up the three staves and holds them up to the moon and then hands them to three wers who have agreed to assist. They each go three equidistant directions to stand at the edge of the sacred area, forming a triangle, dark woods behind them.

The wer who holds the white stave of Artemis, points the stave upward toward the moon while growling loudly: *Io Artemis!*

The rest of the pack repeats this and joins together in a long low up howl.

That wer then sticks the stave securely in the earth. All now "see" Artemis's presence upon the stang as a glowing silver flame.

---

26. *Io Evoe* = Honor, praise! (Greek).

The second person holds up the red stave of Selene to the moon: Growling loudly: *Io Selene!*

The rest of the pack repeats this and joins together in a long low up howl.

That wer then sticks the stave securely in the earth at their feet.

All now "see" Selene's presence upon the stang as a glowing red flame.

The third person holds up the black stave of Hekate to the moon: Growling loudly: *Io Hekate!*

The rest of the pack repeats this and joins together in a long low up howl.

That wer then sticks it securely in the earth and all now "see" Hekate's presence upon the stang as a glowing black flame. Next, the lunar powers will be united through centering of the wild moon.

The beta again takes up the drum for the next part of the ritual and plays light rhythms when it feels right while also participating as he or she wishes.

All return to standing in a circle about the altar and stang, aware of the powerful presence of the three Moon Mothers. The alpha refills the burning bowl with herb and lights it then refills the cup with wine, adding a bit of fruit as well and returns to the center.

The alpha digs a small hole in the earth and holds the wine filled cup to the moon as all up growl AH three times. The alpha growls the following with all repeating:

*Luperca Luperca Luperca!!!*
*Our Wolf Moon Mother*
*Be Here Be Here Be Here!*
*Lupa Dea!*
*FIAT!*

All howl!

Then the alpha passes the cup about the circle and every wer takes a sip and pours a little fruity wine into the hole and then up growls the following:

*Honor and gratitude O Mother Luperca!*
*I am your wolf! Bless and empower me!*
*We are Pack O Lupa Dea!*

All howl!

Now, with pack help, the stang is carefully lifted up by the alpha from where it was without losing the candle. It is then carefully set into the new hole where the wine offerings were poured into the earth. The hole is then filled in with earth by the pack.

The werewolf goddesses are now present.

Every wer present then places his or her talisman or other offering such as a small wreath of ivy, a flower so on or about the stang. As each item is offered in turn by pack members, that wer barks, yips or howls.

When all are done, all then stand about the stang with locked arms and sway and begin chanting HA HA HA while conjuring the Lord of the Forest who flows from the surrounding woods and coalesces about the stang. The alpha low growls the invocation, with all other wers repeating it line by line:

*Lord Of The Forest*
*We call to Thee*
*Sharp Claws, loud Howls*
*Great Beast leap Free*
*By your wild touch*
*So May We Be*
*So May We BE!*
*SO MAY WE BE ... FREE!*

All loudly up howl!

More herbs are lit and the burning bowl and food offerings are all placed about the stang by the alpha and other wers. The candle should still be burning. If low, replace it.

The stang is censed three times by the alpha and the cup is refilled with wine which is offered to the stang with a small pour and a long vibrated HAaaaaa.

Then all bow to the Lord of the Forest, "seeing" him as a very present shadow form arising from the stang.

Then all pick up the HA HA HA growls as they begin to slowly rock together forward and back in sync rhythmically facing the stang, honoring and visualizing the Lord of the Forest so embodied. The alpha then raises his or her paws and growls the following line by line with the pack repeating:

*Faunus Lycan*
*We Call To Thee!*
*Werewolf God*
*Most Ancient Tree*
*Awaken Now*
*Set Us Free*
*Come Dance With Us*
*So Mote It Be!*
*HA HA HA!*

All loudly up howl over and over!

Now begin the esbat revels! The beta really pounds the drum now in wild rhythms and all the wers go nuts as their werewolves are freed!! All dance wildly and howl, bark, yip, chuff, and so on. The wine bottles are passed around along with smoke, food, and so on.

There is much laughing leaping about, no talking, just wild nonverbals! Thus, the wild werewolf rumpus explodes and the rattles, rhythm sticks, clapping barking, paw stamping, and so on become part of the primal music!

As all slide deeper into shapeshifts, the wers growl, sway, stalk about the circle, and create from their primal creativity pantomime and imitate animals, hunting wolves stalking prey, feral animal spirits and whatever erupts from them, always getting wilder and more creative! Howls, growls, and barks become feral songs as the werewolves harmonize and "sing" with occult growing powers and the voices of the spirits.

The barks of the werewolf spirit, the growling of RA RA RAaaa is heard at times as things get wilder, with yips, growls, chuffs, and whines always present.

All are filled with deep Wildness and soon some possessed wers begin to growl out feral invocations of ancient chanted syllables mixed with barbarous tongues.

The werewolves and spirits laugh as the Wildness writhes like a serpent everywhere.

Wers stand forth and let the feral spirits, gods and goddesses flow through them vibrating Ah, Ha, Ma, Ra, Aha and other vibrations that flow from the Wildness through their animal beings. All listen and howl approval as the understanding of this chaotic communion flowers. All this time the wild drumming and other music is still played as instruments change hands.

As the celebration unfolds, wers take breaks, wander the woods, hug trees, growl in pairs, lay on the ground and moon gaze, eat, drink, smoke, meditate or dance with joy.

Wers play together, letting their fur fly, as wild and free as they like.

Make sure all remember the pack rules about appropriacy and consent at all times! The alpha only participates peripherally, keeping an eye on things and gently intervening as needed.

When all begins to calm a bit, and this will occur naturally, the alpha signals with raised claws and a long slow up howl and all slow and stop, returning to a circle about the stang and altar, probably panting with sweaty fur. All lean into each other, locking arms or holding hands and then all up growl HAaaaaaa! three times as loud as possible, a final prayer and thanks to the Lord of the Forest. Then follows a time of receiving blessings

All calm down, drink some water (or more wine), and then raise their paws to the moon and in silence feel the wild but calming crackling energy spinning about the circle.

Without words, the alpha cues the pack, and each wer gathers the Wildness energy to themselves with paws extended outward and then placed that power on their lower body while focusing the wildness power and letting it flow into the loins and lower body rooting it with paws dug into the earth. All growl-vibrate MA and inhale the power.

Without words, each then gathers the soft, loving energy generated by the ritual and also flowing from the forest in extended paws that are then placed on the heart center while letting the loving power of the Wyrd flow through the whole circle of the pack that unites all with a glow of empathy and intuition. All growl-vibrate HA and inhale the power.

Without words or thoughts, each wer gathers and opens to the infinite mystery of this moment in extended paws reaching to the stars and moon, gathering pure consciousness and silence of the unity and illumination all share. Then, all place paws on their head and open and silence their wild minds. In the bliss of nothingness and unity, the power of Way opens everyone's third eye and from one-mind arises silent insight. The pack is one; there is no difference between one thing and another. All then growl-vibrate AH! And inhale the power.

In silence, all absorb all of these energies and place a finger-claw to the mouth.

Then each wer in turn, with non-verbal wer lingo and gestures, offers a final nonverbal prayer of thanks to the Moon Goddess using Ah, then to the Lord of the Forest using Ha and then to the Great Mother Earth with growled MA and touch of the earth. After each wer is done, all the other wers down-howl. At the end, all place arms out and touch paws together with the wers on both sides and all inhale and utter a long, slow, loving RAaaaaa honoring the Werewolf spirit all embody. Then all lock arms and lean in closely and bring all the energy together with three growled AH-HA s and a final explosive howl.

All then down howl and touch the earth with both paws and growl MAaaa ... seeing all the energies conjured sink into the earth.

All stand, shake off the Wildness, and laugh!

Now is a time of quieter joy; other practices and communion and human words may be used.

If the pack desires it or if it has been planned, this is a time to do other practices such as spells, oracle work, skills enhancements, talisman or tool charging, wer healing, and any number of activities found in this book or in *Werewolf Magick*. As always, it is up to the pack.

Those needing peace, protection, healing, or magickal help are now given attention by the pack with full spells or focused energetic touch, chants, and low up howls, with the alpha assisting or making suggestions. Feasting, drinking, discussion visions and ideas, writing in journals are all possible during this chill time. It is good to just enjoy being relaxed, free and fully accepted by your brother and sister wers in this completely safe, accepting, healing, a wildland natural lair. Ah!

When it is time to end, the beta begins a slow drumbeat after a nod from the alpha and the shutdown begins:

The wers who planted the staves return to the stave then planted and each

The wer who is with the Artemis stave pulls it up and holds the white stave of Artemis up to the moon, all visualizing the Goddess flowing back to the moon with love.

The wer holding the stave growls loudly: *Io Artemis Agape!*[27] The rest of the pack repeats this.

That wer then brings the stave to the stang and leans it into the cleft of the stang.

The next wer pulls up the red stave of Selene, pointing it up to the moon, all visualizing her departing with love. The wer holding the stave growls loudly: *Io Selene Agape!*

The rest of the pack repeats this.

That wer brings that stave to the stang and leans it into the cleft of the stang

The last "stave wer" pulls and holds the black stave of Hekate pointing up to the moon- and all visualize her departing with love. The wer holding the stave growls loudly: *Io Hekate Agape!*

The rest of the pack repeats this.

The wer then brings the stave to the stang and leans it into the cleft of the stang.

---

27. *Agape* = spiritual love (Greek).

The energies engendered are visualized contracting back into the altar and stang.

All form a tight circle and bow to the center as the alpha growls and the rest repeat:

*Luperca Luperca Luperca!!!*
*Bless us Great Wolf Mother*
*Our work now done*
*Live in our hearts*
*Moon, woods, earth all one*
*The Great Wolf Spirit lives!*
*Wildness, Wyrd, Way begun!*
*Wild wolves all free*
*One wild pack are we*
*So mote it be!*

All howl!

When all is done, all stand about the stang and rumble for a time as the beta drums slow, vibrating open palm taps, bringing all energy down, down ... down.

The alpha begins to slowly do three AHhhhh HAaaaa vibrations and the pack all joins in, all touching the stang together. The candle in the stang is extinguished by the alpha and all do a low long down-howl and begin to let go of the shapeshift.

All then touch the earth and vibrate MA MA MA with final drumming and all is grounded. All stand and shake themselves and shake away their werewolf forms as mist evaporating.

Things are cleaned up, organized, packed and so on. The last of the wine and food is poured out with barks and yips of thanks. All take their charms off the stang and put them on. Organic offerings like flowers and appropriate food are scattered in the woods. Finally, the stang is pulled out of the earth by the whole pack together with a group HA! Then, still all together, the stang is reversed and the horns are touched to the earth. All visualize the final excess energy flowing into the Earth Mother to empower this place so that it may prosper and remain healthy, then all growl:

*Gaia MA!*
*To You*
*From You*
*All Things*
*MA! MA! MAaaaaa!*

All make sure that nothing that is not natural is packed up, with a final check for anything left behind. Pack it in, pack it out.

Then a big pack hug and howl, and all leave in silence, with the beta slowly and softly drumming as all exit the forest realm, and a final bow to the guardian wolves, powers and spirits, as the lunar doorway closes behind and all go their way.

**Pentagram in Paw**

## Werewolf Pack Seasonal Sabbat Ritual

This pack ritual is suitable for solstices, equinoxes, and other feral or Pagan sacred days such as the fire festivals. This is decided by the pack. At least the solstices and equinoxes should be celebrated by each pack. If separated from the pack or working alone, this ritual can be adapted fairly easily for solo work. It is different from many of our rituals in that it is held during broad daylight, but neither wolves nor werewolves are vampires! Wolves are very active and hunt in the day and there is nothing to stop werewolf magick rituals from being done in the sunshine, though we do love the dark. Day pack hikes, rites, and so on are encouraged. Wolfish Apollo[28] was honored by ancients, as are other werewolf magick solar deities. As with all else, this ritual can be changed and added to as the pack decrees.

## Set Up

Sabbats, like esbats, are held in the pack rally grove or in a wooded sacred place that has been consecrated and empowered. It should, if possible, be held on a sunny day with a fairly clear sky. Fall and winter sabbats may call for warmer clothing and so on that spring and summer sabbats. Plan accordingly. The ritual area, be it the rally grove or another, should be checked out and the layout discussed since this is a fairly complex ritual and may require a bit more planning and organization by the whole pack. Unlike esbats, pack friends can be invited to sabbats if they are trustworthy and interested, if the whole pack agrees.

One decision that will change the ritual is whether the shrine is used. It is wise to use the shrine for some sabbats like solstices and equinoxes, ley liminal moments when the power of the shrine is useful, but as always, it is up to the pack.

## Items Needed

The stang.

The pack drum.

Several seasonal flower or leaf wreaths that are small and hand made.

**Note:** Each sabbat will call for different flowers or greenery, holly or pine for winter solstice for example. All used should be available in nature at that time.

Flowers or greenery appropriate for that Sabbat.

Five natural beeswax candles.

---

28. Sargent, *Werewolf Magick*, 13.

A lot of good, natural food like fruits, bread, cakes, berries and dried or
  cooked meat and a variety of drinks.

Small plates or bowls for offerings to the gods.

Larger platters and so on for the feasting food.

A sacred, natural cup or drinking bowl used for rites.

One of the three werewolf magick staves, depending on the sabbat (red stave
  for spring and summer sabbats, black for fall and winter sabbats, and white
  for liminal sabbats that are neither solstices or equinoxes, traditionally
  called cross quarter sabbats).

Dried rosemary with appropriate flower petals and a small bowl to burn it in.

Pure water to drink.

Small sabbat blessing gifts for all appropriate to the season for all (small pack-
  ets of seeds, shells, decorated eggs, polished stones, chocolates and so on).

A cloth of appropriate color for laying out items on.

Wine or mead of any sorts, chosen for whichever sabbat it is.

The shrine (if being used as the altar).

*Optional:* Any divination system desired, but the werewolf magick oracle is
  best.

## THE RITUAL

With much in tow, the pack arrives at the rally grove or other wild ritual area
on a day close to or on the equinox, solstice or other high holy day. Set up
should begin late morning or midday, depending on how long everyone wants
the ritual and party to run. Trusted non-wer pack friends can help set up and
bring up the rear.

The alpha enters the sacred space first and holds the stang while the beta (or
another) has the drum. As the pack is about to enter the path to the sacred place,
all pause, rumble, and think intently of the image of the Fool tarot card. Each
visualizing him or herself as the Fool but also as the wolf running next to the
fool, the wolfish dog being the Animalself. The beta slowly taps on the drum, all
"see" the fool and wolf becoming one on the great journey still rumbling.

Then, the alpha pours out some sacred wine on the path and growls the following and repeat line by line:

*To our Human selves, To our Animalselves.*
*To the Wildness, Wyrd and Way of ourselves*
*We enter the liminal Shapeshifting Way*
*To honor our wild gods with whom we play!*

All up howl.

All bow to the Lord of the Forest to make the "leap" into the liminal spirit world for this sabbat and all vibrate a log growled HAaaaaaaa honoring and calling that god.

All wait. There will be a response of some kind from the forest, then all may enter.

The pack goes to the center of the place and stands in a circle.

The alpha raises the stang and all up howl three times calling forth the Wildness, Wyrd, and Way. Non-wer pack friends, if present, form an outer ring and observe. They may howl along. The pack then does the up growl banishing rite.

The altar (or the shrine) is set up in the center of the space while the beta ritually drums a slow relaxing beat and all wers rumble during the whole set up from then on.

Ritual items may be laid out as desired and all is prepared: the herb in the burning bowl, candles set up in holders (one ready in the center), the sacred cup has clean water in it, small bowls for offerings to the gods and food for the feast is arranged on various small and large platters and various drinks as well and so on. Flowers, tree greenery, other decorations are also set up and all else. When done, the pack forms a circle around the altar or shrine, still rumbling and begins to sway in sync to the tapping of the drum until the alpha, standing in the center, raises the stang and all becomes silent.

Next comes the invoking of the four quarters: As the invoking proceeds, all the wers will visualize brilliant sunlight pouring down and forming mighty, glowing, werewolf spirit guardians sitting at each quarter.

The alpha holds the stang by the base and thrust it out, horns first, to each cardinal direction in turn, beginning with the east. The alpha growls the following and the pack repeats each line as the stang is thrust to each direction and all howl as each guardian appears! Thus:

(To the East)

*Apollo Lycaeus Empower us! (all howl)*

(To the South)

*Lupercus Empower us! (all howl)*

(To the West)

*Apollo Cunomaglos Empower us!! (all howl)*

(To the North)

*Soranus Apollo Empower us!! (all howl)*

(In the center, pointing stang to the sun)

*Apollo Lycaeus Empower us! (all howl)*

Then the whole pack, open paws wide, calls forth the Lord of the Forest by loudly growling three long HAaaaaa as the alpha sticks the stang into the earth behind the altar (or shrine).

The alpha takes up the cup and walks clockwise around the pack and pours out the water in a circle as all loudly growl AH … three times.

Then the pack with paws to the ground about the altar or shrine loudly growls MAaaaaa three times to honor and awaken the Earth Mother.

The alpha places flowers on the altar and then lights the candle.

Then the pack comes together about the altar or shrine and, arms locked or holding paws, all growl RAaaaaa very loudly three times, leaning into the center and intensely call in the Great Wolf Spirit, visualizing the wolf deity in his fiery solar form.

Then all break apart, howling.

All then do the Praxis Rite, standing in a circle about the altar or shrine.

The pack continues to sway and rumble as the alpha takes the drum and carefully treads the circumference of the area clockwise while he or she slowly and loudly vibrates AHhhhhh … HAaaaaa … MAaaaa … RAaaaa … while slowly drumming and so casts a circle of solar energy about the entire area with a final AH-Haaaaaa! as he returns to the pack.

All loudly reply AH-HAaaaaa!

Then all growl chant together:

*Sun and Moon, Silver and gold*
*The Wildness is young*
*The Wolf Spirit is old*
*As packs all gather*
*We come and go*
*Howling together*
*May wildness flow!*

All up howl several times!

Each wer then in turn approaches the altar or shrine and places a flower or looped wreath on the stang with a few growled words, howls and growls and gestures honoring the primal gods and goddesses of this sabbat. As each item is offered, all others respond with a joyous barking!

If pack friends are present, they can each give similar offerings and pay honor the same way to the gods and goddesses of nature.

## The Casting of the Triskele

Now, the pack friends return to the circumference and the alpha takes up the appropriate stave and goes to the north.

The beta takes up the drum and begins to drum an appropriate beat while the alpha growls loudly:

*Silver goddess three*
*Hidden by the sun*
*Bring down the power*
*O Shining Silver One*

*Open the magick flower!*
*The Wildness has begun!*

The beta continues to appropriately drum during the following, changing the rhythm and pace as appropriate and drums more intensely when the pack loudly growls responses.

Beginning at a place to the north, several steps from the altar, one of the wers takes the white stave and draws a clockwise spiral upon the earth that extends and connects the glowing line to the shrine, seeing the lunar power flow through this image.

As this is being done, the whole pack growls repeatedly growls AH AH AH which peaks when the wer leans the stave on the stang or shrine and raises his or her paws.

Another wer takes up the red stave and, beginning at a place to the southeast on the edge of the circle, draws a clockwise spiral upon the earth that then extends and connects the glowing line to the shrine, seeing the red power of life flow through this line.

As this is being done, the whole pack repeatedly growls HA HA HA which peaks when the wer leans the stave on the stang or shrine and raises his or her paws.

Another wer takes up the black stave and, beginning at a place to the southwest on the edge of the circle, draws a clockwise spiral upon the earth that then extends and connects the glowing line to the shrine, seeing the purple spirit of deep life flow through this line.

As this is being done, the whole pack repeatedly growls MA MA MA, which peaks when the wer leans the stave on the stang or shrine and raises his or her paws.

The beta lowers the intensity of the drumming here. The pack reforms into a circle about the altar or shrine and sways in sync and rumbles loudly.

As the invocation begins, the drumming becomes louder and more intense with the pack echoing, "Arise and awake!"

The alpha growl chants the following while the pack growls and repeats line by line:

*Lady Trikona, Threefold Gate*
*Three Faced Wolf, Lady Fate*
*Blazing Power Of Wild-Earth*
*Wyrd Arise, Together Rebirth*
*Great Forest Sing*
*Earth Mother Quake*
*Great Wolf God*
*Arise And Awake!!!*
*Arise And Awake!!!*
*Arise And Awake!!!*

Drumming stops. All howl! Visualize a glowing wolf eye symbol filling the circle as the Great Wolf Spirit manifests through the pack. glowing with power.

The pack begins to loudly up growl together in rhythm RA RA RA ... first quietly, then louder and louder and begin dancing in place in full werewolf forms and finally howling like mad!

The alpha takes the drum from the beta and begins a lighter, more joyous rhythm and the beta loudly growls the invocation of the Lord of the Forest with all repeating line by line:

*Great Primal Green One*
*By Our Blood Blessed*
*Howler Born Of Sun*
*Lord Of The Forest*
*God Of All Trees*
*Silvanus, Faunus, Pan*
*Hear Now Our Pleas*
*O Lykos Wolf-Man*
*Feral God Frey*
*We Dance Now with Thee*
*Wolf Gold And Wolf Grey*
*So Mote It Be!*

The alpha begins a solid, slow rhythm now. All the wers reach paws out open wide and growl HA HA HA while swaying in sync.

All continue to growl HA, and both the drumming in rhythm and the growl chants get slowly louder. Finally, the growl-chanting and drumming reach a crescendo and all face outward toward the woods and howl HAAAAAA! invoking the wild Lord of the Forest to come. Then, silence!

There will be a sign when he arrives.

When this happens, all howl wildly and now bring the friends of the pack into the circle and get them to join in wolfish rocking and growling HA HA HA with fun and laughter and so on as the beta begins drumming appropriate up beat rhythms as all dance.

As this goes on, the alpha lights more of the herbal petal mix again and has one pack wer carry it, swaying and weaving a bit like, a slow dance about the circle going clockwise, still growling HA HA HA and making sure every wer and guest receives a blessing from the smoking mixture they carry. Another wer is then given the lit candle and does the same.

Finally, the alpha takes up the cup, fills it with wine and does the same, weaving about the circle clockwise, growling HA, offering wine to the stang, and making sure all the wers and humans are blessed with it. Each may sip of the cup or have a touch of wine on their forehead as they wish. In this way, all honoring the feral gods and goddesses of the Sabbat and receive their blessings from werewolves!

When the alpha sees that all the elements have been circulated and all have been blessed, then the burning bowl is brought to the altar or shrine and is offered to the gods about and set down. The same is then done with the candle and finally the alpha sprinkles some wine on the stang and on the altar or shrine.

All then come together, wer and guests, and all repeatedly, howl creating complex harmonies and wolfish songs as they dance about, laugh and the sabbat relaxes into wildness!

Drumming continues as others clap, pound rhythm sticks, get out and play flutes, pipes, and bells and make music as all dance and have fun with laughter and all kinds of wolfish sounds.

The feast begins soon after with wine, mead, beer, juices, spring water and other liquids are poured into cups and handed around until all present have one, then the alpha leads a toast: TO WILDNESS! And all present growl TO WILDNESS! The alpha then growls TO THE WYRD! and all growl back with howls. Then the alpha loudly growls TO THE WAY! and all growl back with howls, downing their beverages.

More toasts or blessings are made by any others who wish to do so, then food is offered to all and all fall to eating, drinking and making merry. The smoking herb is passed about, if it is acceptable, with a loud AH-HA! Which all repeat as it is passed about to those who wish it with added howling or growling they wish.

When the feasting, talking, singing, and so on is done, the alpha cues the beta who begins to drum a simple but fun rhythm and the pack wers pick up rattles or rhythm sticks or begin to clap as the alpha stands and growls the following, all present repeating each line:

*Wildness and Wyrd, now flows through me!*
*Unleash the wolf and so be free*
*By sacred signs: moon, sun and tree*
*Faunus Lycan flows through thee!*

All howl as the howling, barking and rhythmic music explodes with lots of deep rhythmic down growls. A space is gently made in the center of the craziness by the alpha. All the pack wers deepen their trance states and open to the voices of the wild gods and the Great Wolf Spirit, then, one at a time, each wers leaps into the middle of the circle and spontaneously channels invocations, songs, poetry, nonverbal wer chants and so on as they are filled with the Wildness! In response, the rest howl or bark or yip!

When the trance-chants and possessions end, then the alpha leaps into the middle and begins to wildly dance, signaling all to join in. Those keeping the beat can do so while dancing as well! Clothing may fly off, howling, barking, growling, and so on rises and from then on, all dance for a time, clap, sway, leap and spin as wers gently encourage the human pack friends present to join in and let loose. When things begin to relax into conversations, more feasting, and conviviality, the beta picks up the drum and begins a quieter beat.

When it is time to end the festivities, the alpha gives a long, quiet up howl and all the wers of the pack join in. Then each wer makes a final bow and low up howl of thanks to the gods before the altar. Guests may do this as well, and are invited to do so. When offerings are done, small blessing gifts are then shared all around to everyone.

Pack members and human guests, if they choose, all stand in a circle about the altar or shrine, hold hands, and center themselves rumbling. After a time, with a cue from the alpha, all let loose three up howls of joy and then three long, low down growls to calm the wild energies and ground the powers. Human guests can follow along as they like.

Still holding hands, the alpha lets go of one hand and, begins a low growl chant of HA HA HA … and slowly begins a counterclockwise spiral walk that movies out and out, around and around, ever widening until it reaches the circumference the area, then the alpha gently reverses the "snake" and begins to spiral back in clockwise, all *now repeatedly intoning MA MA MA* as they all spiral in toward the center where the altar is, continuously growling MA MA MA … until all again form a circle about the altar. Then *all* touch the earth, growling:

*Mother Gaia!*
*To You,*
*From You,*
*All Things-MAaaaaaa!*

The candle is blown out, the last of the wine poured out, and all join in three loud up howls. The pack then does the end of the Praxis Rite and shakes and growls until the shapeshift trance is gone and then mingles with the guests.

When ready to end things, all together pack up, pick up, and clean up the whole area leaving all as it was. Appropriate natural food is offered to the woodland and animals at the end.

The beta or another lightly drums during as all winds down and, when all are ready to go, it is a time for a group pack hug that may include the pack friends if they wish.

All now leave with gentle drumming and "see" the sparkling motes of the gold and greenish glow of the forest and the earth and the Wildness spiral about them, spreading into the lives and woodland dreams of all who wish to again be wild.

Astral Wer

## Werewolf Pack Astral Temple Gathering Rite

Werewolf magick is about astral, etheric or energetic, lycanthropic magickal activity or work.

Much of the work mentioned so far has been etheric or energetic, working with the spiritual essence or energetic wolf-self, wearing that etheric shapeshift skin and shifting mental modality. Astral work is free of the ego and of the physical and even mental bodies. In dream, we can activate and build awareness into our werewolf form and actually become it and move or work with it out of the body. This is called the Double[29] and is often molded into a wolfish

---

29. Sargent, *Werewolf Magick*, 127.

form and used to travel astrally. Mastering work with the Double in this way aids greatly the magick of astral projection and sending our wolfish spirit self out for distance viewing or working with various energy forces and beings out-of-body.

## Set Up

This is one of those workings that may be done in dream or trance states with some preparation and focus. If you are well-versed in astral projection or distance viewing, it can be done in a secure protective circle or temple of your choice.

There is a special place on the astral plane and in dreamtime for werewolves and wolf-shifters to gather and bond, dance, communicate, make love, play, or tussle as they will.

I have been there. It is quite clear and easy to visualize for those versed in werewolf magick, and when you find it you will know.

Only those in wer or wolf form are welcome and human-forms may be scared away, chased or, I'm guessing, possibly eaten!

## Items Needed

A visible full moon is best.

A safe place that is warm, comfortable and in darkness.

A time when you will be completely undisturbed, a safe quiet place, with fresh air.

A trance, liminal or dream state.

A simple ritual to protect your space and your body.

Three clear glasses.

A glass container of moonwater (water that has spent the night under a full or near full moon or which was charge in an applicable ritual[30]) used for:

- Two glasses of pure water on either side of your resting or trance space.
- One glass of pure water is nearby with lemon in it to drink later and some chocolate.
- Whatever werewolf charm or talisman you have already created.

---

30. See Bonding with the Moon Mothers Rite in Chapter 3.

- A werewolf power candle [31] or another candle that's been charged (unless you are doing dreamwork)
- A mental image of the Moon tarot card.

## The Rite

Magickally banish and protect the area as you like. You may use the oft-used Up Growl Banishing found in the Appendix. Visualize the trident-like algiz rune glowing at the four directions protecting you. If you are not sleeping but doing this as a trance-state ritual practice, Light the candle and offer any prayers or statements of intention you wish, especially directed to the Moon Goddess and the Lord of the Forest who you may call by the name Faunus Lycan.

Algiz Rune

When you are in a full trance or altered liminal state, or just before full sleep, call on all your werewolf magick skill and power you learned from shapeshifting practice to mentally and psychically transform your astral self to the shifted werewolf form you usually "wear" when shapeshifting actively.

Your astral form or spirit will now be in wer form. You see yourself transformed and feel your fur, paws, claws, tail and so on. When you have centered yourself and truly feel your astral body is a werewolf, visualize the Moon tarot card, with some differences. The two towers are now stone pillars, ancient menhirs.

The full moon above them is very large and luminous and there are massive pine trees on either side and all around you. You stand on a rocky path, you are in the mountains, on either side of the path a creek flows away from you, toward the rising moon.

You move forward ... you drift slightly upward, floating.

---

31. Sargent, *Werewolf Magick*, 173.

You pass the stone pillars and, as you do, the moon fills all and you pass into pure moonlight.

You are heading to the timeless Wolf Mountain, the legendary Mount Lykaion.

Soon, as your astral spirit glides forward, you find yourself within a stone henge circle, quite large, amid the mountains and pines. The full moon is now directly overhead. The area is covered in grass and smells fresh and intoxicating. Around the edge of the circle, you "see" blooming wolfsbane.

You are not alone.

Other werewolves of all kinds are materializing or flowing into the stone circle.

In the center of the circle is a larger, flat stone: the altar. Upon it are wild greens, berries, roots and a freshly killed deer, a gift of Artemis. At the foot of the altar is a large stone basin of spring water.

The sky above is clear and full of stars as well as the moon. The air is fresh, clean, and cool. It is filled with the scents of fresh greenery, rich soil and the smells of many wild animals you can now identify.

You are on a wooded plateau of Wolf Mountain. Faintly you see the misty peak of the mountain behind you and you see the wild forests on rolling hills spread out below, shimmering in the moonlight. The gentle pine scented breeze stirs the trees about you. You hear the distant howling of wild wolves drifting in the wind.

Enter and do as you will. As more and more werewolves appear, there is soon a circle about the altar and at some point, growls, yips, and such are stilled.

One wolf—maybe you—will raise his or her hairy arms and begin the howl.

All will join in. Who can say how long it will go?

Then all of you werewolves will dance.

Who can say for how long or in what manner? You will see.

Then, all will pile about the altar, a pack bonding.

Then, you will all fall upon the food and rip, tear, chew, gulp, and lap fresh water. After the wild feasting, all will in turn offer water to the moon above in cupped paws and drink and clean their muzzles, paws, and fur.

The rest of the evening is up to you.

You may cavort with another werewolf, have mental telepathic conversations, seek-out the wisest wer and receive wisdom or spells or curses or special symbols.

You may want to scry into the water basin when it has become calm and full of moonlight.

You may want to leave a sigil or stone or chant upon the altar, arms outstretched to the Moon Lady and the Lord of the Forest about you.

If you have a pack of werewolf magick friends, you can all arrange to meet here and do spell or ritual work here together.

This astral temple is real and the more you visit it, the clearer and more potent it will be.

Someday, you might be able to see and understand the strange runes carved upon the altar thousands of years ago, when Wolf Mountain was blessed and made sacred by the horned wild god with his moon lady.

If you are in full dream, what happens will happen and when you awake, make sure to write it down in your journal.

If you are in a trance or liminal state, when you feel it is time to go, follow this simple protocol.

Back up to the edge of the circle.

Raise your arms up and howl projecting GRATITUDE TO YOU! All the other wers present will howl back.

Raise your arms up again and howl projecting BLESSINGS AND JOY TO YOU!. All the other wers present will howl back.

Raise your arms up one last time and howl projecting FARE WELL, WE ARE PACK! All the other wers present will howl back loud!

Turn and face the wooded darkness. The moon is now behind you but little light is visible.

Begin walking forward through the two stone pillars on either side.

With every step, the scene fades, the light fades, and you are on a gray-lit trail. You hear trickling water flowing on either side. Soon, you are in your ritually protected place. Enter your body.

Awaken slowly, quickly reach for your journal and pen, and write down everything.

Symbols, spells, words of power, omens, and such that you gained from the experience will be very important and useful later on.

As you arouse, sip the lemon water and eat the chocolate.

When fully "back" to yourself, banish your area, maybe burn some sage or rosemary and cense yourself. Afterward, take the glasses of water on either side of you and pour them at the roots of a tree outside.

**Note:** This can be done as a group practice. If so, do the following:

All lay with your heads in the center, outside is best, but in a large, warm room on something comfortable is fine.

Use four glasses of water at the four quarters, not two.

Have a large silver or glass bowl in the center filled with lemon water and a small plate of chocolates. This will be for all to share after. Next to the bowl and the plate, set the werewolf candle to be lit as the rite begins.

It is important if you do this with your pack that you all return, awaken, have some water and chocolate in silence, and write in your individual journals in silence.

Then, go around the circle and each reads their visions and experiences and share what they saw or received or understood. This is all very important. Your pack will weave new magicks and rites from this sort of work with the werewolf gnosis.

When done, banish as you will as a group and do the three howls goodbye howls:

All raise arms up and howl together projecting *Gratitude!*

All raise arms up again and howl together projecting *Blessings and Joy!*

All raise arms up one last time and howl together projecting *Farewell, we are pack!*

Group wolf pack hug, for this is the way of every pack.

Banish then as you will, taking smoldering sage or rosemary about the circle for all to immerse in is a nice ending. Maybe finish with the Up Growl Banishing to be thorough. All the wers take the leftover water outside and pour it with prayers of low up howls and chants of AHhhhh ... HAaaaa ... RAaaa! to the Moon, Forest and Wolf God, ending with a touching of the Earth and a long MAaaa! to ground yourselves.

## Pack Scrying Ritual

Scrying is the ancient art of peering into the astral plane or spirit world through a ritual portal of some kind, like a crystal ball, a dark pool of water, a mirror, or a black mirror. Our scrying rite is used for pack divination to receive omens and messages from the Great Wolf Spirit or from another of our feral deities or nature spirits. Scrying is often used by individual sorcerers and each wer can certainly use this rite to scry alone, but using it with the whole pack brings much increased intensity, magick, and focus. It also offers spiritual information for the whole pack on many levels.

### SET UP

As the pack becomes more attuned to each other, shared Instinct, Intuition, and Insights become more and more common and telepathy, intense empathy and a deep, primal, unconscious binding occurs. These things benefit all pack members, grow the egregore of the pack, and offer more powers and protection. As with any small, tight-knit magickal group, powerful ritual work binds and interpenetrates the individual wers and, more importantly, enhances and empowers each wer's Animalself. Werewolf pack magick, being based on unified and bonded Animalselves, makes all magick and visions deeper and more prescient. Scrying as a pack becomes not just an exploration of the spirit world or communion with a divinity, but also deepens the pack bond on many levels.

This rite utilizes traditional runic Norse magickal words of power from a *seidr* runic master (and my magickal brother) Shade Vedhrfolnir who approved of and supported *Werewolf Magick*. He passed away last year, and his posthumous book is cited and in the bibliography. May Odin the great God of Wolves guide him to the realm of heroes.

Conjure Wheel

## Items Needed

A black scrying portal. This can be fashioned of ceramic, glass, or wood painted or stained black. The best portal is a black mirror, which is often a circular piece of glass or, best, a large (on to two feet) clock face glass whose concave side has been carefully painted black.

The following rune conjure wheel should be ritually drawn or painted on the back of the item and this portal should be empowered with a Talismanic Blessing Rite before the scrying session.[32] Once charged and blessed, it can be used as many times as needed by the pack as a whole or borrowed and used by individual members. It also is kept by the alpha along with other pack tools. It will grow in potency and power the more it is used.

A bottle of pond or lake water collected by a pack member on or near a full moon with a simple impromptu werewolf magick thank you honoring the Moon Goddess and the spirit of the lake.

Some sea salt.

---

32. See the Blessing Ritual for Werewolf Magick Tools in the Appendix.

A private natural gathering place, with a crosspath if possible, but three inter-
   secting paths is best. The rally grove is perfect, of course, but another will do.

The black stave of Hekate, the white stave of Artemis and the red stave of
   Selene. All three staves will be laid around the scrying bowl or mirror in this
   order. The "right one," depending on the moon phase when this rite is held,
   is placed to the north.

An herb that aids scrying (cut with a ritual knife on a dark moon with a simple
   prayer and offering to Hekate and then dried). Mullen, wormwood, rue or
   dried willow leaves all work well individually or in a mixture.

A burning bowl.

Journals and pens.

The stang.

The ritual pack cup.

Very dark wine (a small sprig of wormwood can be added to soak in it).

A ritual plate with all natural food.

The pack drum.

A tall beeswax candle, black if possible.

A black altar cloth or a flat stone or wood altar.

The best time for scrying is when the veil between the worlds is thin, on the
   dark moon. However, depending on the goal, scrying can be done on the
   full moon or waxing crescent moon. The moon phase chosen for this is
   shown by which stave is placed to the north behind the portal.

For focus, an original werewolf magick icon or glyph can be drawn on a piece
   of bark or natural paper and used to focus on a particular subject. Briefly,
   here are the choices as shown in the Appendix, or the pack can create its
   own specific symbol or sigil for the scrying:

   *The Triskele:* Calling Wildness, Wyrd, and Way for visions concerning the
      growth and power of the pack and how to solve issues.

   *The Wolf Paw:* For solutions and strength concerning choices, overcoming
      difficulties, pack dynamics or power.

   *The Werewolf Fangs:* For visions concerning attacks, protection, banishing,
      or righteous cursing for those harming the pack.

*The Eye of the Wolf:* For visions from the Great Wolf Spirit or the Lord of the Forest regarding important work or decisions or just to learn something very necessary.

*The Claw Slash:* Divining which enemies or negative forces may be problematic or interfering with the pack or seeking visions on how to repel and banish evil.

*The Pentagram in Paw:* To learn of occult powers, special spells, arcane rites and guidance in our feral magick from all the werewolf magick powers.

*The Lit Stang:* For direct communion with and visions from the Lord of the Forest, the great horned god of Wildness, good for visions on increasing Animalself work and anything having to do with the wilderness, animals or the environment.

*The Triple Moon:* To learn deep astral wisdom concerning shapeshifting, spell work, emotional and physical ecstasy and all moon magicks.

*The Wolf Triquetra:* For direct visions from the Great Wolf Spirit and the egregore of the pack, especially on how to guide or better the pack and gain more power, ability and unity.

Finally, all participating wers should be somewhat familiar with scrying or divination trance work before the rite is done. A lot of information on scrying exists in books and on websites, several will be noted in the bibliography. Any pack member who has shown great skill in this art can take time to discuss it and to coach the whole pack on how to scry. It is expected that every pack member will excel in a variety of occult skills and that all will share and mentor one another, this being an important point of a pack!

## THE RITUAL

In silence, all go to the place where the scrying will be done carrying all the items.

One pack member carries the staves and another carries the bottles of the sacred water that were gathered. The alpha carries the drum and stang.

Once all arrive, a simple altar is erected to the north of the center, with all items on it, except the portal and scrying symbol. The alpha or another then lights the candle on the altar along with the herbs in the burning bowl and wine is poured into the cup. When done, all gently up howl three times.

Then the portal with the symbol on bark or paper atop it, is placed in the center of the sacred area by the alpha and all stand about it and, turning face out, do the Up-growl Banishing. Then, facing inward again, all do a long, slow version of the Praxis Rite with the alpha tapping the drum in a soft rhythm in sync with the shifting rite.

When done, the pack sways and growls HA HA HA as the alpha walks clockwise around the pack casting and sealing the circle.

The alpha rejoins the pack and, still tapping on the drum, now sets a rhythm while the swaying pack rumble-growls repeatedly as all become more deeply entranced and the shifting deepens. The alpha then stops drumming as the pack continues to rumble and sway, lays the drum down and goes and gets the staves and brings them back and lays them down about the portal, with the correct stave to the north and altar and the others finishing the triangle. When done, their paws are raised, and all low up howl three times, welcoming the Moon Mothers, and then all sit down about the portal in attentive silence.

The alpha takes up the symbol on the piece of bark or paper and holds up to the pack. All begin a quiet deep rumble while the scrying sigil is then passed around clockwise to each wer who stares at it deeply and imprints it and hands it to the next wer. When it returns to the alpha, he or she lifts up the portal and places it on the ground in the center and then carefully places the portal on top of it to center the energies in the circle. Still rumbling, all close their eyes and clearly hold and visualize the symbol they imprinted for this scrying session. After a few minutes, the alpha low-growls RA as a cue and all open their eyes and lean forward and together up growl RA RA RA! three times, sanctifying the space and invoking the Wildness, Wyrd, and Way to open the astral gate for scrying.

All then begin to gently rock forward and back and rumble as they slowly slide deeper into shifting trance and stare into the depths of the portal and the alpha joins in.

The rumbling soon fades into silence and all open their third eyes and focus on the portal and through their Animalself, project first the symbol that had been imprinted, and let it sink and disappear into the void.

As this happens, all growl AH-HA...

Then, all dive into the portal in silence, seeking visions.

All is silent for a time as the pack psychically slides down into the portal.

Each wer feels the energy of the woods, the earth and the moon swirling about them and filling them like a loving breeze and helping them open and dive deeper into this astral dimension. Then, suddenly, visions will start appearing and erupting. The alpha quietly begins rumbling when this psychic shift is felt and all begin to rumble. The alpha deeply growls the following and all growl repeat the following:

*Tawo Lathodu!*[33]
*So Begins this Rite!*

(pause)

*Ulf Hamingja!*
*Wolf Magick Manifest!*

(long pause)

*Ulf Alugod!*[34]

All growl louder together: *Ulf Alugod!!*
All howl this together: ULF ALUGOD!

Then silence as all stare deep and open to the visions that are becoming vivid, intense, and potent. All begin rumbling as they are filled with the magick and visionary consciousness arising from the black depths. They become open

---

33. Norse terms followed by translation from Norse to English, both spoken in the ritual.
34. Good Wolf (Spirit) arise!

to the spirits and the power flowing out of the depths of the portal. If this is not successful or doesn't happen, then the portal is closed and the rite is ended.

This continues in silence until the alpha feels the energy beginning to fade and knows that the visions are receding. Then the alpha takes up the drum and begins to tap it and rumble growl to help the visions withdraw and help all the wers come back slowly into their bodies. As they do so, they join the rumble growl until all are rumbling and the visions flow back into the portal and begin to fade into the darkness from which they came. Then the alpha begins to deeply down growl in earnest and all join in as powers contract and sink into the vessel and the alpha's drumming becomes stronger until, with one strike, the portal is closed as the alpha loudly growls AH-HA! AH-HA! AH-HA! which the pack echoes in response. The portal is closed. This ends the session.

The pack then returns to rumbling, thus bringing themselves back into their bodies and earthing themselves. After a time, with the pack still sitting and rumbling, the alpha rises, picks up the portal, and moves it to the altar, leaving the symbol face down. The alpha returns with the container of water and then walks about the outside of the circle, dribbling water counterclockwise behind the pack and sprinkling each grumbling wer as well to help bring them back to their bodies and finally sprinkles his or her head and body. The alpha then takes up the symbol, burns it in the center of the pack circle and pours water over the ashes so it all sinks into the earth.

The whole pack then growls MAaaaa. All then stand and raise their arms and howl three times while the alpha bangs the drum loudly, once for each howl. All shake their bodies and let the energy left over fly free. The alpha then loudly growls the following and the pack repeats it:

*Ulf He Gina!*
*Holy Wolf Power is Finished!* [35]

Then all stand and again shake vigorously and stamp paws growling MA MA MA as the last bits of the shifting and trance flow into Mother Earth. And each wer lets his or her Animalself retreat inside them and all come back to

---

35. Norse terms followed by translation; both spoken during the ritual.

being semi-human. The last part of the Praxis Rite can then be done to finish the process.

Then all then sit and relax, drink some wine or other liquids, eat some food, smoke if appropriate and more of the herb is lit in the burning bowl and all cense themselves as they like. At this point, everyone should take some quiet time to write their visions into their journals as they drink, nibble, and so on.

When all are done with noting their visions down, each in turn tells about their visions, the alpha being the last. The pack then compares, discusses and decides what they think the visions mean or portend or teach the pack in terms of what was asked. Special attention should be given to similarities in symbols and visions! This is an indication of success.

This is a time now to relax, eat, party, sing, play, whatever the pack desires. All will be a bit drained however, so a mellow time is expected. When all agree that it is time to end it, the pack goes to the altar and thanks the gods who protect them by together growling:

AH (Paws in the air toward the moon)

HA (Paws out toward the forest)

RA (Head back, claws out, honoring the Wolf Spirit)

MA (All touching the earth)

The candle is blown out, all made safe and packed up, leftover natural food, offered to spirits and woodland critters, and a final check to make sure all is clean and free of debris.

When all are ready to go, the pack stands in a circle and all hug and rumble together with a final howled AH-HA! The pack then goes forth in silence. All should pay attention to their dreams that night and note them down to share at the next gathering.

## CHAPTER 5

# PACK RITES AND RITUALS
# OF TRANSFORMATION

————————————— )( —————————————

In researching werewolf magick I was floored by how many amazing were-wolf rituals and sects there were. Thanks to many ancient historians and anthropologists and historians, we know more than I would have believed possible about things like werewolf induction and possible initiation rituals and festivals. *Werewolf Pack Magick* grew out of my desire to try and revive these old rituals as best I could with whatever information I could glean from historical documents and personages like Swedish priest Olaus Magnus who wrote about the following induction rite [36] so clearly that it was fairly easy to revive, rewrite, and update in my own way. Most of the following rituals are mostly my creation and worked and reworked by myself, but based on what was noted in the past as real werewolf magick.

## Rite to Induct a New Pack Member

*"To become a werewolf, the werewolf-to-be has to share a mug of beer with an experienced werewolf who has to recite a certain spell while doing this."*
—*Olaus Magnus, 1555* [37]

---

36. de Blécourt, *Werewolf Histories*, 209.
37. Ibid.

## Set Up

Pack members may have some concerns about sharing one mug of beer at these times, even if all are vaccinated (which would be best). A brief conversation should be had, also with the newbie, because personal sharing in this way is a key part of the rite. One solution, though impersonal, is to share the group beer among several small cups, though with all the close howling, I wonder if it makes a difference. This is up to the pack.

When a person wishes to join a werewolf magick pack, he or she must be vetted and accepted by the pack before the actual pack initiation ritual. He or she must be checked out for a time by a pack member, vetted, and found acceptable. After that, they must casually meet the rest of the pack in a neutral setting and generally fit in. Once the pack has agreed to seriously consider the newbie for full initiation, this induction rite is the next step and is scheduled as close to a full moon as possible. A meeting of the pack with the newbie is arranged at the old school tavern which, if possible, reflects feral beastie aesthetics. If the newbie is really interested, a copy of *Werewolf Magick* should be given to him or her if they don't have it and it should be read by the newbie before the induction. After this social induction rite, the newbie has a month to commit to initiation or pass on it, as does the pack. Hanging out in the meantime, even coming to a pack ritual as a guest, is recommended during this "probationary" time.

## Items Needed

An awesome beer mug with a wolf image on it. Extra points if it is crafted in
  the shape of a wolf's head. This will be given to the new inductee at the
  end of this short rite.
As rustic a tavern or pub as you can find with really good beers, ales on tap.
  If you can reserve a larger table ahead of time, great, if not a wer can go
  ahead of time and stake one out.
Possibly a designated pack member driver or drivers, depending on how much
  drinking may occur. Cabs, Lyft, or Uber are excellent options as well.
Appropriately rough wolfish clothing you can wear (wer?) in public without
  people thinking it is Halloween.

## THE RITE

The pack arrives at the tavern a bit early and sets up at a large (hopefully) rough-hewn table with a seat reserved for the new "wolf cub" next to the wer sponsoring him or her. Once the newbie arrives and is hailed with a hearty howl and seated, an excellent beer is ordered in solid mugs, as dark and as natural as possible.

Those who don't drink can, of course, order something else.

When all have ordered at least one delicious beverage, small talk should begin to give way to more serious pack and werewolfery talk.

The new initiate is asked three times by three different people if he or she is sure about joining and asked why. Conversations indicate that it is a serious commitment involving friendship, trust, loyalty and magick.

The new-wolf is informed that they have to be tough, caring, committed to unleashing their Animalself and independent. They should also be deeply attracted to nature and wish freedom from the prevailing cultural norms and restrictions.

With this in mind, the newbie is questioned about their personal interests and skills and how they feel about nature, wild animals and werewolf magick. When all this has been discussed and all the newbie's questions have been answered by the pack, with much teasing and laughing and a bit of bonding, the alpha calls for silence with a growl and asks for a vote on a *provisional* acceptance of this new wolf into the pack. It is stated that the vote must be unanimous for the newbie to get in.

Each wer then votes in turn about the table, raising his or her beer and up growling if they vote yes, those voting not sure put their mug down and cross their arms. One wer will do this as has been secretly planned beforehand, and this one predetermined not sure vote will then grill the wolf pup about werewolf magick, the rules of the pack, and some concerns until that doubtful wer is all convinced! Then all, including the new potential wer, howl together and bang on the table growling HA HA HA!

Another round is called for and soon the pack members begin to gently tap their mugs or fists on the table in rhythm while rocking side to side and rumble, shifting somewhat until the circle is crackling with the werewolf energy.

The special mug with a wolf on it, is then placed in the center of the table by the alpha with the best dark beer or mead poured into it. All continue rocking in sync and shift to up growling as the banging and the up growling and simple shapeshifting get louder and louder.

The alpha then holds this filled wolf mug up and all present howl, and paws out, filling the cup with wild green visualized energy. Then all goes silent.

The alpha then growls the toast and all *but* the new potential wolf cub repeats each line:

*Fang and claw, howl and tail*
*We prowl together, never fail*
*Faunus, Fatuus, Fatuclus* [38] *Free*
*By kiss of cup we join with thee*
*By earth and stang, moon and sun*
*By feral bond, The pack is One!*

All howl!The alpha sips from the cup and passes it to the next wer and so on around the table, all drinking a sip, the last pack member leaves beer, the wolf mug and hands it to the pup and tells him or her to repeat the chant as the alpha growls it again slowly.

The alpha does so and the new wolf repeats each line (with prompts if necessary) and when done, all howl as he drains the last of the mug completely.

The wolf mug is then filled again and goes around again, each pack member sipping and toasting the new wolf pup, he or she growling what words they wish!

All answer with an up growl! When done, the alpha wolf grins and stands and growls:

*By kiss of cup you'll joined us too*
*For now we have accepted you!*
*Together we share the werewolf "curse!"*
*You're with our pack, it could be worse!*

---

38. These are the wolfish gods invoked at Lupercalia.

All howl and laugh! The wolf flagon is then given as a gift to the new wolf, now a pre-initiate wer of the pack. In return, the new pre-initiate wolf should pay for one of the rounds of drinks!

All howl, laugh and have another round as they like and then jabber werewolf lore, jokes and stuff to excite, scare and amuse the newest pack inductee who at this point can ask any questions he or she wants.

This is also a time to discuss the actual initiation ritual and chat about how the pack works and so on. If the new wolf has in fact read *Werewolf Magick*, he or she should begin doing the work as per the alpha's guidance or mentored by another wer in the pack before the actual initiation since shapeshifting will be required! The new inductee is told they have until the next full moon to decide whether they want full initiation, but informative get-togethers beforehand can and should be arranged with the alpha or with another wer.

When all are ready to go, all stand and rock side by side and down growl together, including the newbie, until the alpha raises paws and all slam paws on the table and growl MA MA MA grounding and ending the rite. All stand, howl, tip well and, with laughter, all go forth and likely take an Uber home.

## Werewolf Pack Initiation

*"Evanthes … writes that the Arcadians have a tradition that someone chosen out of the clan of a certain Anthus by casting lots among the family is taken to a certain marsh in that region, and hanging his clothes on an oak-tree swims across the water and goes away into a desolate place and is transformed into a wolf and herds with the others of the same kind for nine years; and that if in that period he has refrained from touching a human being, he returns to the same marsh, swims across it and recovers his shape, with nine years' age added to his former appearance."*

—Pliny, *Natural History* 8.34.1[39]

39. Pliny the Elder, "Natural History 1–11."

*"…these texts seem to describe an ancient ritual…*
*whereby adolescents were initiated into hunting/warrior parties*
*(the 'wolves') before returning to society… "* [40]

This initiation is a way for the initiate to ritually shed the restrictions and bondage of the human-self and thus let go of human limitations while gaining focus and confidence. This empowers the release of the Animalself, like a kind of psychic prison break! This ritual also bonds the initiate deeply with the pack members—Animalself to Animalself—personally, emotionally and magick-ally. It's a powerful, individual, liminal initiation, but also an important rite for the whole pack. The ritual should be done on a hot, clear day in summer or early fall, during the waxing moon, and as close to a full moon as possible. The liminal gateway is noted as a lake but in this ritual, for safety, a pond is recommended. Another choice is a wide, shallow creek or small river that can be safely forged with footwear and maybe a walking stick as well. The water in the pond should be fairly warm and comfortable! Waiting for this sunny day in summer gives the new wolf initiate time to master werewolf magick and the practices of shapeshifting as explained in the book of the same name. The time between the induction rite and the initiation will likely be filled with dis-cussions, camping trips, doing werewolf shapeshifting rituals, and so on. [41] As an inductee who has stated their desire for initiation, the newbie should attend some regular pack rituals during this time and is always encouraged to partic-ipate and ask questions, all before the actual initiation. In this way, the initia-tion, which requires some shapeshifting, will be a success.

## Set Up

Before the initiation, the pack needs to find a small, clean, safe, and beautiful pond that is easy to swim across, or a wide, shallow creek that can be easily forged. It should be in as wooded and secluded a place as possible since a lot of howling and some nudity will be likely involved. There should be a path around the pond as well or an easy ford for the wide creek for set up on the

---

40. Colavito, "The Werewolf in Ancient Greece."
41. Sargent, *Werewolf Magick*, Chapter 5.

other side. There should also be an accessible place to enter the lake or wide creek that is near a large tree. There must also be an open area across the pond or wide creek where the ritual will ritually finish that has space for a small safe fire pit.

If a pond is being swum across, the initiate must be an excellent swimmer and a pack member who is an experienced swimmer will swim all the way across near the initiate for safety. It can be the alpha or another wer, one with lifeguard training is optimal. If there is any trepidation by the initiate during discussions, doing the rite with a wide, shallow, creek is a fine option. All of this, and a check of the upcoming weather, which should be sunny and warm, should be done and discussed before the ritual.

Finally, a couple of pack members will need to prepare the ritual space across the water where the initiate will "land" before the ritual begins. If not possible, then they will have to walk quickly to set things up and start a small safe fire there during the initiate's liminal water "crossing."

## ITEMS NEEDED

A towel or two.

A new simple set of clothes, black, provided by the pack or the initiate.

A set of dry clothes for the alpha or co-swimmer as well.

A red scarf to hang in a tree as a marker.

Fresh water in containers.

Brandy or another rich liquor in a small unbreakable container to warm up the after swimmers (or waders) are done

Dried rosemary and a burning bowl and a lighter

Other sacred herbs of your choice

Each pack member brings their own small sharp ritual knife and one can be brought for the initiate

Ritual drum

Easy to pack natural food like meat jerky, nuts and wild edible berries or whatever you all wish.

Three fresh oak leaves.

The pack icon from the shrine (or the whole shrine)

The stang, the three staves, and a ritual bowl or chalice

Found materials for a simple found-stone or wood altar

### THE RITUAL

All arrive at the path the pond or creek "launching" place together at an agreed upon time, midday is best.

All gather, a big group hug, a howl, and all hike in silence or with rumbling to the pond (or creek), meditating on the importance of the initiation.

Once there, the alpha reviews the steps of the ritual and confirms the place where initiate and alpha will swim across the lake.

Once there, a tree where you will begin your swim (or creek forging), is noted.

During the set-up there will be a small (legal) fire on the other side of the lake and a red scarf to aim for. These are reviewed as well as basic safety rules.

Arriving at the lake or pond, the pack unpacks supplies while the initiate relaxes. When all has been prepared and all know their responsibilities, then the rite begins.

The pack gathers around the new initiate in a circle and then face outward and do the Up Growl Banishing to protect him or her and all present.

Then all face the initiate and all place a paw on him or her and then, including the initiate, all up howl three long howls announcing to all the Wildness, Wyrd and Way to empower and protect the new initiate. Next, all throw their paws in the air and loudly up growl RAaaaa! to invoke the Wolf Spirit and acknowledge that a new wolf is to be initiated.

The alpha offers a little food and some flowers into the pond or river for the spirits of this place and the waters, asking for blessings and success as all growl:

*MA (for Gaia)*

*HA (for the Lord of the Forest)*

*AH (for the Moon Mothers)*

*And a final loud RA (for the Wolf Spirit, paws over initiate)*

Then all, including the initiate who should have mastered this by now, do the Praxis Rite together facing the water.

All pause for a minute and meditate on the beauty of this lovely place. The pack rumble growls together as all reach out with their minds and feel the living trees, plants and wild creatures surrounding them, for all are part of this. Stare into the lake and feel its power and energy. Feel the love and Wildness you share.

At the cue of the alpha, all raise arms and up howl your joy and welcome, then the initiate alone growls the following:

*Spirit of the sky, remember!*
*Spirit of the forest, remember!*
*Spirit of the lake, remember!*
*Spirit of the sun, remember!*
*Spirit of the moon, remember!*
*Spirit of the earth, remember!*
*I come to transform in Wildness!*
*I come to reclaim my Animalself!*
*Spirits of the sky and forest,*
*Of earth and water and light*
*Spirit of the wolf*
*Fill me with your might!*

The initiate is prompted to pour out a bit of brandy into the lake, then splashes abit of water on him or herself, growl shouting:

*Versipellis Est!*
*Versipellis Est!*
*Versipellis Est!* [42]
*FIAT!* [43]

---

42. *A werewolf is here!*
43. *So be it!*

All pack members up growl *Versipellis Est!* In confirmation, it echoes across the pond or creek!

All then wait in silence for the response from the Lord of the Forest. It will come and all will quietly up howl honoring this omen.

At this point, at least one pack member begins to go to the other side of the pond or river as quickly as they can with the items needed. It is best if at least one wer is there before the initiate crosses the water to start a small fire and set things up.

The pack members remaining gather about the initiate and growling loudly, like a pack of wolves, playfully claw and growl at the initiate as he or she strips off most clothing. The alpha or the wer who will accompany the initiate across the water now also strips and both hand their clothes to a pack member for safe-keeping. This wer will carry these items around the pond or creek, catching up with those who are already there preparing the site.

Then, with a raucous howling the initiate followed by the guardian alpha (or other wer) enters the pond and begins to swim or enters the creek and begins to carefully forge the waters.

The rest of the pack is busy now finishing setting up the ritual area across the water where the initiate and guardian; will land, hanging the red scarf on a visible tree to show the swimmers (or those fording the river) where to aim for as they build a small fire.

The rest of the ritual space is then set up. A natural found altar being a found stone or log is set up and everything is laid out as is desired with the shrine and stang upright behind the small altar where the tools, drinks, food, and so on are laid out, as desired. The three staves are stuck into the earth or sand about the fire pit, forming a triangle, the white one nearest the shrine, then red and black.

The pack should then strip as naked as they will, but for amulets and such. They may also decorate their bodies with natural paint, mud, and so on with magick symbols and such. Primal creativity is encouraged. Get as wild and feral as you like!

While this is going on, the beta or another wer takes up the ritual drum, keeps an eye on the swimmers, and gently plays the drum, tapping slowly and calmly in time to their strokes or as is appropriate. The echoing drum transforms the whole area into an otherworldly magickal space.

If a wide shallow creek is being used, the initiate must forge across but may use a walking stick to balance. At the center of the creek, they should splash water over themselves and visualize the shift and the internal invocation. All else is the same.

From the start of the water crossing, the initiate should rumble and deepen his or her shapeshifting trance while also being careful about the crossing while silently mentally repeating in their mind the chant *Versipellis est*, and visualize something like the following:

With each stroke (or step), the wilderness is gently dissolving your restrictions in the water that flows about you as your inner wolf spirit Animalself gently arises in your consciousness as your human self recedes. In this relaxed trance state, you physically focus on the joy of swimming (or forging the river) with great focus. You feel your body shifting with calm ease as you flow through the water. Your growing wolf fur feels lovely, your paws make it easier to move forward, the intense vitality of the wildness all about you fills you with a flood of spiritual and physical life energy. Your animalistic happiness and the physical movement fills you with great joy. You are just a happy werewolf in water, in nature, fully present in this sacred moment…

When the initiate gets to the other side, he or she emerges in full entranced, werewolf form, feeling furred, feral, primal, and happy to burst forth with full intense howls which all those waiting echo with joy and with barking, laughter and hugs and pats on the back while offering towels to the initiate and the wer who also crossed the water. The beta pounds the drum in a crescendo and then puts it down and joins the fun.

From this time on, all joyous werewolves are in liminal sacred space and no human words are to be uttered by all until the next invocation by the alpha. All may yip, howl, whine, chuff, growl, gesture and so on but may not speak even one word. All must remain fully in wer mode and stay as naked as possible, only using a towel to dry as needed or putting on new clothes as needed. The pack then stands or sits about the fire rumbling, barking, yipping, playing and laughing as they like. The initiate, pure animal now, and being very hungry and feral, is offered food and wine and water from the altar first and then the rest is shared among the pack, all being devoured wildly and when done, the initiate howls with glee and all join in. Then all wash up in the lake (or river) and splash about, swim, relax, smoke, drink as they like. If it is warm, all can swim, splash and so on while remaining naked. It is who we are after all.

After a time, the alpha calls all back to sit around the fire. Then, everyone gets up and gently sways in sync, going deeper into the shift and intuitively feeling the change in the pack with a new member. Then the alpha grabs the bowl, sharp knife and antiseptic wipes and growls RAaaa!!! Three times and all respond loudly each time.

At this cue, the whole pack, including the new member, begins to then rock forward and back all together and low-growl with each forward rock RA RA RA…calling on the Wolf Spirit to descend and fill their circle. The alpha takes the knife and gently cuts some of the initiate's hair off and throws it into the fire with the oak leaves.

All howl RA! as the past restrictions of the initiate are burned away and the new wer is set free!

Now the low growl chanting of RA RA RA continues, without the swaying.

The alpha cleans the knife with the wipe then pricks his finger with his knife and drips blood into the bowl. Each pack member takes up their own knife and does the same while the alpha holds the bowl. As each member does this, he or she loudly growls RA! Invoking the Great Wolf Spirit as all continue the chant. The initiate is the last one to do this, and when he does so, all loudly growl RA!

The alpha then stirs the blood with blood with his cleaned knife, then uses the knife i to place a drop of blood on the shrine icon as all the wers become quiet and the alpha intones MA, HA, AH, AH-HA with the pack repeating each growl-chant honoring the gods and welcoming with them the new pack member in the presence of the Great Wolf Spirit.

The alpha then leaves the knife on the altar and returns to the initiate with the bowl of pack blood and all stand in a circle about the fire as the alpha then marks the initiate with blood from the cup on the forehead, then on the chest and then on the fire center, just under the navel and all howl.

Then all begin the low RA RA RA chant again as the bowl is passed about the circle clockwise and each pack member marks themselves in the mixed blood in the same way: head, heart, fire center, and then howls with all joining in. When done, the alpha pours the rest of the blood into the fire and washes it out in the water and all begin to howl wildly and growl RA over and over. After a time, the alpha growls loudly *as all repeat:*

*Consumatum est!* [44]
*It is finished!*
*lupus novo natus est*
*A new wolf is born!!!*

All howl a lot and dance about madly and then all hop into the water with laughter, joy and play, splashing each other with wild abandon.

Then there is a group hug with the initiate in the middle and all howl. The new wer is now a member of the pack! It is done. Now people can growl human talk if they wish.

The red scarf is ceremonially given to the new pack member and also the new clothes and any other gifts pack members wish to give to the new wer. Brandy is shared and growly toasts can be given and so on.

Then it is party time. People can get dressed or stay naked of course. Play and swimming is encouraged. The brandy and other things are passed around, more food is eaten, and fun is had. The new initiate is encouraged to express what they have experienced, what omens or visions were received, and so on. All talk and share their inner feral thoughts as they like.

Preparing to return to the mundane world, all should sit in silence for a time and just listen, let the Wildness speak to the pack, let the Wolf Spirit grant wisdom or visions, let the initiation and bonding settle.

After a time, the alpha takes up the drum and taps it lightly and slowly, speaks into the back of the drum and with whatever growled words flow out, invokes the Wildness and the Great Wolf Spirit and thanks the primal powers.

---

44. All Latin phrases followed by English translations; both recited during the ritual.

He continues then to keep a slew quiet rhythm while each member does the same with fer or many growled words, including the initiate.

Then the last part of the Praxis Rite is done, all shake intensely like the creatures they are and then all plant paws on the earth and growl MA MA MA letting most of the shift fade into the Mother.

The site is then cleaned up so it is as it was and the fire is carefully extinguished and cleaned up so no trace is left. As this is done, each member takes a bit of the fire's ash and puts it on their third eye and the alpha can take some to use for spells and such, it being very powerful. Then rest of the ashes are thrown into the water as the initiate growls the following and all repeat:

*Lupus Ego Sum-Fiat!* [45]
*Now I'm a Wolf, So May It Be!*

All howl!

Then all walk back together, the new wolf wearing his or her new clothes and the red scarf.

There is meditative mood as all continuously rumble with every step as the intense wer energies sink into the earth as each wer lets go of their Animalself and returns to human, but as a stronger, tougher, smarter more primal human!

Soon all are back to where it began, there is a final group hug and howl, then silence for a moment as all settles. Then everyone goes home, or maybe continues the party elsewhere? It is, as always, up to the pack.

## Pack Rituals of Mating, Birth and Death

There are key transitional and liminal moments of every life for every family, clan or group, in our case, our pack. The pack is a magickal clan and a family of choice. Pack members take care of each other in life and death and other times of change. This is the way of wolf packs as well. What follows are rites to commemorate, bless, support and empower fellow pack members and their kin at these powerful and pivotal moments of life.

---

45. *(Now) I am a wolf! -So may it be!*

## *Werewolf Pack Mating Ritual*

When wers wish to sanctify their mating, this ritual is done with the pack and other friends of the pack present, if that is the will of those who are mating. It is both wonderful and powerful to celebrate the finding of love, and this is a special bonding that is honored within the pack. There are no limits or restrictions as to who is getting mated, their gender, how they identify or even how many are involved. Wolves don't care so why should werewolves?

### Set Up

This is a suggested ritual, but of course those mating can and should change anything about it as they wish or even scrap it and create something new. Non-pack "friends of the pack" can be invited, especially if one or more involved are not wer, it doesn't matter: love is love. The wers being mated bring to the rite a braided cord or band made of natural materials that they worked on together. Woven into it is some of their hair and, if they are very serious, a bit of blood and sexual fluid as well. Other items like holy stones, charms, beads and so on may also be added as they like, It is completely up to those mating what this will look like and contain. The braid should have three lengths of yarn or cord to braid together representing the Wildness, Wyrd, and Way. The braid when done should be about two feet long. This will be wrapped around the wrists of the couple.

Together, the mates should prepare a vow of union in any form they wish for the mating rite as well as a short invocation of powers of nature in whatever way they wish.

The mating ritual is held in a pack gathering place in the woods, away from civilization as much as possible. Before the actual ritual, the shrine will be set up to the east before those being mated and guests arrive. The alpha will officiate unless those being mated wish to choose another pack member to do so, though much of the ritual will be done by those being mated.

### Items Needed

The shrine, decorated with flowers

Rich, natural incense to burn made of natural materials, rose or lavender or
  any scent the couple chooses

A burning bowl and lighter

A simple altar, as natural as possible, that is at least four feet high. It can be made of natural found wood in the area or brought in

Red candles for the shrine and altar

The drum (optional)

## If Desired

Plentiful wine or mead and other drinks like tea, juice and so on.

A large picnic put together for the pack and laid out before the shrine with silverware and plates and cups.

A small bottle of pure mead for the mating cup.

Natural red grease paint or water-based paint; All the wers will decorate their bodies as they wish with signs, icons and images of joy and love

All will wear their werewolf magick jewelry and so on and dress as they like to fit the occasion.

## On the Altar

Small burning bows with incense

A large red beeswax candle

A special cup with at first pure spring water in it, later mead

Red flowers and a small pile of red petals

Place for the braided cord to lay

A place for the stang to stand or be laid

Musical instruments if people wish to play them for dancing, especially the pack drum (optional)

## The Rite

A mood of civility reigns. Pack and guests mingle and laugh and drink and party as they like for a time. All greet each other and then, when the rite is about to start, all gather near the altar except for those being mated. When all is set up and ready, the alpha makes a long low up howl and maybe the beta gently pounds the drum to announce the beginning of the rite. As all come to the area, the pack stands closest, about the altar, leaving room for those being mated to enter and stand before the altar. All other guests stand as they like.

Those being mated hang back in the trees and wait to be called, but their finished braid has already been laid on the altar. Once all are ready, the alpha raises his paws and welcomes all, states the reason for this rite, and gently prepares the non-wer visitors what will occur. Then the alpha asks all to raise a howl for this event:

All then up howl in a melodious manner, striving for harmonics.

The pack then goes to the edge of the area and does the Up Growl Banishing and the Praxis Rite.

Then, they face the altar and up howl long, happy howls while swaying. Others may join in if they will. Those being mated now enter and stand before the altar.

The alpha lights the candle, and the incense and makes sure the water is in the cup.

The alpha takes up the stang in one hand and the incense in the other as the pack begins to slowly and quietly vibrate HAaaa over and over in harmony as the alpha first censes the couple with the incense while growling HAaaa and then walks clockwise around the whole circle, censing all present with more vibrations of HAaaa.

While the pack continues quietly chanting HAaaa, the alpha repeats this process with the candle, letting all feel the flame, then with the cup of water sprinkling a little water on each person, then emptying the cup at the base of the tree. Then, the alpha takes up some of the petals, and gently tosses some on each person, last upon those being mated which a long slow vibration of AH … HAaaaaa. Then a moment of silence.

Then, the stang is given to the couple to hold together, one with left paw, the other with right, as the alpha fills the empty cup on the altar with mead.

The alpha and pack raise paws and the alpha growls the following lines with each wer repeating, all up howl after each line. Others present may join in as they like:

*We call the gods, animal spirits, ancestors, feral teachers and all wild things that play*

*(All howl!)*

*We invoke the Wildness that is our true home, the Wyrd that binds us in love
and the Way of primal joy!*

(All howl!)

*In the heart of joy, with the blessing of Mother Nature, we honor, bless,
empower, and embrace this union with love, will and Wildness!*

(All howl!)

*Now those who bring their love together now, speak truth from that love!
Those being mated then together read aloud whatever vow or statement they
had wrote together and all listen intently.*

The alpha then takes up the cup and vibrates AHhhhhh-HAhhhhh!
The pack all repeat AHhhhhh-HAhhhhh!
Then the alpha then hands those being mated the cup of mead.
They take it and, each in turn, holds the cup and carefully gives some to
the other to drink until it is mostly empty, then pours out the last bit onto the
earth. Then they lovingly kiss and howl together!
That is the signal for all present to howl a lot with gusto!! With such group
howling, lovely harmonies can be made!
Then the alpha takes up the mating braid and holds it up and growl-chants,
with pack echoing:

*MAaaa! Blessings of Gaia*
*HAaaa! Blessings of the Lord of the Forest*
*AHaaa! Blessings of the Moon Mothers*
*RAaaa! Blessings of the Great Wolf Spirit*

Then the alpha carefully places the braid over the wrists of the mating
couple and loops up each end to lay on top of the wrists, vibrating *AH-HA!*
The alpha then gently takes up the stang and touches the bound wrists,
growling:

*Lord of Wildness and Mother Earth*
*Lady moon, and wolfish sun*
*You are joined with Love and Mirth*
*What once was separate now is one!!*
*FIAT!*

The couple again kiss and howl or as they like. The pack howls and whoever else likes, barks, growls wildly, and dances about as the drum is now
played with verve!

If the mated ones have rings, they place them on each other's fingers, with
help from the alpha as needed, with words that only they can hear as the howling and wildness continues and increases about them. The braid is then placed
back on the altar by the alpha as the wild rumpus party really starts, with continued drumming and music making. Feasting, dancing, laughing, howling,
hijinks and craziness and a fair amount of partying then ensues.

When things wind down a bit, the alpha calls for attention and a modicum
of silence and the pack then stands about the circle and rumbles and sways.

Those mated now together approach the shrine and say or growl words of
thanks and gratitude and may quietly ask the nature gods being honored here
as well as the Wolf Spirit for a special boon. Then they turn and face all, bow,
and all let loose the biggest howl with all madly joining in. followed by a big
feral group hug. The bind braid is then given to the mated ones by the alpha
with a bow and off they go, with more petals being tossed on them. Guests
may linger and party, but at a certain time only the pack will be left. Then, the
final part of the Praxis Rite is done, all shaking and laughing!

All clean up the area and all else, shut down the shrine and stow it, pick
up everything and scatter some ecologically appropriate food, flowers, and
petals into the woods for the gods, animals, and spirits. When all is ready, the
pack does the Up Growl Banishing, then places paws on the earth and growls
MAaaa grounding all the leftover energies to Gaia then, a group hug full of
love and joy and all go.

## *Werewolf Pack New Birth Blessing Rite*

A birth or adoption is intensely sacred to the gods, spirits and the pack. Whether it is a new baby, an adoption of a child or even if one is adopting a pet, such new love is the eternal power of the life that Gaia gives, the Lord of the Forest mentors, the Moon Mothers nurture and the Wolf Spirit protects. This ritual marks this penultimate time of joy and happiness and honors the manifesting of a new spirit in the world as well as the commitment and strength for those who will care for this new life which the gods of nature help to thrive.

### Set Up

This rite is held during the day but twilight is best. The new life blessing should be held as deep in nature as possible, but allowances should be made for the newborn. Doing so at the rally grove is best but any wild place, even a wooded yard, is fine.

The parent or parents will be present as well as the whole pack and any pack friends who are invited by the parent or parents. All are wearing something green, the newborn should have a green wrap as well. Decorations of greenery will be set up as well.

### Items Needed

A natural altar of some kind

Green oak leaves (if possible) and evergreen boughs to cover the altar

A fairly large cup or bowl of pure, natural water placed under or next to the altar.

A one foot wide ceramic or wood blessing bowl that will be given to the parent or parents for the newborn or newly adopted

Some pure spring water

A little sea salt

A fresh oak leaf (or twig)

A fresh hawthorn or mountain ash (rowen) leaf or twig

A sprig of cedar or pine

Dried sage of any kind

A burning bowl

The stang

The drum (optional)

A beeswax candle that is natural or white on a small plate or holder.

*If desired:* Food for sharing as well as whatever drinks are appropriate

## The Rite

The pack enters the area first, sets up the altar in the center facing east and covers it with leaves or boughs. Then the pack places the blessing bowl on the center, the candle on the right side and the small burning bowl with sage on the other side. The gathered leaves or twigs are gathered behind the bowl. The stang is placed across the top of the bowl. The feasting food and drink are set up separately at the north edge of the space. All this can be done before others arrive, but if they are there, they wait to enter the area until the following is done: The pack turns outward and all do the Up Growl Banishing. The pack gathers about the altar and all do the Praxis Rite. Now, the ones with the newly born or adopted enter first, followed by any others invited. The pack drum, if present, may be lightly played by the beta or wer.

The alpha lights the sage and candle and cues the pack to stand in a circle about the altar. The alpha takes the burning sage and walks clockwise about the circle, growling AH-HA and censing the pack and the area before returning it to the altar.

Then, the pack all face the altar with paws out and bless the altar and space with single long growls:

*MAaaa! (Touching the altar)*
*HAaaa! (All hold open arms, paws out to the woods)*
*AHaaa! (All touch the side of the bowl)*

Then, while the alpha pours the pure water into the bowl with a pinch of sea salt.

*RAaaaaaa!*

All raise paws while the alpha sprinkles some salt water in a clockwise circle upon all presnt as well as on the area, thus invoking the Wolf Spirit's protection.

The pack then pulls back to the perimeter and gently sways in sync while rumbling.

The alpha gestures to the parent or parents who come first and bring their newborn or adopted one. Other guests then follow into the now sacred circle and up to the altar.

Parent(s) are facing west over the altar with the alpha facing them while holding the stang in one hand and the oak leaf, hawthorn (or rowen) leaf, and sprig of cedar or pine in the right hand, growling:

*By the Wildness, Wyrd, and Way*
*By all the nature gods that play*
*New child, new star, new blessed mirth*
*Be now filled with love of Earth!*

The pack and only others who wish then gently and melodically up howl.

The leaves or tugs are held together and the alpha swirls them in the water clockwise and gently growls:

*One for strength and bravery*
*One for protection, all evil flee*
*The last for health and wealth,*
*So may it be!*

All the pack repeats *So may it be!* And then gently and melodically up howls with joy.

The alpha gestures to the parent(s) to come forward with the new one and then gently lets a few drops from the leaves/twigs touch the top of the new one's head and gently growls the following which the parent(s) and pack repeat line by line:

*O newborn star (____name____)*
*Be blessed by Earth*
*Be full of love, joy and mirth*
*By the Moon, Earth, Forest and Sun*
*You and the Wildness Will A One!*
*Io Evoe*


Then all present up howl gently and melodically and also joyously.

Now is the time to sing, feast, admire the new one and hang out.

With permission, each pack member is encouraged to give their own gentle blessing to the new one with words or werewolf lingo as the social event continues.

When things are winding down, The pack comes together in a circle and they and the guests form one circle around the parent(s) and newborn or newly adopted and all hold hands and, as the alpha growl-chant the following lines, each repeat as they will:

*MAaaa! Gaia bless and protect!*
*HAaaa! Lord of the Forest bless and protect!*
*AHaaa! Great Moon Mothers bless and protect!*
*RAaaaaaa! Great Wolf Spirit bless and protect!*
*AH-HA! May this new star shine and play*
*Filled with happiness every day!*


All up howl gently. The rite is over. The parent(s) with the new addition to the clan depart after being given the (now) empty blessing bowl as a gift for the new one.

The pack cleans up everything as usual, scattering or burying the leaves/twigs used in the rite and offering some appropriate leftover food to the forest spirits and animals.

When all is as it was, the pack comes to the center and does the ending of the Praxis Rite (if they wish) and then all do the Up Growl Banishing.

All place paws on the earth and growl chant MA over and over to let the shift slide down into the earth along with any leftover energy, then all go forth with joy and mirth!

## Werewolf Pack Rite of Farewell

Wers are intensely bonded with nature and their Animalself and as such are deeply integrated within their ecosystem. The transition of death is thus seen as a natural return to the wellspring of nature from which we all came. Death is a transcendent journey and our Animalself becomes the wolf-psychopomp who guides our star on that journey, as it has done for millennia.

When a wer brother or sister passes, it is a deep sorrow and visceral pain for the whole pack. You all have been wild and wolfish together, sharing communion with your deepest primal Animalselves. The deceased pack member will be remembered and honored by the pack whenever it meets and a piece of his or her werewolf jewelry will be permanently tied to the pack stang. He or she will be honored at every pack gathering. It is even possible that their wer Animalself could become a guardian wolf spirit of the pack. That is up to the will of the deceased.

### Set Up

This can be done in the regular werewolf pack rally grove or the whole pack can go camping in the wilderness at an isolated campsite and make a real wake-event out of it. It could be a place the deceased wer loved. Though the items needed and the rite follows, it can and should all be discussed by the pack ahead of time to change things as the deceased wer would have liked. Things he or she loved should be included, all of this is very personal and should be. This is a time of sorrow, remembrance, and letting go. But it also imbues a belief that the spirit and love of the deceased is eternal and present and that this matters. Wherever this is done in the woods, there should be a safe fire pit for a small fire or a portable fire pit as well as room to plant a new tree.

> **Note:** During the rite that sacred tree *is treated as the deceased, spoken to, hailed, cried over and so on.* When toasts are made, a small bit is given to the tree and at the end, when it is planted, a bit of the food, tobacco, and other items are laid at the foot of the tree.

## Items Needed

A small native tree sapling that is healthy and ready to plant. If the deceased
had a special tree, that would be best, but if not, then the whole pack can
choose the "right" tree.

A lot of the deceased wer's favorite food, drink, smoke and so on

Some wer item that is potent from the deceased, like a piece of jewelry or a
magickal tool

A piece of clothing that has the scent of the deceased pack member on it.

A black cloth

Dried leaves of yew, cedar and oak

A burning bowl

A sacred cup

A large, natural black candle

A small safe fire pit or or a portable fire pit set up to the south. (If neither are
possible, a ceramic bowl with chunks of camphor in it will work.)

A black cloth for the altar

The stang which is stood upright behind

Food, alcohol, tobacco, other smoking herbs and other mementos of the
deceased as

A photo of the deceased

Containers of pure water, other drinks

Appropriate flowers

Any other items deemed appropriate

## The Rite

When the pack arrives, all stand in silence and hold hands. Then at the cue of the
alpha all begin to rumble in sync, blending their energies and consciousness and
Animalselves, sharing the sadness and their love for each other and the deceased
with the in-out breathing and rumbling. After maybe ten minutes, the alpha
raises paws and all do the same and release a long, mournful, sorrow-filled up
howl.

Then all as they like, rumbling, set up the altar to the north. The altar is
covered with the black cloth, and also has the candle, a cup filled with water

and a burning bowl with dried leaves on it. The stang is standing upright behind the altar with the deceased's jewelry or other item hanging on it. The deceased's photo should be on the altar as well. The drinks, food, and all other items are placed on or around the altar as well.

The firepit is set up to the south and prepped for a small fire and the small tree is placed in the center of the space.

And one or more werewolf magick items owned by the deceased should be placed on it, even some of the wer's cremated ashes or hair, anything that makes it an icon of the deceased. During the rite, the tree will be empowered and then honored as a link or channel to the deceased and honored as such.

When all is ready, the pack stands in a circle about the tree and, facing outward, does the Up Growl Banishing.

Turning to face the tree, all then do the Praxis Rite (visualizing the deceased wer with them).

All then go deeper into the werewolf shapeshifter state, led by the alpha growling a visualization.

Then, in wer-form, everyone locks arms and low up howls their sorrow and grief, intensely and as often as the pack wishes, unleashing their sorrow and tears. When the grief settles and the howling shifts to long mournful slow howls and soon all fades to a deep sorrow and then a calm rumbling.

The alpha then growls a few words regarding this gathering and the deceased as the rest of the pack yips, barks, chuffs, howls as they will.

Then the alpha growls and all repeat line for line:

*We are one, We are pack*
*In life's green and in death's black*
*Together loping forward*
*Together prowl and track*
*We bond in life and love and play*
*A clan, a tribe, in every way*
*In our hearts YOU will stay*

*The pack is one*
*The pack is free*
*In life and death*
*So shall it be!*

All howl with full intensity.

All the pack then sways in sync and up growls together, visualizing green energy filling the circle, dispelling the dark sorrow, as a wer picks up the small tree and the alpha takes up the stang and draws a pentagram symbol in the dirt in the center. Then the container of the small tree is placed in the center of this star, representing the eternal light of the deceased.

Pentagram

The alpha then uses the stang to draw a circle around the whole area as he does so, the rest of the pack growl-chants MA while the alpha does the same.

Another member takes up the cup of water and sprinkles it about the circle clockwise while all growl-chant AH.

Another pack member lights the leaves in the burning bowl and walks it about the circle clockwise as all growl-chant HA.

Then the alpha carries the lit candle about the circle as all growl chant RA. The alpha then uses the candle to light the prepared fire in the firepit as all continue to growl chant RA RA and then all throw up their hands and howl, for the fire is a gateway for the departed.

The alpha replaces the candle on the altar and joins the pack. Then hold hands in the circle facing the tree and begin to sway together side to side in sync and rumble as all intensely visualize the deceased wer standing in wer or werewolf form where the tree stands.

This is a quiet time of remembrance and communing with the loved pack-mate. It may last as long as needed until the wave of love and sorrow ebbs. Then the alpha begins to quietly up growl the name of the deceased and the rest follow suit as all see deceased more clearly before them and feel love, gratitude and loss while growling his or her name. As this gets louder, and clearer, all release their arms, raise them, and begin also howling, barking, growling at will. All begin slowly walking-swaying-prowling clockwise about the tree as they like. Now all visualize that they are dancing with the shade of the deceased who is now present. The liminal gateway between life and death is manifesting and now all becomes intuitive and spontaneous. Pack members may cry, laugh, rock, growl to the deceased words of love and remembrance, or enter a deep trance where they speak with the dead, whatever they feel is right guided by the Animalself direct experience, all thinking silenced.

As the trance deepens, water, wine, food, tobacco and other things are consumed and shared with the deceased who is now very present and of course with each other.

The fire should be kept burning by whichever wer sees the need.

When the frisson fades and the liminal space closes and the visions become distant, the alpha brings all back together about the tree and leads all a loud group "howl-a-thon" that can weave sadness, joy, up howls, down howls and so on as the group mind intuitively honors and says farewell to the lost loved one.

A bottle of the deceased's favorite wine, liquor, other drink, and favorite smoke is brought out and passed around, all being offered to the tree honoring the deceased by name *for he or she is present.*

Next, each wer in turn growls the deceased's name and then offers a short personal eulogy *to the deceased.* The rest of the pack softly up howls after each eulogy is done.

Then, all sit rumbling and commune with the deceased as the sacraments are passed around. Once this is done, the piece of clothing with the scent of the deceased is slowly passed around and each wer smells the scent of their lost packmate and holds it in memory as they bid their packmate goodbye in silence. When done, the alpha takes this cloth it to the fire and burns it and all raise their hands and howl a long "letting go" howl which ends with all seated, paws and forehead on the earth with the tree in before them, chanting MA MA MAAA and letting go of the sadness while holding onto the love.

Then everyone stands, shakes, growls HAaaaaaa! And so begins a time of feasting and rejoicing, telling stories about the deceased, playing music, smoking, drinking, roughhousing, games and so on, in short, doing things the deceased loved. Whatever is eaten or drunk, a small bit should go into the fire for the deceased.

When the party winds down, the alpha gathers all into a big group hug and growls as all repeat line by line:

*We howl for sun, moon, forest and earth!*
*For All that is wild; death, life, love and rebirth!*
*In sadness and joy we howl now today*
*Living the Wildness, Wyrd and Way*
*We plant now in honor this sacred tree*
*May our wer-kin __deceased's name__ always run free! (All howl)*

Then all together the pack chooses the best and safest place to plant the tree, then all plant the tree together while rumbling. The hole is dug and mementos from and for the deceased are placed in the hole with barks, yips, growls and down howls. The tree is planted carefully and watered all together as all meditate on the deceased and then the alpha puts out the fire and mixes some of the ashes with water and pours it out at the base of the tree.

All down-howl then each touches the tree and says goodbye as they like.

In silence the area is picked up, all things packed and no evidence left. Excess food may be scattered into the woods or taken home. All is as it was. All then do the up growl banishing.

Finally, there is a group pack hug and a long, slow, heartfelt howl as all remember that life is short but love is forever. All place hands on the earth and let go of any remaining energy into Gaia as all together growl MA MA MA, then stand, shake together and leave that lovely place to return to the mundane in silence for a time.

Note: The pack may and should return to this place to honor *the deceased's tree* together or alone as they remember their lost wer kin on special days or as they like That tree will continually be a touchstone and gateway for the deceased and thus a place to honor or speak with one who is still loved, still a packmate.

## Pack Rite for Communing with Werewolf Shades

This spell is for communicating with any wer friends or loved ones who have passed on, but especially for pack kin or others, even useful to contact shades of the ancient werewolf cults to gain knowledge. The goal is to receive advice and helpful omens. It can be done by the pack where deceased pack members have been ritually honored as the previous ritual described, or at the shrine on appropriate days such as Samhain or Day of the Dead. The ancient werewolf cults had strong connections with helping and working with the shades of the dead [46] and we follow this lineage practice. Any wer can do this rite this by themselves, though when dealing with shade, there is safety in feral numbers!

### Set Up

Many of the ancient werewolf cults worked with the dead and the Wolf Spirit is a psychopomp. [47] This can be done on any dark moon or, more intensely, for all Hallows or Samhain. It should be done in an atmospheric wooded and natural place, a crossroads, especially in a graveyard is the best place to do this.

### Items Needed

An appropriate wild place or appropriately sacred spot at sunset (the grove where the pack plants memorial saplings is perfect).

A black candle.

Dried yew leaves and a burning bowl.

---

46. Sargent, *Werewolf Magick*, Chapter 1.
47. Ibid.

A small dish and cup of food and drink for the dead: Fruit and nuts & dark
wine or beer.

Appropriate dark wine or beer for the honored dead and participants.

Images representing those being honored.

The stang.

The black Hekate stave.

The black scrying mirror (optional).

Shifting triggers (optional).

A small flat stone used as an altar is set up facing West. The black candle, burning bowl with dried yew, the upright stang, images (if any) the food and
wine offerings and the black stave are set up on the altar.

## The Rite

All do the Up Growl Banishing. All stand in a circle and touch the earth growling MA several times while silently calling on Gaia and the spirits of the under-
world for aid.

All reach up to the sky and visualize the dark moon, growling AH three
times, calling on Hekate.

All reach out to the dark woods and the liminal realm of the dead and
growl HA invoking the dark Lord of the Forest.

All then all stretch paws forward toward the altar and growl RA three times
calling on the dark Wolf God as psychopomp to convey carry the dead to this
place.

The pack sits before the altar and all rumble growl and sway, seeing the liminal gate opening. As they do this, the alpha lights the black candle and lights
the dried yew and then takes up the black stave and uses it to draw a circle
about the pack and altar. Then the alpha pours out some wine on the altar,
growling:

*Dark Lord of Wildness*
*Feral Shades of the Dead*
*Lord of the Forest*
*Of hallows, of dread*

*Open the mystery*
*Below and above*
*Hekate help us commune*
*With those whom we love*
*Mortuis Honor!* [48]

All now sit and begin deep rumbling and rocking forward and back in sync and so begin shifting and opening to the dead. All quietly up howl three times, honoring and calling forth the dead you seek as well as the answers you see. After a time, all should begin "seeing" the shades being called arising from the herb smoke or in the scry mirror if that is being used.

All commune as they will, remembering everything shown, said and so on.

After a time, the alpha taps the earth three times with the Hekate stave and then sticks it in the earth. This is then time for those wers who are able to channel the words of the dead as they speak through them. Also, those getting visions can growl them.

When done, the alpha takes up the stave and slowly pounds three times on the earth with it as all down-howl three times, "seeing" the spirits sink down into the netherworld.

All rock and rumble for a time and come back and when this is done, the alpha growls:

*Mortuis Honor!* three times and all repeat.

Then conversations, partying in honor of the dead and sharing of experiences is done as all note down in their journals what came.

When done, all stand up, blow out the candle, scatter the yew ashes, and do the same with the food and drink offerings. All is packed and made as it was.

All then do the Up Growl Banishing, then all growl *Mortuis Honor!* and up howl three times their love and blessing and thanks to the honored dead, and then go.

Thus, the dead are honored.

---

48. *Honor to the dead!* (Latin).

# CHAPTER 6

# PACK MAGICK FOR PROTECTION, HEALING, AND PURIFICATION

As with any group, the pack offers strength in numbers, but also magickal protection, healing and purification. Always larger and more powerful than the sum of its parts, the pack, more than most groups, is a loyal clan that has every wer's back emotionally, physically and magickally. This is why larger predators avoid wolf packs, *For the strength of the pack is the wolf, and the strength of the wolf is the pack.*

## Pack Protection and Banishing Rite

Like all outlier magickal groups, the pack as well as its members may be affected by negative people, events, energies, curses, bad luck and so on as the wild power and work of the pack increases. Our culture is deeply disconnected from nature and filled with fear of all that is Animistic or feral. As with all who strive to accept their place as fellow animals within the ecosystem, we become both overt and unconscious targets of the anti-life prevailing culture that ignores ecological collapse and worships money and power over life. werewolf magick changes you and alters and enhances your wildness. It offers a way of walking within the spirit world of nature as an animal who *really belongs*. By shifting and discarding the prevailing cultural programming, each werewolf mage attracts negative forces of that programming, no matter how circumspect they may be. As you shapeshift you revive your Animalself with every step, moving further into the primal world. This scares and repels those who fear us eco-warriors, which includes most who buy-into the current cultural norms.

## SET UP

This rite is thus for the magickal, emotional and physical protection of the pack and its members. All Packs must anticipate some conflict and of course wild wolves are being slaughtered simply for being the wolves they are. It is wise for us to think on this fact, though never with fear or paranoia. Like wolves who are absurdly feared, we are defensive and not aggressive. We will protect ourselves and our brother and sister pack members to the end, right? This simple rite is for this very thing; protecting the whole pack or a pack member who is being assaulted on any level, mental, physical, magickal, emotional or psychic. This rite should be done in the woods as usual, at the rally grove if possible, but it can be done in any natural area as needed. A backyard with a few trees and some privacy would be fine, but really anywhere is OK if the pack feels a psychic attack is happening or if a member has already been harassed. This rite is best done at the dark of the moon but can be done anytime as needed.

It can also be part of an esbat if it is a general protection rite for the whole pack for specific issues or for general pack protection. Better safe than sorry. The goal is quick response and protection. Attack one pack member, you get a whole pack on your ass. One for all, all for one.

## ITEMS NEEDED

A mixture of a small pinch of dried red pepper flakes, sage, and a small bit dried pine sap

Charcoal for incense

A small safe bowl or incense burner to burn the charcoal in that is safe to pick up

All bring their werewolf pack daggers

Sea salt

A chunk of camphor

Some spring or other natural water, river, ocean, lake etc.

A bowl of natural material for the water

The sacred pack cup

A small bottle of deep red wine in which several dried hot peppers have
   been soaking.

A fresh oak leaf and a thistle or holly leaf

Several red natural candles or a small central fire if outside

A small natural red cloth

One of the werewolf warrior's long red staves or the black Hekate stave

The stang

## THE RITE

All meet and gather at the appointed time and place and when all are assembled, the alpha calls for silence and all is quiet and all hold hands.

All begin to rumble and all send energy around the circle filled with love and protection and unity. Then all call on the Werewolf Spirit with a furious RA RA RA that gets louder and louder and ends with a howl.

Then a small altar is set up in the center of the circle, even just a red cloth is fine. All items are placed there including the bowl in the center filled with the gathered sacred water where the oak and thistle leaves are placed. The red candle is lit as is the incense and some red pepper wine is poured into the cup. All take part in creating the altar while rumble-growling, building up a wolfish intensity.

Then, all stand in a circle facing inward. If one wer is the focus of this rite he or she may sit before the altar. When the blessing is given all receiving it should prepare to strip naked or at least leave the upper half of their body to receive it.

The alpha picks up the black stave or long warrior stave in one hand and the stang in the other and begins rhythmic up growling as all join in, all swaying back and forth with each up growl. The alpha strikes the side of the stang with the stave with each growl and slowly walks clockwise around the inside of the circle and looks into the eyes of each pack member as the red circle is cast. The rhythmic down growling becomes louder and more intense as everyone focuses their will on protecting the pack and each pack member and all howl together, with stang raised. Alpha then places the stang standing upright behind the altar with the stave laid before the altar.

All then do the simple Up Growl Banishing.

All then do the Praxis Rite invokes his or her most pissed off Animalself which projects fierce energy and scares away all negative energies.

When done the alpha raises his dagger and all do likewise and all turn around, facing outward, point them outward and lunge and howl as one, projecting fierce protective power. All raise their knives straight up and loudly growl RA! Calling on the power of the Werewolf God and then all plunge their knives into the earth at their feet, calling on Gaia to affirm their protective work with a loud MA!

All turn and face the center as the alpha picks up the bowl of smoking incense and holds it as each wer censes him or herself and loudly down growls visualizing bright blessing, cleansing and protection. If the rite is for one wer, they are censed last after the alpha, with all holding out paws and down growling protection.

The burning bowl is placed back on the altar. Then the water bowl with leaves in it is picked up.

The alpha picks up the water bowl and the pack reaches forward with a paw and all together support the water bowl, grow-rumbling in unison and then, in unison, loudly up growl RA RA RA ... while charging the mixture with visualized intense red glowing wolfish energy. After a time, the RA growl becomes a constant low rumbling of Ra Ra Ra as all who are to be protected now strip (at least the top half) and place clothes behind them at the edge of the circle. The RA-rumbling continues and furious energy builds as the Wolf deities fill the circle until the alpha raises the bowl and all go silent.

Alpha growls the following with all repeating line by line:

*Tooth And Claw*
*Fang And Blood*
*Fire And Storms*
*Earth And Flood*
*Avert Attack*

*Dark Evil Flee*
*Protect Our Back*
*Wolf Powers Three*
*All Enemies Destroy*
*So May It Be!*

All howl with full intensity and release the spell as all continue to RA-rumble and sway and the alpha goes about splashing water from the bowl with the oak leaf all over each wer and making the runic sign of Algiz for protection on each wer's back also with the leaf. The alpha then does this for him or herself last and pours out the rest of the water on the ground to the south. Then all howl over and over and visualize the flaming red protective power and glowing Algiz rune on their bodies as they tense their whole bodies in full werewolf form, with claws and arms open and full of flaming fury at whatever or whomever has attacked them.

Then all torn around and attack-lunge, projecting spouting wolfish red bolts of lightning to the evil doers and scream RA as loud as they can, releasing the Great Wolf Power to take care of its pack.

All then Turn back around and gently up howl and then rumble and sway together, calming down, letting go of the spell and letting the red power fade and the light of peace fill each wer's inner wolf for a time. When the alpha takes up the stave and taps the floor three times, he growls FIAT! And repeat that word. And then all can relax.

Water may be toweled off fur, flesh and floor, clothes may be replaced all sit and rumble and the spicy wine is passed around for all to partake of as they wish and the alpha (or the one who was attacked) pours some out onto the earth for the wolfish gods and howls a wish for justice and protection which all echo.

This has been intense, so the pack takes time to party and lay about and relax, as naked as they wish. All take time to bask in the love and protection of the pack, it is a cold, cruel world. After a time, at the alpha's cue, all take up their daggers from the earth and stand together in the center facing in. All raise daggers and touch their dagger points together and growl loudly:

*Pack Is One*
*Pack Is Free*
*Harm One Harm All*
*All Enemies Flee*
*By Fangs And Claws*
*So It Shall Be!*

All howl and raise their knives. Still holding daggers, all then turn about and do the basic Up-Growl banishing, thrusting forward daggers and claws with each of the nine growls.

Then all sheath their daggers, place paws on the earth and down growl MA MA MA seeing all excess energies, and there are a bunch, sink into the earth.

All face each other and shake off the shifting and do the last part of the Praxis Rite to bring themselves back to human-ish.

All then get dressed if they need to and pick up the site as usual, packing all things, leaving it as it was, in silence. Finally, when all are ready to go, all come together in a big, long loving healing rumble hug and then howl! If this was done for one pack member, then that wer is in the center. Then all leave together.

## Werewolf Spell for Renewing Vitality

### Set Up

This spell can be done alone or, more intensely, in a pack.

The energy of the Werewolf Spirit, especially in solar form, can imbue you with tremendous vitality and a new burst of energy when you are run-down, recovering from something or need some new energy for whatever reason. Don't reach for an energy drink or espresso, do this instead!

### Items Needed

A leaf of fresh basil

Your werewolf magick talisman (even better if it is a shifting trigger)

A large, healthy tree or, better, a small group of trees.

A bright sunny day with the sun up in the sky

## THE SPELL

Lean against the strongest tree and sink into it, worn out as you are. Close your eyes and quietly up growl nine times and visualize a ring of bright yellow fire about you, banishing all negative energies and stresses away.

Now, rumble until you are fully relaxed, breathing deeply, feel the energy of the tree, the earth and especially the sun fill you as all the stress flows from you.

Then, hold the basil leaf up to the sun and low-growl:

*O Lupercus Deus!* [49]
*Sun Wolf of power*
*Begone weariness and pain*
*In this sun-lit hour*
*So your energy I may gain!*

Quietly up howl as you look at the sun briefly and see the Sun Wolf smiling down upon you and filling the basil leaf you hold up with intense power.

Then, eat the basil, chewing it slowly as the Wolf God energy fills you with light and power. When done, inhale with a RA sound several times as you bask in the sun with paws up and the fiery solar wolfish power fills you with each in-breath.

When you are all charged up, thank Lupercus with paws up and do a long, low up howl as the renewed energy fills you and your weariness dissipates. Finally, paws together, honor the Solar Wolf Spirit by growling:

*Ut luceat magnus lupu!* [50]
*May we shine as the Sun-Wolf God!*

Now, go kick ass and have fun.

---

49. *O great wolf god!* (Latin).

50. *May the great wolf shine!* (Latin).

## The Fire Rite of Warrior Werewolves

*"The Indo-European religion included initiatory cul-societies of warriors ...*
*This cult tradition of a band of wizard-warriors roaming outside society,*
*sometimes shapeshifting into animals has survived ..."* [51]

As mentioned in Chapter 1 of *Werewolf Magick*, the connection between warriors and the Wolf Spirit in various shape shifting cults across many cultures is well documented. The linguistically reconstructed term in Proto-European for this kind of wolfish martial shapeshifting through consciousness is **WLK-wYA,** or "wolfishness, martial rage." There are many later examples of warrior werewolves such as the Norse *Einherjer* or Odin's warriors and berserkers, and the *Haomavarka* or *Haoma Wolves*,[52] a cult of werewolf warriors from what is now Persia. Roman soldiers were led into war under wolf standards sacred to the god Mars[53] and there are many other similar examples. The intense ferocity, loyalty, dedication and strength of wolves and wolf packs have always been admired and imitated by many werewolf warrior cults.

### Set Up

First, let's be clear on the purpose of this rite. werewolf magick, is not about macho ego-pumping, needless aggression or unnecessary fighting, imitating the reality that wolves rarely battle each other except for dire necessity and tend to avoid conflict whenever possible for the good of their pack. Yet staying strong, powerful and in readiness protects the pack, strengthens the will of all members, keeps reflexes honed, builds discipline and thus enhances self-esteem as well as ability to protect oneself and one's pack.

In this spirit, this ritual is used for strengthening the physical and etheric fire within the wers of the pack to enhance positive and protective qualities. The focus should be on balance, extending and using the gut fire center and improving agility and will. This will strengthen, empower and give confidence

---

51. Jackson, *The Compleat Vampyre*, 13.

52. Ibid.

53. Sargent, *Werewolf Magick*, 17.

for each wer in the daily struggles and strivings of life and help all bond with the pack and each other. Plus, as every role-player knows, this is fun.

Discipline and focus are useful in every area of magick and life and this is sometimes lost in the cavorting, partying, romping and playing of the pack. This brings a bit more intensity and clarity to the Animalself and reinforces the idea that as wers we also heal, help and protect those weaker than us by standing up to abusers and bullies. This is our way.

Prepare ahead of time: Short sparring staffs of wood or bamboo, found and prepared by each pack wer ahead of time. Each staff should be the length of a walking cane, around four feet long and no wider than one inch thick. They should be cleaned smooth of bark and so on. These sparring staffs are then painted or stained red, using natural colorants if possible. Each wer is responsible for crafting his or her own sparring staff, thus owning the concept of being a werewolf warrior. Each wer should decorate their staff with appropriate werewolf icon symbols that are original or chosen from the symbols in the Appendix. Of course, other appropriate werewolf magick images can be incised, scribed or pained on each wer's staff as they feel is right desired. Each staff will be charged and empowered in this rite and in itself becomes a tool of power for each wer who crafts one. They can be carried and used in other rituals such as the werewolf parade that appears later on. All wers can appear for the rite having painted markings and symbols on their skin using natural colorants, using werewolf magick symbols or others in red if they like. It is appropriate magick for this rite and will look cool.

All should keep in mind that this is a rite and the alternate striking of each other's rods is ceremonial, meaning not forceful or aggro at all. You are ceremonially sparring with your kin, not enemies. If a wer gets a bit overly enthusiastic, *the alpha will point and growl*, meaning *cool it!* All know ahead of time that safety is primary in the rite.

**Note:** In this rite the alpha is noted as the referee of the event, but if another wer wishes to do so in lieu of participating in this rite, he or she then temporarily takes the office of alpha and all it entails for this rite. If so, then the alpha can and should participate as a player. Finally, if there is an odd number of warriors then the alpha shall make sure that with each partner change, the odd-wer-out gets a chance to enter as one steps out.

## Items Needed

The rally grove of the pack or another wild place blessed with werewolf magick.

The makings of a safe and acceptable small fire.

Gathered branches to use for the fire, the best being oak, yew, hawthorn, pine, fir or holly or any other wood associated with protection and strength.

A red beeswax candle

The pack shrine can be present as well, with all that it entails. (optional)

A simple altar (if the shrine is absent.)

A red cloth for either the altar or the shrine, whichever is chosen.

A handful of raw garlic cloves

A bag of dried red peppers

A small branch of dried oak leaves

A small packet of dried brambles or thistles

A burning bowl.

A bottle of vodka or rum infused with three small dried red peppers should be present, more peppers can be added if all are brave.

For those wanting something else, a thermos of strong black tea with one or two peppers added

A feast of natural food for after the rite, up to the pack, it is important because afterward all will be hungry!

Many containers of pure drinking water to aid hydration, all will be encouraged to hydrate

The wers should fast before the ritual and wear red, if they wear anything

## The Rite

All enter the sacred space growling loudly in full regalia and then stand about the edge of the space rumbling and swaying in sync continually as things are set up and the fire is built but not lit by the alpha.

The altar is in the south and out of the way, the small firepit is in the center of the circle about which all the action will happen.

As usual the stang is set up standing behind the altar or shrine. If the shrine is present, the red cloth is placed upon that and so that becomes the altar and all items are placed there.

When all is set up, the alpha cues the pack and all howl and raise their staffs and then gather silently about the fire pit in the center, still rumbling and swaying in sync side to side.

They all begin to enter a light trance state and *shift to low rumbling RAaaa RAaaa RAaaa* repeatedly. This continues for a time until the alpha raises a paw and all then

*Facing each other, all do the Praxis Rite, but with deeper growls and more intense actions.*

The red candle on the altar is then lit by the alpha who loudly growls:

*Sumus Lupus Dei!* [54]

As the cloves are passed, each warrior wer takes one and growls the following before he or chews it.

*Sumus Lupus Dei!*

The alpha puts *only three* dried red peppers and pieces of thistle or brambles in the burning bowl and lights it. As it smolders, the alpha walks clockwise about the circle up growling RA RA RA in a rhythm as all wers continue swaying and rumble growl RA RA RA as well, tapping their staffs on the ground in unison. All are now in a light trance and are visualizing all negative powers, evil spirits and their own negative issues being driven away. The smoldering pepper/herb mix is then placed on the altar and the alpha joins the circle and sways for a time then raises paws and howls and all join in. Then all stand in silence and visualize the following, the alpha may growl this visualization if desired:

---

54. *We are the Wolf God* (Latin).

*A ring of red-eyed spirit wolves now encircles the pack, protecting and empowering us as kin and banishing all evil from our rite. Slowly these wolves change into a ring of red flame.*

At this all the wers up howl over and over again, getting louder and louder and tensing their bodies until alpha raises paws and all the wers thrust their long staves up for a final howl and go silent.

The alpha raises his or her arms and all wers pause, staffs planted on the ground as the fire is lit and by the alpha, then the alpha raises arms and growls the following as all repeat line by line, staffs planted on the ground but leaning forward toward the fire. Then all intone with arms raised as the fire grows:

*Io Evoe Lykaios!*
*Hail and honor to the Wolf God*
*Salve Lupus Dei!*
*Hail to the Wolf God*
*Io Evoe Ares!*
*Honor to Mars!*
*Ayibobo Ogou!*
*Hail to all Wolfish warrior gods and spirits!* [55]
*We call on you!*
*Bring power, strength, ferocity*
*Loyalty, Love and bravery,*
*So may it be!*
*Sumus Lupus Dei*

All raise and extend their staffs to touch the tips to the fire and loudly with intensity growl.

*Lupus Dei Vult!* [56]

Then all howl.

---

55. *Io Evoe* (Greek), *Salve* (Roman), *Ayibobo* (Haitian) are all honorifics roughly meaning *Honor to___ or Hail!*

56. *The Wolf God wills it!*

In pairs, about the fire, all the warrior wers face each other with space between pairs the alpha gently arranging them. All hold their staffs like a katana (Japanese sword) with both hands ¾ of the way down the staff. It should be held slightly slanted to the left.

When the alpha *loudly* up growls RA! All warrior wers bark RA and gently strike each other's staffs seven times *alternating right, left, right, left,* tap-tap-tap-tap…barking RA loudly each time, being careful not to hit each other of course. This will be synchronized as the alpha bark RA as well and set the rhythm. The first time is a bit slower for all to get the rhythm of the left/right/left/right practice.

The Alpha raises paws and all pause while a couple of dried red peppers are thrown on the fire then all loudly growling *Sumus Lupus Dei!* Thus, they **are** invoking *ferocity!*

Then all the *outer* wers move clockwise, the inner wers stay put. In this way all get new partners. Again, wers face each other, staffs out as before and all pause.

When the alpha up growls RA! All warrior wers bark RA and repeat the alternate left-right-left right staff striking as before seven times, as before. This is synchronized by the alpha's barking RA as before. At this point, all should have it down and can be a bit quicker, the alpha watches carefully, ready to slow or correct anything.

When done, more thistles or brambles are thrown onto the small fire by the alpha and all growl *Sumus Lupus Dei! for protection*:

Now, partners change again to new partners as before and all face each other again in pairs. Holding up their long staffs as before, the alpha barks RA and the warrior wers bark Ra and again strike each other's staffs seven times, right, left, right, left and so on, synchronized by the Alpha's rhythmic RA barks.

Then the alpha throws oak leaves onto the fire.

All howl for strength and then loudly growl *Sumus Lupus Dei!*

All raise their staffs on the air loudly growling RA RA RA with the alpha joining in until the alpha cues a howl and all the wers extend and tough tips of all their staffs above the the fire growling over and over, louder and louder *Sumus Lupus Dei!* Until the alpha howls and all join in.

Then all partially lower their staffs and, now each holding the bottom of the staff with their right hand, each gently lowers the end of the staff to the wer on the right who then grabs it with *their* left hand. In this way a circle of staves is now made connecting all the wers with the fire in the center. The alpha takes up the bottle of peppery liqueur and pours a bit into the fire, while loudly growling the following which all growl-shout-repeat in response:

*The pack is a mighty tree!*
*Intensity, love, loyalty*
*Strength and bravery*
*United as one, so may it be!*
*Sumus Lupus Dei (all howl)*
*Sumus Lupus Dei (all howl)*
*Sumus Lupus Dei! (all howl)*

All then laugh, howl, and relax. All the staffs can be stacked near the altar and the drum should come out for the alpha to pound on as all the warrior wolves pass the spicy liquor and water around then and let the energy fly as they run and romp around the the fire with lots of fur shaking, leaping, dancing, jumping, howling, barking and so on.

The bottle of pepper liqueur is then passed around with more howling, barking, yipping and laughing as containers of water are also passed around too! (Hydrate!)

When things calm down, the alpha raises arms and howls as all form a circle about the fire.

Then, each wer in turn, stands before the fire and growls their own invocation for a werewolf warrior blessing for the good of pack and themselves, then that wer steps back a few steps, runs and then leaps over the (small) fire as all howl. The alpha leaps last.

Then turns and all howl as the alpha offering a blessing for the whole pack, pouring pepper liquor into the fire and growling:

*Sumus Lupus Dei!*

All repeat this loudly then howl!

When every wer has gone, the alpha is the last to go and growls a final blessing for all the pack and all howl *Sumus Lupus Dei!* Finally, all gather their staffs, return to the fire, together hold up their staffs touching tips high and then together briefly dip them into the coals of the dying fire as the final invocation is made by the alpha while all the warrior wers growl RA RA RAaaaaaaa.

*For the mother*
*The Wolf God roars*
*Protect each other*
*The firebird soars!*
*Stronger than we know*
*Loyal wolves we be*
*Feral and powerful*
*For all to see!*
*Our will is one*
*Thus we roam free!*
*Sumus Lupus Dei! Fiat!*

All growl **FIAT!**

Now it is time to relax, hang out, eat like mad, hydrate, drink, party, horse around and play fight with their staffs- carefully! (until some gets whacked) and dance about as all like until all come down from the adrenaline.

At the end, when the fire is completely out, the alpha puts out the red candle and raises paws and all do likewise and All point staffs up and growl AH to the Moon Mothers.

Then all carefully turn and point staffs outwards to the forest and growl HA to the Lord of the Forest. All then all again touch staff tips together growling RA to honor the Wolf God then all lay their staffs on the earth, pointing at the fire pit and down growl MA MA MA slowly and deeply, letting all excess energy flow into the earth while also sealing this blessing into themselves and their staffs. When done, the pack, still holding their staffs, do the end of the *Praxis Rite*, releasing the Animalself.

All then turn about facing out and do the Up Growl Banishing.

Then it is clean up time, some more hydrating, and careful pick up.

The fire, as usual, should be carefully doused with water and all cleaned away so that no trace remains.

When all is as it should be, a group hug and a final howl and all leave with a swagger.

## Lunar Eclipse Pack Purification Rite

Several times a year the full moon is devoured by the Great Wolf Spirit, who changes the lunar sphere red as blood and all goes dark. Lunar eclipses are powerful for many reasons, but in the world of werewolf magick, they mark a time of release, letting go, banishing and purification. This is envisioned as a solo working but could just as easily be done with the whole pack with very few changes, All could have copies of the rite to read the Latin conjurings or the alpha could lead and all repeat, up to the pack.

### Set Up

As each wer is developing and expanding his or her form in spirit, so the process is enhanced and speeded up by magickally letting go of those spiritual and psychological hindrances and flaws that suppress the Wolf within. These often-red full moon eclipses are gifts given by the Wolf Spirit, the Lunar Lady and Lord of the Forest so that we may bathe in the red lunar power and so dissolve all restrictions to our will and so better release and integrate with our Animalself. All this shield be meditated on as the eclipse approaches.

### Items Needed

A wild and secluded place where you can view the lunar eclipse and howl.

A personal shifting trigger talisman if you have one (see Chapter 3) or any werewolf magick talisman.

A small container of pure spring water

Each wer has a magickal knife

Sterilizing wipes

## THE RITE

All arrive under the full moon just before the eclipse begins.

All announce themselves and offer praise to the full moon by howling three times, paws raised.

Each wer, in turn, then pours out a little of the water and calls on the Moon Mothers with a long growly HAaaaaa!

All in a circle turn outward and do the Up Growl Banishing (Appendix)

All then turn to the center with the water container in the center and do the *Praxis Rite*.

This is done slowly and intensely, like waves on a sea, taking a long time to enhance and extend the shifting with a shifting trigger item if you have one, or other techniques you have already learned such as accessing your fire center (See the shifting section in *Werewolf Magick*).

All conjure forth their Animalself and shift, intensely invoke and visualize astral wolf forms, take as long as you need until you are fully, wildly feral. At this point the moon will begin to darken from the eclipse, at this all raise your paws to the moon and loudly growl:

*Lupus Et obscuratus Magna*
*Remove humanum problems*
*Luna lupus ad gloriam!* [57]

Each wer reaches up to the moon and feels Her rays of light and power fill wer forms completely until both are completely integrated, each wer and this cosmic lunar goddess.

As the eclipse proceeds, all deepen their trance states and feel the shifting, changing moon and shadow mirrored in each shifting body as each wer's consciousness becomes clearer, darker, larger. Let go and embrace the transforming

---

57. *Great Wolf eclipse! Remove my human problems! Honor to the wolf moon!*

alchemy unlike any you have felt before! As the Wolf Spirit devours the moon so too is your human self overwhelmed by your joyful Animalself!

Then all growl:

*O gloriosa eclipsis lunae lupus;*
*Et do facultatem, ut benedicat mihi*
*Luna magno lupum vorat*
*Et angustiis meis comedi!* [58]

As the eclipse comes to completion, all complete their full assumption of this primordial werewolf form and raise paws into the air at the reddish orb above as all chant:

*Per lupus deus Faunus, sic esto!*
*By the Wolf God Faunus, so be it!* [59]

Each wer lets go of human consciousness completely and simply sinks into the mystical liminal experience of the personal lunar transformation that is happening.

Each wer lets go of any insecurities, negativity, neuroses, fears and everything that needs to be banished!! Each wer is in a deeply primordial werewolf form, all of this while the human ego sleeps in the umbra! Do the deep work, standing or sitting. Drink the water and feel the power of the moon cleanse, and heal you.

When the moon emerges from the black-red shadow, all rumble growl for a long time as each feels the transformation that has been invoked becoming focused and manifest, like a serpent, shedding a dead skin. All restrictions and negative aspects that are no longer needed dissolve. When all feel that release, the alpha or another wer digs a hole in the center of the circle and each were takes out their knife and points it at the moon and all howl letting go!

---

58. *Oh glorious Wolf eclipse Moon. Bless and empower me! As the great wolf devours the Moon.*
59. The Latin words are followed by translation; both are recited during the rite.

Now each wer takes their knife and cuts off a lock of hair and drops it in the hole, as all intensely growl MAaaaaa! This is repeated until every wer has done this.

Then, each wer uses a wipe on the knife and on a finger and then pricks his or her paw and drips a drop of blood into the hole, when all have done this, then all together growl RAaaaaa!

Pass the water counter clockwise, each drinking some, until the last of the water is poured into the hole, then all deeply growl AHhhhh!

Then all together fill in the hole intensely and together loudly growl ending with a loud HAaaaa!

All then place paws over the now covered hole and growl loudly AHhh-HAaaa! AHhh-HAaaa! AHhh-HAaaa! thus sealing the rite.

Then all dance! All that has been released scatters by the grace of the werewolf gods and the power of the black, red, white moon! Dance, laugh, party as you all like until the moon is again full and shining. Then, when ready, all come together in a group hug, hold hands, and then spiral out counter clockwise with the alpha or another leading and all stomping and shaking and letting the shifting trance sink into the earth with long growls of Maaaa Maaaa Maaa … and then shake like wet wolves and leave that place, do not look back!

So may it be.

## Pack Magick Healing Rite

Pack members get hurt in many ways. Surviving physical, mental and emotional pain is a badge of werewolf honor, but also leaves deep hurt that can last. The pack can and should offer healing for any pack member through love and magick, that is what a pack is for.

### Set Up

This is a simple rite to be done anytime a pack member is really hurting for whatever reason. It should be done after a dark moon to help the wer recover. Though the power of the pack together makes this a most potent rite, any wer can do it alone with adaptations or for a wer friend who is not a pack member. It can also be done on the astral by coordinating times if pack members are separated physically. Even Zoom could work!

**ITEMS NEEDED**

Some dried rosemary, sage and lavender mixed together

A burning bowl

A ritual bowl or large cup

Fresh spring or other natural water.

Some sea salt

A green cloth for the altar or as the altar.

A green robe, shawl or cloth for the injured wer to wear

Green beeswax candles

A wooded, calm, vibrant, natural healing place, the pack's rally grove is best if possible.

A freshly cut willow branch (cut with permission from the tree spirit near a full moon).

An appropriate blanket for the wounded wer to sit or lay upon.

A sacred cup

Fresh juice

Containers of fresh water to drink

**THE RITE**

This Rite is done at sunset finishing in the darkness and all arrive at the place and remain in silence or expressing themselves with wer lingo.

All are wearing something green, including the wounded wer who arrives and is then lovingly wrapped in the green shawl or cloth. The alpha holds the stang and leads the way into the rally grove with all following, the beta bringing up the rear, gently tapping and rubbing the drum.

A place for the wounded wer is set up with the blanket to sit on and a container of fresh water to the east and the altar is set up in the center facing that wer. The simple altar is created with the green cloth on it or the cloth itself can be the altar. On it is a green candle in a holder, the burning bowl filled with some of the mixed dry herbs with some of the herbs placed in the large bowl with the sea salt. This bowl is central to the altar and has the willow branch and the stang draped across it. Next is the banishing.

When ready, the pack, minus the wer being healed, forms a circle. First, all do the Up Growl Banishing. Then all do the Praxis Rite.

The wounded wer does this silently/internally where they are sitting, while opening to the magick at play and accepting the energies.

When the area is clear and sacred, the alpha pours the water into the bowl that already contains some of the herbal mixture and the sea salt. All begin to rumble and sway and, with paws extended, visualize healing green energy flowing into the bowl. The alpha takes the stang and places the end in the bowl and all begin to down growl HA HA HA over and over, empowering the water and the whole space with green healing energy.

When the alpha lifts up the stang, all growling fades. The alpha goes to the wounded wer and hands him or her the stang to hold. The candle is lit and the bowl is now filled with pure water. There should be a comfortable place for the wounded wer to sit.

Then the alpha has the wounded wer arise and, taking the blanket, escorts him or her to sit before the bowl and altar after laying down the blanket.

Then all stand about the altar and the sitting wer and, paws out send blessing power while the beta taps out a slow, appropriate tune. All growl:

*Lord of Forest and Green of Tree*
*Ha ha ha (deep growling)*
*Gaia Mother we call to thee*
*Ma ma ma (deep growling)*
*O pain and sorrow, may you flee*
*Ra Ra Ra (deep growling)*
*Pack Healing and Love!*
*So May it be! (deep growling)*
*AH AH AH*

All howl three times, including the wounded wer.

Then, the pack members pull back in a rough circle and silently retreat into the surrounding woods, just a short way, leaving the wounded wer before the altar.

The wounded wer, using a hand, takes up some of the water from the bowl and uses it to bless their hands, head and body, especially where the hurt is centered.

Then that wer takes up the willow branch and meditates on the sorrow, pain and trauma he or she is dealing with and opens and releases it while waving the herb smoke over the body with the branch while rocking and grumbling and so on, all without words. When he or she is ready to release as much as he or she can and is ready to receive healing and love from the pack he or she begins a series of low, keening, pain-filled up howls which signals pain and sadness.

At the sound of this, the pack members who are standing in the woods begin to echo the low, sad howls with their own sad up howls. As they do so, they slowly move into the sacred space from all directions and feel and share the wounded wer's pain as they sorrow-howl over and over, long drawn out howls, and merge their sad low howls together with that of the wounded wer until they all become one song.

All open their hearts to their hurt pack member as they come closer and a deep magick occurs: All are low-howling becomes one howl, all share and feel the pain, what hurts one pack member hurts them all, and in this way love and healing begin to dissolve the pain as the whole pack takes it on.

The pack then sits or kneels about the hurt wer, all gently laying a paw on him or her, continuing this deep hurt-howling magick until the hurt wer lets go of all the pain they can with a long, deep AH-HAaaaa and then all pull back and remain sitting in loving silence.

When the hurt wer is ready to release as much of the suffering as possible, he or she turns to the water and, with help from the pack if needed, gently uses the water in the bowl to wash his or her body, especially where the hurt is centered. Ideally this is done naked, but that depends on the wer being healed.

As this washing happens the rest of the pack sways and begins a rhythmic HA HA HA growl with hands out, projecting green healing love and seeing it wash the hurt away.

When done, the wounded wer takes the small willow branch and ties it into a simple loop as the rest of the pack goes silent.

The hurting wer then utters whatever growling words he or she needs to say to help heal and release the suffering and places the willow twig loop over the horn of the stang which he or she holds and stand up proud holding it high with intensity and up howls as strongly as possible letting go of the hurt and the pack rises and joins in the howling. When done, the wounded wer remains standing and the pack surround and embrace him or her and all rumble together for a time and become one pack with one heart.

Then all sit and relax and listen in silence to the wounded wer who may need to speak or growl or howl ... whatever they need.

When done, the healing wer takes the willow loop off the stang and drops it into the bowl and together they all turn the bowl over and let everything flow into Gaia, taking all the suffering the magickal release with it with one long growl of MAaaaaa.

All now separate, begin to rock and finish Praxis Rite then all place hands on the earth and growl:

*Ma ma ma*
*Mother take it*
*Ma ma ma*
*Mother make it*
*Ma ma ma*
*Wild and free*

The rest of the pack then does all the clean-up and packing and so on as the healing wer sits in peace then, when ready to depart, all stand and wrap arms about each other and the alpha growls and all repeat the following line by line:

*Our pack is one*
*One family*
*By moon and Sun*
*And every tree*
*Feral and joined*
*We all run free*

*One heart, one mind*
*So may it be!*

All low up howl.
Go in silence and love, surrounding the recovering wer.

# Pack Spell to Calm Wer Chaos

Pack work is high energy, wild and free and, of course, feral af, which is the whole point. The Animalself brings freedom from restrictions but also brings animalistic energy, mostly great, sometimes chaotic. If things get a bit sparky, overly rambunctious, or contentious, use this pack spell to calm and chill things out.

## Set Up

This spell can be done at any time things seem to be wonky with the pack, but during a new crescent moon is best. It can be done during the day or at night. It is best to do this near naked naked since all will get pretty wet. Such shared soaking and openness of this kind elicits more bonding and focuses all to be in the moment while letting go of crankiness or other negative feelings. This is the spell to do if there has been bickering or raw feelings in the pack. The alpha or any pack member can call for this spell to be done if things have gotten raspy, slightly contentious or a bit unbalanced. Of course, talking about these things before this spell is a good idea so the spell will clear the air as it washes over all. Since a free use of water is involved, the large bowl could contain warm water and being able to get dry and warm up, maybe inside, is a possibility depending on the weather.

This spell can be done anywhere outside that is private, but the rally grove or another natural, wooded place is ideal, keeping in mind that things will get wet.

## Items Needed

Some dried sage and lavender mixed together and a burning bowl (sage should
    be home-grown)
Each pack member must bring one white carnation
A small branch an apple tree
The stang

Towels

A pure white cloth

White candles if light is needed

Wers should wear minimal or no clothes during the rite and also bring another
set of clothes

## The Spell

After conversations, all enter the area where the spell will be done in silence
and wait.

The white cloth is laid down as the altar and the alpha sets up the items.

In the center is the bowl of water. The stang is leaned against the bowl to
the west, and the burning bowl with herbs is to the east.

When ready, all gather in a circle about the items and do the Up Growl Banishing with white carnations in their paws.

Then all turn around, facing the center and rumble and sway back and
forth in sync for ten or more minutes and meditate deeply on releasing resentments, hurt feelings, negativity, confusion and so on as all link energies and
sway together until the circle is filled with peace.

The alpha then lights the dried herbs in the burning bowl and carries it
about the circle, censing and growling:

*Out tout throughout and about*
*All good come in, all evil stay out*
*So the joining has begun*
*AH-HA, the pack is one.*

All repeat line by line and then continue rumbling

The alpha then places the burning bowl back where it was, tosses his white
carnation into the bowl with an *AH-HAaaa!* The whole pack growls AH-HAaaa
as the alpha joins the circle and rumbles and sways as in sync with the whole
pack for a time.

When ready, any wer who feels the calm unity growls AH-HAaaa and
tosses his or her white flower into the bowl as the rest of the pack echoes the

AH-HAaaa and continues rumbling and swaying. This process repeats in the same way until each wer has released their carnation into the water and all stand rumbling and swaying.

At that point, the alpha and then the pack begin to shift the simple rumbling to AH-HA over and over, mouths just barely open. It slowly gets louder and the pack feels the unity growing and all chaos and division fade away.

As this chant builds, the alpha then takes up the apple branch and uses it to stir the bowl of flower water while the AH-HA growl continues and then uses the branch to sprinkle some of this water on each member of the pack. while growling the following line three times, louder each time as all the wers repeat each line:

*Amor et pax et simultas! Unum lupos!* [60]

Then all the pack members up howl wildly and completely release their issues, resentments, irritations and so on while lurching forward, thrusting their paws into the big bowl of flowery water and splashing it wildly on each other howling, laughing, barking and so on until the bowl is empty and all are soaked. Then all link arms or hold hands and howl mightily!

Then, a bit calmer, all down-howl three times, renewing their psychic bond.

When done, all growl *Unum lupos!* Three times.

The spell is done.

Time for fun howling, laughing, relaxing, talking through things and partying as desired. And also using the towels to dry off! Spare clothes that were brought can then be worn.

When done, the last of the flowery water is poured out onto the earth with a final AH-Haaaa!

All place paws on the earth and growl a long MAaaaaa to earth everything.

As usual, clean up, pack everything and leave, though the flowers could be gathered by the alpha and placed in a vase before the shrine to seal the spell.

---

60. *Love and peace and togetherness, (we are all) one wolf!*
*One Wolf Spirit.*

# CHAPTER 7
# PUBLIC PACK WEREWOLF EVENTS
———————— ❯☾ ————————

The following werewolf pack magickal events are a chance for wolfish out-reach and wild fun. They are designed to be open to friends of the pack as well as other fellow travelers who have interests in occult, Pagan or Craft prac-tices or are just fun open-minded free-spirits.

Believe it or not, there were a number of pagan werewolf festivals in the ancient and medieval world, several mentioned in *Werewolf Magick*.[61] One of our goals is to revive some of these amazing werewolf celebrations because they are powerful feral Pagan traditions that, as wers, we should revive and honor. It is amazing that such Pagan, Animist werewolf-oriented traditions were preserved and celebrated into the Christian era, even if many of the ori-gins were forgotten. What follows are two such revived and revised werewolf fests, revived creatively from found historical information. I plan to share more in the future, there are many left to play with. Such revived werewolf magick events can be made open to werewolf-sympathetic friends or even to the public if the pack wishes. Even today in Europe, primal feral festivals, like the infa-mous Krampus Lauf and others are held with "becoming" Animist spirits and acting wild![62] All of this is now seen as harmless fun and it seems some ancient feral shapeshifting traditions have not completely died out but become big ani-malistic parties. Following are revivals of two of the oldest werewolf festivals I know of, the first being from ancient Rome, the second from Medieval Europe.

---

61. Sargent, *Werewolf Magick*, chapters 1 and 8.
62. Guardian writers, "10 traditional winter festivals in Europe."

## On Lupercalia

One of the greatest werewolf cults and festivals in the ancient world was the festival of Lupercalia (Wolf Festival) held in Rome beginning in the 6th century BC,[63] but the festival was so ancient that even the Romans were not sure when it began. The main god was the Faunus, the Roman Pan, who was also lord of wolves and his priests were called Lupercai or werewolves. Sound familiar? The festival conflates older pre-Roman myths and the founding of Rome by Romulus and Remus who were nurtured by the divine female wolf who seems to have been an older wolf goddess. It was a wild four-day party where Lupercai priests first held secret rites in a cave, stripped naked, were anointed with blood and goat milk and, wearing only bits of bloody goatskin, ran amok in Rome whipping semi-naked women and men with goat skin strips to increase fertility! It was an infamous week of wild debauchery and carousing. The festival was so popular that even when Rome became Christian, the bishop couldn't stop it and so made it a festival for the virgin Mary! Some say that it shifted into Valentine's Day, dedicated to the saint of love![64]

This pack recreation is quite tame today since what were common Roman orgiastic public displays, like wild drunken orgies in the streets, would for sure lead to arrests nowadays. What follows is a fairly accurate but much tamer revival run by the pack and enjoyed by a group of fellow wild friends, Witches, Pagans and other heathen-types who are game for a rocking werewolf festival.

## Lupercalia Werewolf Magick Festival

### Set Up

The best location for this would be a cave in the woods where no one will intrude, but that is a bit hard to find. If this is open to others, a nice grove in a wooded park that is accessible to pack friends and others should be chosen. The pack could even reserve a wooded park pavilion or picnic area. If this festival is going to be more of a really wild party, it can be held in a wooded backyard of a pack member or friend of the pack. If it has been blessed and used for werewolf magick, so much the better. It is important that the two chosen

63. History.com editors, "Lupercalia."
64. Knowles, Elizabeth. Oxford Dictionary Of Phrase and Fable, 654.

to be the anointed Lupercai (werewolf priests) need to be experienced wers with great shapeshifting skills as per werewolf magick before leaping about in a wolfish trance state in sandals and goatskin loin cloths! There is a lot of stuff that needs to be gathered together or prepared to put on a public event like this. The entire thing should be blocked out and practiced a few times, like a short play, to avoid muck-ups in public.

Before the festival day invited guests are encouraged to dress as Roman as they like though they may wear what they wish, but when the dancing and running begin, participants should show at least a bit of flesh to get the blessing from the werewolf priests!

The Latin translations of the rite, found at the end of the rite, should be gone over with the attendees before the ritual begins, so there is some understanding of the invocations. Copies of the rite can also be handed out before attendees enter the ritual area or put online in a way that is accessible for cell phones for those who want to join in.

## Items Needed

A clear area surrounded by trees

A stone or stump to use as the altar

Two safe tiki torches with non-toxic burning oil in them, place on either side of the altar

A small amount of goat milk

Two goat skins, with fur, large enough to wear about the waist

Six cords or thin ribbons of goatskin, at least two feet long that are cut from the edges of the goat skins

Wolf hair (if possible) or dog hair

Dried rosemary

Dried bay laurel

Dried rue and chips of oak wood

A burning bowl

A ritual knife with a sharp point

Antiseptic wipes

A small piece of natural white cloth and one of red cloth, both new

Two ceremonial cups appropriate for werewolf magick (one for goat milk, the other for wine)

The stang (here representing Faunus Lupercus, the horned and hoofed wolf god). This may be the stang generally used by the pack rituals or may be a larger more elaborate festive stang.

A statue of the horned wolfish god Faunus, but any Pan image will work

A large bottle of red Italian wine with a sprig of fresh rosemary in it

Biodegradable cups for the crowd

Costumes! All pack members participating faux togas or simple tunics of red cloth or red over white with loose black pants. The pack can be less or more creative, but the alpha should be really decked, being the lead priest! Fake fur can be incorporated in all costumes as well.

Paint on werewolf magick symbols as desired

The pack drum

Other instruments such as bells, rattles and so on as desired, pan pipes being very appropriate

## THE EVENT

As the fest begins and celebrants begin to show up, the torches are lit and the dried rosemary is placed and lit in the burning bowl.

On the altar is the upraised stang with the thongs hanging from the cleft, the two cups, one with wine and the other goat milk, the disinfected knife, sterile wipes and on two oak leaves, also small piles of wolf (or dog) hair and goat hair taken from a hide, respectively.

The pack stands about the ritual area looking serious and rumbling while beta or another holds the pack drum and begins a ritualistic simple rhythm that references Roman music if possible.

When all is ready, the alpha up howls and the attendees enter.

The pack gathers in a semicircle, facing the altar, as alpha faces the pack and the entering attendees who gather behind the pack as the drum plays and pack rumbles.

When all are present, the alpha welcomes all with a call of *Sal-ve, Sal-ve!*[65] then howls and urges the guests to howl along. The alpha then quiets the crowd and tells them a bit about the Lupercalia festival and also about werewolf magick. Then the alpha models and mentors the crowd on how to up and down howl and up and down growl so they can participate when cued to do so. A little practice may be in order.

The alpha then briefly explains to the crowd that the pack is going to first banish away all evil spirits and then enter a werewolf trance state before the actual ritual begins and that all are welcome to join in if they wish to do so by observing and imitating the pack!

The pack faces the crowd and begins grumbling and swaying in sync until everyone is doing it. The alpha then loudly growls as the drum is pounded "Ut auferat malum! Begone all evil!"

The pack then growls this as well

The drum is then put down and the pack then slowly and loudly does the Up Growl Banishing, crowd joining if they like.

The beta or another then takes up the drum and lightly plays a simple rhythm.

The alpha takes the smoking rosemary and carries it around the whole area so that each wer and each attendee can wave the scent on them to purify them. Pausing before each person, the alpha low up howls and all howl as the person receives the blessing.

The drumming stops as the alpha raises hands for silence and then growls loudly:

*Sumus Lupus Dei! We are the Wolf God!*

The pack all repeat this with growls, attendees may do so as well if they like.

Then the pack, facing the crowd, slowly and loudly does the Praxis Rite while the crowd is encouraged to copy their actions, growls and so on. When done, everyone howls!

---

65. "Greetings!" (Latin).

The alpha then tells the crowd; "Now we will invoke the gods and goddesses of Lupercalia, please repeat with us if you like!" The beta or another drums until the ritual begins, then stops and joins the pack.

The magick is unleashed. The alpha takes up the cup filled with wine and growls the following as the pack and the crowd, repeats:

*Ave Faunus Lupercus*
*Ave Inuus*
*Ave Feronia*
*Ave Lupa!* [66]
*Deos ad salutant nos feram!* [67]

The alpha then holds up both cups and pours some out on the earth and loudly growls

*Ave Faunus Lupercus!* [68]

Then all repeat and howl!

Dried rue and chips of oak wood are added to the burning bowl by the alpha to create a tiny fire in the burning bowl on the altar while all are howling and slow drumming begins by the beta or another.

Each member of the pack then in turn comes up and takes a little of the goat hair that is on the altar and adds it to the fire while making a special wild wish, saying,

*Ave Faunus! Ave Lupa! Bring me_(wish)_____ Fiat!* [69]

All up growl loudly after each wish!

---

66. Faunus is the Roman Pan, Inuus is a God of Fertility and sex, Feronia is a goddess of the woods and flowers, Lupa is the wolf goddess, all are Roman and were invoked in the Lupercalia.
67. We salute the gods of the wild (Latin).
68. Hail Werewolf Faunus!
69. Hail God Faunus, Hail wolf Goddess Lupa, bring me (__) So may it be done!

The alpha makes sure the fire is kept burning as the attendees who wish to make a similar petition to the old gods come up one at a time and do the same. The alpha can whisper the Latin phrase for each to repeat if needed. makes their petitions.

When done, the alpha places dried bay laurel leaves on the flame and growls loudly FIAT! And all up growl in agreement.

All return to where they were. The alpha raises paws, the drumming pauses, and the alpha says "All repeat as you like!" Then the alpha growls:

*Faunus Lupercus*
*And all Wolfish kin*
*Fill and Bless us*
*As we call the wolves in!*
*Now flows the wild fun*
*May all wildness begin!*
*Now the werewolves run*
*Each with toothy grin!*
*Ave Lupercai!* [70]
*Ave Lupercai!*
*Lupercai Sumus!* [71]

Wild drumming now begins!

All howl loudly and the pack dances in place shouting out *Lupercal Esti!* At will and helping pass out cups of wine to all as the alpha fills them with a hearty *Lupercai est!* The party has begun. pack wers should deepen their shifting trance state and take on the persona of a werewolf, howling, growling and being wild and getting the newbies involved! When the energy and power has reached a peak and the wine is gone, the drumming pauses and the alpha growls for attention and takes up the two goatskin thongs in one hand and the goat skins in the other skin stands before the altar and howls and all join in. Then the alpha growls the following and all repeat:

---

70. Hail werewolf priests!
71. We are (all) werewolf priests (now)!

*Salutant nos Lupa Dea!*[72]
*Faunus! Innus! Feronia!*
*Feral gods of Lupercalia!*
*Now the choosing, now the blood!*
*Now the blessing, now the flood!*
*Joy and love and fertility!*
*As we play, so may it be!*

All howl!
The alpha growls loudly to all, looking about, arms raised:

*Oh Lupercai, Oh Lupercai who will it be?*
*To bless us all and set us free!?*

Somber drum playing begins by beta or another.

Two pack members who are prepared for this role, come forward and bow before the alpha. Each is already wearing a goat skin loincloth under their toga and so they simply removes the togas and place them to the side and howl!

Meanwhile the rest of the pack members are howling and growling or barking in rhythm, getting the attendees to join in, as the two Lupercai come closer to the altar. The alpha begins to sways and up growls and deepens his shapeshifting trance and the Lupercai join in as do the pack to. Bringing full werewolf energy forth as much as possible. The attendees hopefully join in.

Then the alpha raises arms and all calms a bit and he or she takes up the small sharp dagger, sanitizes it with a wipe, and pricks his finger, then anointing anoints each Lupercai on the forehead with his "wolf blood" carefully with the flat of the dagger loudly growling:

*Lupercai est!*
*Lætificet nos, et felicitatem!*[73]

---

72. We salute the goddess Lupa.
73. Werewolf priests are you! Bring joy and prosperity! (Latin).

They both laugh loudly! The rest of the crowd laughs as well while the alpha wipes the excess blood on the red cloth.

Then he take up the white cloth, dips it in goat milk and wipes the blood off their foreheads, saying:

*Lupercai est!*
*Lætificet nos, et felicitatem!* [74]

The two werewolf priests both laugh loudly!

The rest of the crowd laughs as well while the alpha wipes most of the goat milk and blood off their foreheads with the small the white cloth and places it in the burning bowl.

The alpha then takes the goatskin cords off the stang and, bowing to each Lupercai, hands then three each, loudly growling

*Wildness, Wyrd, and Way*
*Bless us here and now today!*

Then the alpha raises his paws and loudly growls the following, as the pack and any attendees who wish loudly repeat:

*Omnia Lupercai!* [75]
*Lætificet nos, et felicitatem!*

Now, the beta or another takes up the drum and wild drumming begins as everyone howls over and over wildly and dances with the werewolf priests, the Lupercai, lead the revels in a circle dance, yipping, barking, howling as they like in pure feral form.

All other participants should then soon show some skin be it arms, backs, legs, butts or whatever parts of their body they wish!

---

74. (Same).

75. All (here) are (now) werewolf priests.

The two Lupercai then bless each person by gently whipping them with a cord, growling

*Fortuna Tibi!* [76]
*And then howl*

When everyone has been (gently!) whipped by the goatskin cords and thus blessed the wild dance may continue, maybe some other instruments joining in as well played by pack members. Cups of wine can then be handed out by the pack members weaving through the crowd to all who want some and all continue dancing.

The alpha may start simple chants such as *Lupercai Sumus* (We are all were-wolves!) or *Fortuna Tibi!* (Good fortune!) that the whole crowd can pick up and chant, along with lots of howls and up growls of course!

After all who wish have been, literally, (gently) whipped into a frenzy and things calm a bit, the alpha joins the mob and raises the arms of both of the Tarzan-like Lupercai werewolf priests who then shout several times, with all who wish joining in, *Magna Lupercai!* [77]

The two Lupercai howl back *Fortuna Tibi!*

Everyone howls. All hug, fist bump or pat the Lupercai on the back and then they go up to the altar and then hang their goatskin cords on the stang and place more rosemary in the burning bowl making sure it is lit and smoldering. Then they put their toga-costumes back on to stay warm!

Now is a time for more wine, laughter, conversations, dancing, joy and partying.

Music can be played on drums, pan pipes and so on or appropriate primal dance music be played on a system for all to dance to.

When the party's winding down, the alpha takes off the blessed "whipping cords" and then ties one about the trunk of the stang to empower it and holds it aloft as all howl. Here it will stay. Then the alpha carries it about until the festival ends.

---

76. Good fortune to you!
77. (These are) Great Werewolf Priests!

The beta or another again drums slowly, as all present gather in a circle before the altar, the pack members closest. The beta slowly pounds the drum.

One wer digs a shallow hole in the ground before the altar and other wers go get the the burning bowl full of ashes and the cups of wine goat milk from the altar and bring them to the dug hole.

They are then poured into the hole as the alpha says the following and all repeat:

*Gratias tibi Faunus*
*Gratias tibi Innus!*
*Gratias tibi Feronika!*
*Gratias tibi Lupa!*
*Gratias tibi Lupercus et Lupercai!*
*Deos ad salutant nos feram!!!*
*Fiat!*[78]

The hole is filled in and *all* present touch the earth and growl MA MA MAaaaaa!

Earthing all the energy and giving it to the great Mother Gaia. The alpha touches the covered hole with the tines of the stang as there is a final *boom, boom, BOOM!* on the drum and a last massive howl-a-thon with all present.

The pack stands about the filled in hole and, facing outwards, they get the whole crowd to do likewise and all go do the Up Growl Banishing and end with a howl, paws in the air!

Now the alpha should ask everyone to help pick up stuff, police the area and so on and may also mention to the now leaving attendees that if they had fun and are interested in werewolf magick to let one of the pack know.

---

78. Thank you god Faunus, Thank you god Innus, Thank you goddess Feronika, Thank you goddess Lupa, Thank your werewolf priests and priestesses; We salute the gods of the wild! So may it be! (Latin).

# Winter Werewolf Prowl Parade

There have been and still many feral or Animistic festivals held in Europe and so were mentioned by Church authorities as specifically werewolf festivals! They were held in the depths of winter, often during the darkest time before Christmas when hungry wolves roamed the woods. Some of these were clearly very old festivals that likely dated from before the middle ages. There exists a lot of folklore involving this pre-yule occult time of prancing feral demi-gods and shapeshifters sometimes called *misrule*. The following reconstructed and revived werewolf "parade" ritual festival that follows is based on a terrifyingly fun midwinter gathering event and procession of werewolves in Livonia, what is today known as Lithuania.[79]

The story as told by Medieval Christian authors is this: The darkest time of year, before Yule, belongs to "the Devil" or "Old Hornie," "the Dark Man" among other names. This feral Lord of the Forest comes calling in the form of a fearful wolfish limping child who prowls at this deep winter time amid the heavy snow and winter darkness to call to him werewolves in hiding! He comes from the darkness of the night, a wild limping child of frightening mein. Some say he limped because he had one hoof and one human foot, just as Krampus does, but who can say? He strides through cold fields and snow-covered paths, piping on a flute or pounding a small drum and carrying a whip and staff, going from one isolated farmhouse to another *where he knows werewolves, who secretly live as human farmers, live.* He pounds on each door, demanding to be let in, with a growl. If ignored, he forces his way in and in a commanding voice calls out the human werewolves demanding the shapeshift! If they refuse to change into their werewolf forms he magickally makes them change by beating them with a whip or his staff. Then they then have no choice but to and join his unholy parade! The Christians feared this darkest time of year before Christmas the darkest time as the spirits, imps and wolves who owned this time of chaotic misrule time, but to the werewolves, it was the holiest time of the year. As they wound from farmhouse to farmhouse, cajoling or forcing the werewolf farmers to shapeshift and join them, this wolfish parade grew and also

---

79. Baring-Gould, *The Book Of Werewolves*, 56.

began to be joined by ancestors, wandering ghosts, the wild werewolf dead and all kinds of wintery faerie and nature spirits making this procession one of old Pagan powers as well as werewolves.

The procession, led by this mysterious limping devil-child whose shadow shifted and changed, went from village to village, collecting more hidden werewolves. Imagine! All the werewolves and ghosts and spirits howling and pouncing, yipping, barking and prowling through the snow. Their howls were said to be the roaring winter storms and all true Christians who heard this locked their doors and prayed in fear while this wild dark parade roamed through the empty fields and down the snowy roads.

Once the parade was full-up, the fun began. They would break into closed taverns and devour all the food and drink all the beer and have a grand time scampering about the fields and forests. They sometimes ate livestock, as wolves do, *but never humans*, for this was forbidden. The cavorted, feasted and had a great time, prowling, partying and playing into the deep night.

Then, at the hour of sunrise, the church bells rang for it was Christmas morning, and so the new Christian god ended the werewolf revelry and all the spirits and the werewolves returned home before it became light, changing to their human forms. It is said that the mysterious limping-wild child god hid his horns and hooves and staff and whip and returned to his sacred dark place of wildness and mystery, driven forth as Christmas day dawned.

This legend is old and there are many variations and I've woven a few together. In my mind it indicates the survival of a Pagan werewolf cult amid Christendom and even today it's shadow can be seen in several folk festivals and parades that celebrate the wild spirit of misrule that was indulged in before Christmas. What fun it could be to join the werewolf mages cavorting with the spirits of Misrule! And so, this revived parade fest was recreated. Awooo!

## Set Up

This recreated version of the festival-parade is held in the depth of winter, just at or before either solstice or Christmas, as the pack decides. It can include pack members, pack friends and any others the pack wishes or it can even be open to all who want to come, like the local Portland Krampus Parade is.

The Werewolf Prowl Parade is held in as natural an area as possible, as the pack wishes and wherever the wolfish shenanigans involved are tolerated!

Before the Winter Werewolf Prowl Parade, the pack and any others involved should have a several meetings to discuss and decide on all aspects of this, including the winding procession path, the logistics of how the "Horned-Wild-God-Devil" will gather each participant along the way, where it will all end up and how the final howl-filled party will be run. The final destination could be a friendly rustic tavern or someone's house or farm with room to mingle and party.

The ideal place to end the parade should involve a fire pit for folks to warm up and a table of food and drink. The pack and other core crew should also set times to gather and do tasks like make fur-covered costumes and so on! Depending on how many the pack wanst involved in this madness, it can be small and intimate or large and boisterous, but all need to be decked out as wild werewolves or other spirits!

## ITEMS NEEDED

*Costumes & props*

One for the dark "limping child" a.k.a. the "Lord of the Forest" or "Horned Devil" should have a cool horned werewolf costume for sure, with staff and prop whip! This can be played by the alpha or another. It should be really scary.

All pack members and other participants should get decked out in feral or werewolfish costumes. At a minimum furry cloaks, capes, and masks. The general rule of using natural items is suspended here, faux fur material, artificial masks and so on are fine and these costumes can be used every year. Costumes can have sound makers like bells, rattles and so on as well.

The Horned Devil will carry a staff-whip, that is, made of natural wood with three strips or cords of leather or goatskin attached to the top and hanging down. It should also be decorated with bits of holly, evergreen branches, bells, werewolf magick symbols or whatever the pack feels is fun. This will be used to humorously and gently whip every werewolf participant as they are forces to change and join the procession.

*Other things needed*

A few hand-held lanterns. The main lantern held by the the Horned Devil or
 another can be electric with holly tied to it, but other werewolves if possible should carry similarly decorated candle lanterns.

Musical Instruments:

The pack drum should be present and lead the way behind Horned Devil,
 carried and played ceremonially by the beta or another. The other pack
 members and friends involved can also play feral music on small drums,
 flutes, bells, rattles and so on as they prowl about.

A final gathering place for the end-of-parade party. It should have a fire pit or
 fireplace. It is traditional to emerge from the darkness of winter into the
 light and warmth of fire!

Lots of previously blessed mead or dark beer should be available, the more
 traditional the better, homemade is best.

Simple werewolf winter chants that can be created and chanted or sung during
 the parade should be growled as the procession prowls about as well. Think
 of these as Pagan Yule werewolf carols to stir up the unseen forces to join in!

Here are three you may use, but feel free to make up your own:

*1. Off we wander off we prowl*
*We leap and bark, stomp and Howl*
*The dead and sun soon will rise*
*See it in our flaming eyes!*

*2. Gather now all wolves and kin*
*To sing the darkest winter in*
*Ice and snow, frigid hail*
*We laugh and play as humans quail!*

*3. Ole hornie calls and we must ken*
*To leave the grayish world of men*
*With paws and fur and yips of glee*
*Cavorting about the great world tree!*

## The Parade-Fest

The parade starts at one pack member's home, where the the Horned Devil, and the beta with the drum get dressed up and go forth at the time arranged, following the route planned so as to grab all the werewolves along the way!

They arrive at the first place agreed upon with drumming and growls and howls to pick up the pack member werewolf who is waiting there. The same short skit-rite follows as each pack member and other "werewolf" is forced into the parade:

The Horned Devil howls loudly and knocks three times with the staff upon the door of the place where the werewolf (or werewolves await), then loudly growls:

*Come thou forth into the night*
*Thou art called by shadow and light*
*Humans shift to werewolf might!*
*Awooo!*

The skittish human wer pack member opens the door and whines in reply:

*I cannot prowl this darkest night*
*I shun my wolf, I'm filled with fright!*

The limping Horned Devil steps in, growls loudly and then gently strikes that wer (or wers if there are others gathered there) with the whip of goat-skin cords. The whipped human-wers put on a big show of being chastised and howl and then slip on their werewolf costumes or furry coat and then all howl with glee.

Shots of fiery liquor or small cups of mulled cider may then be consumed by all with laughter and howls.

Then all follow the werewolf devil out, swaying and growling.

As the stride forth the the Horned Devil, in the lead, one of the werewolf carols is chanted by all (can be call and response) and as drums and other music is played with all swaying in sync, up growling and shapeshifting. The parade continues in this way as a loose, ongoing approximation of the Praxis Rite, all as they go sliding into their liminal shifted state of werewolfery.

All continue on the route from place to place, rocking and growling in sync, unleashing their Animalselves and shifting and howling, barking and so on, like any gathering of werewolves! The same short skit-rite is repeated at each place visited, along with the sips of warming liquor or hot cider, as the growling parade and the Horned Devil gathers up other "skittish werewolves," everyone howling with each new member added.

Keep in mind that the wers being gathered up in this process are likely pack members but can also be non-pack members who have prepared to join this fun. Later on, it can even be strangers who get excited about this furry parade of wild werewolves and get pulled into the madness and join in.

It can also just be a small private pack-only parade through woods and fields, that is up to the pack. Regardless, it is joyous, wild, loud and encourages laughter, chants, shifting while prowling and having fun while staying warm.

Many stops and shenanigans later, the now this larger Winter Werewolf Prowl Parade finishes the route agreed upon and arrives at the final party destination be it a pack member's house, a picnic shelter with fire pit or an open-minded pub with a fireplace.

A fire of some sort should be lit, wherever all can gather surrounded by simple Yule decorations. Food and a variety of drinks should be wild and plentiful!

As the fire is lit, simple wild rhythmic music is played, some sprigs of holly and evergreen are thrown in, and one or more of the werewolf winter carols will then be growled by every werewolf altogether, call and response or handed out and read, while standing around the fire, with yips, barks and howls thrown in! Then a short impromptu and somewhat chaotic Praxis Rite is done with all present, pack or not, led by the alpha Horned Devil werewolf.

There should be at least lots of in sync growl-rocking, howling, the chanting of MA, HA, AH, RA and AH-HA is done, but this is misrule, so it can be very different and free form and fun while still giving everyone a taste of the werewolf trance state

Watch how the whole vibe changes!

The blessed mead, dark beer and other libations are shared with toasts and howls as well as plentiful food of all kinds, whatever the pack has planned.

As the partying, chants and some more wolfish carols are sung, the rowdiness will get wilder as everyone, including newbies, will shift further into feral werewolf trance states. Howls and yips, barks and laughter rise and finally, when the last blessed ceremonial bottle of mead or beer is almost empty, it is given to the "werewolf devil" who pours the last into the fire with spontaneous words of offering to the gods, spirits and honored dead, and then all howl as one.

Then in silence, all begin to sway and growl rhythmically as the "werewolf devil" throws more sprigs of evergreens, holly and, if possible, mistletoe in the fire and a bit of the festival food, The "werewolf devil" then growls the following loudly, with all pack members repeating line by line:

*Honor to the werewolf dead*
*Honor to the wolfish living*
*Blessings to each wolf and shade*
*At this time of feral giving!*

All yip and bark.

Each in turn then steps up to the fire and growls a blessing for the season and for any who has passed and also a blessing for the pack and all who have gathered. All present answer with low howls, yips and barks. When all who offered blessings are done, everyone throws their paws up and howls for the new light of the year and all begin chanting HA HA HA and begin a wild rumpus solstice circle dance until the lame "werewolf devil" waves his whip and all howl and laugh and chill out. Traditional Pagan music (The Lord of the Dance) or even EDM can then be put on and all can dance, party, hang out, have fun, eat and make merry.

Later on, as things get quiet, people (especially wers) can begin telling spooky wolf and werewolf stories. This is also a time for ghost stories and strange lore about this liminal time and also a dark-of-the-year time for telling tales about wild friends who were true to the old ways and those who have passed and are missed.

When all is done and the party's over, all do their best to clean up and organize the chaos as is right. Then, all cleaned and ready, the "werewolf devil" calls all together to form a circle, planting his staff in the center which all grab or touch. All chant MA MA MA, earthing the energy of this wild event, sending it all down to the sleeping earth, ending with a long growled **To Gaiaaaaaa!** Then, the staff put aside, all lock arms and howl loudly honoring this joyous event and the Great Wolf Spirit that pervades it.

Finally, the "werewolf devil" growls and all repeat, line by line:

*From darkness now we birth the Sun*
*With burning hearts wild and free*
*Wolves and shades, we dance as one*
*Happy Glad Yule, to we and thee!*

Big group howl!
All can go home as they came or leave as they will.
A glad Yule and a werewolf Happy New Year, dear readers!

## Raising Wildness Earth Healing

What follows is a werewolf magick Gaia healing ritual practice that is open to other "greens" who want to join the pack in these eco-workings, all worshippers of nature are welcome. It is up to the pack to reach out to fellow Earth-centered occultists, mystics and others to join in this work in whatever way seems fit. While the ritual is part our special magick, healing Gaia is a universal goal and all who wield magick and energy in spiritual work can work together with the pack to directly heal nature, one tainted area at a time.

The healing of our planet, one area at a time, is more crucial now than at any time in our history. Without ranting about the impending environmental disasters even now unfolding, the question is this: What can we do? Supporting environmental groups like Defenders of Wildlife, WWF, The Environmental Defense Fund, and so many others is very important, but hands-on action is crucial. Joining environmental groups, saving wolves and other wildlife, and joining in protests are all positive actions. We who are involved in magick have a very special calling in this regard, we need to start focusing our practices, rituals, meditations, spells and action-backed-prayers and chants to saving our planet! This ritual was not just written for those doing werewolf magick but also is for any Pagans, Witches, Buddhists, Thelemites, Tantrikas and all others who believe in causing real, significant changes in the world through will, love and focused energy and power.

If saving Gaia is not the most important goal of magick, then what is?

The most powerful ritual practice everyone involved in magick can do is to actively help nature heal is to magickally reinvigorate and renew areas of wild nature that are being destroyed. An important work of wild feral magick is to aid Gaia in repairing damaged parts of any ecosystem and to energetically open up blocked access of that land to the deep power of Gaia, the Green energy source of life.

Particularly potent natural areas have energetic taproots to the raw green energy of the Earth Mother's. Places where this vibrant source-energy fountains forth can be clearly felt and enjoyed by those directly connected with the wildness in the most untouched, natural places. Those of us in communion with nature feel that such Earth-centered holy places exist around the world.

Such true, healthy sacred wilderness areas are becoming rarer as our human sprawl, ignorance and greed devours, pollutes and destroys nature. Just as habitat destruction and overpopulation destroys the delicate webs of ecosystems, so too does it infect and destroy access to the sources of human health, vitality and wellbeing. As toxins, over development, and human abuse of natural areas expands, the green power of Wildness fades and we are left with sterile and dying once-vital natural areas.

These damaged, neglected and poisoned places breed depression, anger, and despair and lack of natural vitality influences humans to numb themselves to survive. This is fed by the great lie that we are separate from nature and that nature is simply there for humans to devour, rape and destroy at will. We are animals and we can only truly thrive and be mentally, emotionally and spiritually survive within nature, like all other animals.

What can we do to help nature as wers and guardians of the Wildness, Wyrd and Way? We can join environmental groups, protest these horrors, donate to environmental causes and preserve and enhance green areas we have control over. As werewolf adepts we can also take direct magickal action by finding pockets of threatened or suffering Wildness and help them heal. This includes damaged and abused tree-filled parks, nature preserves and any green spaces filled with trees and wildlife that are still striving to remain healthy. As wers we can use our magick to find, understand and then magickally help heal these places with energy by reopening the flow of green power from the living earth we honor as a Goddess, Gaia. Opening up the clogged or severed "veins of life" that feed wilderness areas with Her green vitality, we can help revive an. *This is a great use of all magick*, so others outside the pack should be invited to help.

### Set Up

The purpose of this ritual is to open up "green Gates" of fountaining Gaia energies of a particular green area and so aid the healing and revival of a damaged and suffering natural place. The only prerequisites are that the damaged areas chosen must have at least a few trees, have some animals and are not completely dead.

If the pack lives in the country, this is an easier task of course, in a more suburban or urban setting is more challenging but also more important. We can become like our coyote brothers and exist within such an environment while doing what we can to make it better. Places that are overrun, damaged and hurting *can* be revitalized and re-energized with wild magick and the pack should consider doing this a regular practice. It is good feral karma and we are guardians and avatars of Gaia after all. Yet to reverse damage done by hordes of humans takes a lot of primal magick effort.

First, the pack meets and does some research and then identifies natural areas that are accessible and in need of this revival magick.

Next, plans and strategies for implementing this eco-revival magick should be reviewed and discussed along with this ritual.

The pack then scouts these targeted damaged wild places, making sure to look for a large grandfather or grandmother tree, meaning the largest healthy tree that can be a focus for the revival magick because it is offering the deepest taproot down deep into Gaia.

Also, the pack should also learn more about ley lines, the energy webs (a form of the Wyrd) that make up Gaia's nervous system. Such lines of earth-power will often crisscross the areas the pack wishes to heal. Where ley lines cross are centers or nodes of the "fountaining Wildness" that erupts from Gaia making them vital or sacred spots. In ancient times sacred circles, springs and sacred sites like Glastonbury Tor in the UK were established on these ley line nodes for these reasons and this was very a common practice in the ancient world.[80]

Finding maps of ley lines in your area sounds difficult, but it isn't impossible! Surprisingly Seattle, where I live, has a ley line map online and bless the folks who did it. Your area may offer such a map as well. If not, the most psychic member of your pack can wander a targeted area to be healed and feel where the ley lines are. Dowsing works well for ley line hunting as well. When in doubt, use the largest tree as your ritual node in the area you seek to heal.

## Items Needed

The stang: It can be the usual pack stang that has been reconfigured for this ritual or, if your pack is planning to do this ritual often, a new special eco-healing stang can be crafted on the full moon. If so, it should be made of mountain ash (rowen,) hawthorn, birch or oak. Earth healing symbols are painted or carved on the stang and can be chosen from the symbols in the Appendix of this book or created by the pack.

A sacred powerful stone that will be wedged into the V of the stang. It should be a found crystal or crystalline stone that a peck member found and which has an innate power to it.

Several vessels of pure water, best if they been charged in past pack rituals.

A full or near full moon.

A tree seedling, must be native to the area.

---

80. Simon, "What Makes Glastonbury so Mystical?"

Hair to be cut from each member of the pack and a small sharp knife to do so.

Dark red wine with blood or sexual fluid in it.

Another natural uncut crystal or stone for healing that was found by a wer.

Five small twigs (hand size) from a birch or oak depending on the intensity of the work.

A text that describes the ogham (Celtic) tree alphabet. On the five small twigs a pack wer will inscribe either the ogham glyph Beith: ⊤ on Birch twigs for reviving or the ogham glyph Duir on oak twigs for more damaged areas that require stronger healing power: ⊥⊥

A full moon at sunset.

A place the pack has chosen to heal: if done in a public park or reserve, watch the closing time, presence of strolling humans and so, adjust accordingly.

## The Ritual

All go to this wounded natural place, carrying the items needed. Before entering, all touch the earth, let your Animalself arise and low down growl MA MA MA mentally reaching down into the earth and opening yourselves to Gaia and to the "genus loci" or spirit of this place, feeling the pain and damage. Project your empathy and love flow into this spirit, emphasizing that you are wer, not human. Stand and enter the area in silence, staying very psychically open while expanding your energy field and bonding with the ecosystem.

Separate and wander clockwise about the whole area to be healed, gently touching and feeling and empathizing with everything while noting the toxic or damaged places. Open to all around you, breathe deeply, and *listen.*

All then come together about the largest tree or other chosen node (place) that will be the center of the work.

Once there, items are placed about the stang. Then all stand and hold hands and deep breath and rumble while together filling the area with the united pack energy and together all up howl long and slow, letting the spirit(s) and powers of this place know your good intentions and that you are an ally. Wait for a response, it will come.

Quietly and slowly do the Praxis Rite and shift gently into your wer forms. Feel the human "skin" slide off and your feral wolf-selves rise and wrap about you until y'all are in wer consciousness. You are now revealed as children of Gaia, not one of the human despoilers, a green ally, and all your magnified senses will likely be horrified at the damage done here.

All turn around and lock arms while holding paws up and facing outward with claws.

All then do the Up Growl Banishing but stay locked and in place, though strain with every growl. This is a spiritually damaged and toxic place, this banishing is done as a whole pack together for full strength and impact!

All release arms and up howl to the spirits and powers of this place, releasing both anger at what was done and promise of healing. The alpha claps three times with all joining in and growling the following:

*Genus loci and spirits of this place*
*Great devas of tree and plants*
*Water, earth, and sky*
*We come to heal and help.*
*Join with us in this work, flow through us,*
*Let us see what you see*
*And be what you are*
*So you will heal. So may it be!*

All down-howl and touch the earth or the tree.

The alpha takes up the stang and all begin to low rumble HA HA HA continuously and the right place is found for the healing stang to be planted, this will be the node previously identified. If you and using a large tree as your nexus the stang is leaned against the tree, if at a different spot, then the stang is gently pushed into the earth and all throw paws up and softly up howl three times announcing the beginning of the work.

All reach up to the (maybe visualized) moon and draw its power down into the stang and thus the earth while deep down growling AH AH AH as you feel your fur tingle with the flow of lunar energy. The beta or another then walks about the area or tree pouring a trickle of wine while all growl:

*By the blood of beast and vine*
*O Great Selene*
*Your lunar power flows to the Great Mother*
*Gaia, your daughter heals you!*
*Great Selene, come and heal your Mother!*
*AHhhhhhhhhhh!*

Sway back and forth all in sync and see this lunar power flow down through the wine Into the earth, nurturing and healing flowing out into the wild area, the stang a kind of tuning fork transmitting this energy into the Earth. At the alpha's cue, throw paws up and quietly down-howl while lowering paws to the horns of the stang. Do this three times.

Still touching the horns of the stang, all inhale deeply and then low up growling a call to the Lord of the Forest to come and join this healing from more vital woods nearby with deep up growls of HA HA HA. As you all do so, all visualize horns sprouting on your heads, becoming longer and shaggier and interspersed with green leaves. Foot paws turn to roots that go deep into the earth. Then all low-howl and center all the feral magick you have manifested as this primal being down through the stang which is now glowing intensely with green energy.

With eyes closed, all growl and rock backward and forward together while still touching the stang:

*AN HA! AN HA! AN HAaaaa!*
*Joining the Mother and the Daughter*
*The Lord of the Forest Here Now Dances!*
*The Wildness and Roots Reach Deep*
*Guiding Wolf Power, Reviving and Healing!*
*The Flowing Love of the Lord of the Forest!*

All up howl and release the Lord of the Forest possessing them to flow into the earth, howling and long, low up = howl of:

*HAaaaaaaa!*

All see the green and silver energies flowing into Gaia, the three weaving together to support the Earth and this lang and all the spirits here gathered now about your glowing stang.... Expanding outward, embracing the whole area.

The pack has now woven the powers of the Wildness, Wyrd, and Way, so it is time to re-establish and reopen the damaged spiritual tap root from Gaia to this place and so let loose a fountain of Wildness on the astral and physical planes.

All stand about the stang or tree and move back seven steps, facing where the stang is. All begin to rumble and sway in sync, going deeper into the werewolf magick trance and into the earth as well. At a cue from the alpha, all slightly open their mouth and deep down growl RA RA RA... and, continuing this growl-chant, slowly move as one counterclockwise and begin to spiral toward the stang as you go slowly and carefully as one. The closer you get to the stang in your spiral-stalking, the louder and more intense the RA RA RA gets.

At the same time, all are visualizing their fiery belly center glowing and filling their whole body with intense flaming energy as all also empower their werewolf forms. Once all come to the stang all stop, touch the horns of the stang, and loudly growl RA RA RA together and let all the fiery wolf power flow down into the earth to open up the clogged and damages channel of Earth energy, thus unleashing all the lunar and Lord of the Forest power as well into the heart of Gaia, freeing her energy all. Stand silent for a time until you feel an eruption coming from the now freed energy!

As this new geyser of Earth energy explodes upward, the alpha up growls Ah HA and all join and continue up growling AH HA over and over as they spiral stalk clockwise away from the stang, visualizing a mighty fountain of green Earth energy erupting and spraying over the whole area! (**Note:** If the tree is the node, this is visualized as erupting up through the tree and its branches).

You will feel it and howl and sit or lay on the ground letting all your conjured power flow into this wonderful geyser. Sit or lay down and feel this deep joy and healing of Gaia falling like green rain upon you and the whole wild area, up howling as you like, with joy and laughter. This open channel of healing may not be strong at this point, but it will get stronger and wilder and can always be renewed by more pack magick in the future. If it is a very damaged place, doing this several times will help.

After a time of sitting or lying about and letting go, all stand and gather in a circle and rumble.

The knife is held up by the alpha who cuts off a small piece of his or her hair and the knife is passed counterclockwise to the next wer who does the same until all have done so.

Next, the four primal elements will be conjured from the four directions. All will honor the taproot and stang, then the alpha will raise the sapling to the north and invoke and then three other wers who volunteer will invoke the south, west and east as indicated. The collected cut hair is thus given by all to the wer who will conjure the east.

All rumble and close their eyes and focus on the stang and intensely visualize and feel the stang glow with power and, like a tree, send down energetic roots of light into the earth and green energy rushes upward like a geyser that sprays the area from the stang. When this is felt, the alpha growls the following and the other wers, eyes still closed, repeat it line by line:

*As green fountains up, all becomes clear*
*Gone contamination, banished all fear*
*Gaia rise like a flower in this holy place*
*Poisons and dis-ease, begone all trace*
*Renew all animals, trees and springs*
*Earth power arises, all healing brings!*

All long, low volume up howl.

All visualize and are filled with the vibrant energy of the green geyser of healing, envisioned even now.

Next, the alpha raises the sapling to the north and growls the following and all repeat:

*We called forth the spirits of mountains, trees and Earth*
*to rise up and glow with the power of rebirth*
*Every stone and every see*
*Reborn and renewed, so may it be!*

All long, low-volume up howl.

Another wer holds up the crystal/stone to the south and growls the following while all repeat:

*We call deep magma power and fiery light*
*Solar, glowing Wolf Spirit, eyes alight*
*Bring protection and healing, for the greatest and least*
*Prospering and freedom for every bird and beast!*

All long, low-volume up howl.

Another wer holds up the wine bottle to the west and growls the following while all repeat:

*We call forth a healing flood,*
*Spirits of river, pond, lake and sea*
*Bring joy in the cleansing*
*Great waters setting all free!*

All long, low-volume up howl.

Another wer holds up cut hair to the east and growls the following while all repeat:

*Spirits of cleansing wind and storm*
*Blow away all that's tainted and worn*
*Energize, revitalize and bring fresh life as is*
*Gaia's winds awake, banish all strife!*

Now the alpha takes up the stang (with inset stone) and the pack rumbles and finds a place to plant the new sapling where it will thrive. When all agree on a place, wer claws and the stang is used to make a hole. Then the hair, the stone / crystal and a little wine with a lot of water is poured in, then the sapling is placed in the hole and all gently plant, with all repeating MA MA MAaaa and gently lending a hand.

Then all sit about it and continue low vibrating MAaaaaa MAaaaaa MAaaaaa with eyes closed visualizing the healing spread from this sapling for a time until it fades, then all simply rumble, very low, very slowly as each works his or her magick to make this rite work.

At a certain point the alpha will "see" that the work is done and begin long, slow down-howling and soon all join in, letting the magick sink deep into the earth.

All sit in silence for a moment and let go of the potent work that was done, sense the new feeling of the place, breathe in and out slowly, all together and bathe in the newly revived fountaining power zone just created until all stary howling at the cue of the alpha!

Now is a time to pass the wine and water, whatever else around the circle for a time, relax, and maybe chat a bit comparing experiences until the magick has settled.

Then all stand and the alpha growls and all repeat:

*By the Wildness, Wyrd, and Way*
*Woven in power here today*
*We empower this place of open gate*
*Giving blood, fur and magick, new life to create*
*Wildness take root here, never be gone*
*May our conjure make right what humans made wrong*
*We call forth green magick with bright prayers three*
*By Moon, Earth and forest, so may it be!*
*By blood, skin and fangs, claws and blood*
*New wave of green life, rise up as a flood*

*All wers and wild things sing now to thee*
*By our deep feral love so may it be!*

All do a final loud howl! Touch the small sapling and offer it growled blessings as they will and pour out more water upon it.

Then all do the end of the Praxis Rite and, all bending down in a circle, place paws on the earth and chant MA MA MA, ever honoring Her.

Group hug, packing up everything, leaving things better than they were (pick up any trash found as well as what the pack brought) and then all leave in happy silence.

Coda: A pack member who lives nearby should come every couple of days, especially when things are dry, and water the sapling as it acclimates.

The pack should then plan to help other nearby natural areas in need of healing and reviving!

# CONCLUSION

———— ❯☾ ————

If my last book, *Werewolf Magick,* was the result of an explosive initiatory ripping asunder of my mundane and magickal reality, this book has been more of a slow erupting revelation that, as a werewolf mage, I am not alone. When I was creating my last book I was doing werewolf magick almost completely solo. I kept shapeshifting, scribbling and doing my wild magick every full moon as I let the results flow into my computer, wondering if I was on the right track or was nuts. As I was writing *Werewolf Magick,* I thought often of how I'd like a pack and so I also began to write about what pack magick rituals and practices might look like.

During this time the gnosis of reintegrating with my Animalself and reconnecting with nature was working for me and was healing me and I intuitively *knew* it could work in a group, that was all I knew, but I took copious notes. I know our gods and spirits guide us and liminal doorways open when we are ready, so I trusted in that and that is how things went. I knew from my experience at Pantheacon that this potent magick can really enthuse and light-up people in groups like a rave. Ecstatically! Wildly! It also showed that I was not alone in this. Then, later on, *Werewolf Magick* began to sell and soon it seemed to be everywhere and soon the dam broke. A flood of wolfish communications hit me from social media and interpersonal encounters. The many hidden wers and their kin had found me, something I had not expected! I am still communicating with dozens of people who *get it but didn't know what was stirring within them.* There are now wers working werewolf magick in Brazil, New Zealand, Wales, Portugal and UK among other places and, of course, all over the US!

Many have stories similar to mine, of feeling their Animalself trying to arise. So many people have written to me, and many more have gotten the book! Almost every day I get messages, emails and mail, it floors me. I see all of them (and you) as my kin, my fellow wers, part of my larger pack and I love you all. I am always available to correspond with you!

I now realized that werewolf magick was not just my path. It is becoming a powerful magick for a whole lot of people, whether they just dip into it or go all-out with it. When *Werewolf Magick* was published, I'd just moved into a small house with its own woods so I was often doing my crazy-ass naked howling growling werewolf magick there every full moon, kinda waiting for cops to show up, I am in Seattle after all. It has been almost three years and not a peep or a siren, and I *am* loud. Maybe the neighbors think it is something else. Last summer a neighbor stopped to chant when I was gardening and mentioned that coyotes had reappeared in our neighborhood. After chatting for a while, I suddenly got it. *I was the coyote!* This seemed a very good omen.

This wild magick was really evolving, but what would it manifest? I soon got a bunch of interview offers for podcasts and a few video chats and of course wolf packs came up. The interviewers were at first all skeptical of werewolf magick but ended up becoming very open and even excited about this new magick. It pushed me to write pack magick rituals and more, *if you build it, they will come* I thought.

(I have a page with links to all my interviews at werewolfmagick.com for those interested.)

I felt the pack magick vibe rising with every interview, and then I was invited to present at a few festivals, to lead just-written werewolf pack magick rituals virtually (due to COVID), and even via zoom *the crowds went wolfishly wild* and wanted to know more, but none were close to me. Then I met some lovely people through a magickal friend of mine. Over a meal in my wooded yard, they all let me know they were interested in and drawn to werewolf magick. Then they asked if I was interested in doing werewolf pack work with them? AWOOO! Of course, I was overjoyed. We still gather and do werewolf pack magick rites together on full moons to great effect. That pack magick influenced me greatly, of course. My writing and revising of this book accelerated, enhanced by doing pack rituals with fellow wers. So, our nascent pack has begun to coalesce as we progress together. And it works. pack magick is, as I'd hoped, like a wildfire. Trance states erupt faster and easier, the ascendency of the Animalself is faster and more intense in a pack than solo. There have also been some sublime discoveries for me, like the melodious tonality of a group of wers in full shifted trance state howling together, raised voices entwined and powerful etheric interconnection when we rock and growl in sync. The sheer joy of shapeshifting with a group is utterly freeing and magnified as is the intoxication of the full moon and quiet zen-like stillness and silent, subtle peace so rarely found when groups of humans gather. I now know that pack magick is powerful, healing, integrative magick.

I've written many occult books, all of them labors of love, *but this book…!*

Through the Great Wolf Spirit who saved me from a potentially fatal disaster, I have rediscovered a very important, very primal and very gnosis gnosis that helps people and, I hope it can help people rip through the wall that separates them from nature and leads to a more natural, joyful life.

I now clearly see that the real goal of werewolf pack magick is to free ourselves from the misery of being separated from nature. In my deepest trance states, I have come to know this truth. We must reconnect with Gaia viscerally and deeply, as the animals we *are* and rediscover a way of life that includes nature, and wildness as our daily reality to save our world. I have stayed with tribal peoples in many countries, hung out with shamans and curanderos and brujo. I have ridden elephants in jungles and camels in deserts, and in many places I visited this reality of being wholly one with the ecosystem is all very real for cultures that are sadly being devoured by the modern world.

As an older wolf now, thinking about what will be after I'm gone, it is my greatest hope that werewolf magick, and similar varieties of feral magic, will spread and help halt our ecological self-destruction. I howl and pray to the feral gods that, long after I'm gone, this magickal path will help in some way revive a way of living as part of nature has mostly been forgotten.

No matter what, Gaia will most likely survive the coming trials, but will homo sapiens? We are not the masters of earth and heaven as we have been told, our species does not have a divine mandate to rule here. It is time we rejoin the natural world, one howl at a time.

Be well and stay Wild! —DS

> *"This we know: the earth does not belong to man, man belongs to the earth.*
> *All things are connected like the blood that unites us all.*
> *Man did not weave the web of life, he is merely a strand in it.*
> *Whatever he does to the web, he does to himself."*
> —Chief Seattle (more correctly, Seathl)
> a Suquamish chief who lived in Puget[81]

---

81. Posted by Dr. Hardy, http://www.csun.edu/~vcpsy00h/seattle.htm, uttered 1854, original published 1931.

# APPENDIX A

# OFTEN REPEATED RITES AND REFERENCED ITEMS

- Up Growl Banishing
- Praxis Rite: Revised and Expanded
- Blessing ritual for Werewolf Magick Tools
- Expanded List of Tools Items and Ingredients
- Werewolf Magick Icons Oracle

## Up Growl Banishing

This can be done in a pack or solo.

If in a pack, all stand in a circle and face outward.

All begin to rock back and forth and rumble (deep low growl, mouth closed) and call forth the Animalself and let it rise to the fore as the human consciousness retreats.

After a time, all open their mouths a little and begin to deeply and intensely growl as they visualize being bigger, stronger and more intense werewolves, full of power and determination.

All are now rocking backward and forward and growling together in sync.

This builds and the growling gets louder and more and more intense.

There is a pause and the growling stop, this is a cue from the alpha.

Then, all raise their paws and visualize being in attack-mode and lunge intensely as one, paws up, claws out and loudly intensely up growl, projecting a powerful force like a mighty psychic roar that is visualized sweeping away all that is negative and unwanted, be it spirits, miasma, or lingering negative energies.

This is done nine times. To nine directions around the circle. Each lunge and power-growl are done on a forward rock, on the rock back all inhale and then repeat.

If you are solo, you do this by slowly moving counterclockwise about your sacred space and lunging nine times to nine different directions until you return to your starting point.

If you are in a pack, all stand equidistant in a circle, then face outward.

All stand in place and lunge and growl nine times or two. All lunge and growl, then all shift to the left and repeat until, nine growls later, all have returned to the same place.

When the nine growl-blasts are done all how loudly until that area is clean!

## Praxis Shifting Rite: Revised and Expanded

This is a preliminary part of many spells in rituals and spells found in *Werewolf Magick*. It can also be done as a stand-alone rite anytime to enter a light werewolf shapeshifting trance but it is often used at the beginning of more complex solo or pack rituals. It would behoove you to memorize it so it can be done extemporaneously, maybe out hiking.

### Set Up

Keep in mind that the longer, deeper and slower you do this, the more powerful it is. A ten minute Praxis Rite will give you a light trance, but in pack I've discovered that a thirty minute Praxis Rite can elicit a deep shapeshifting trance and as such is a great stand alone rite.

### The Rite

Begin by deep breathing, relaxing and banishing all mental activity, focus for a time on awakening your Animalself. See it rise up from the dark depths of your inner mind, arising from the dark cave it sleeps in. As you breathe deeper and deeper, shake your whole body like a canine and go up and the balls of your feet, hunch over and listen to your whole body. Place your hands on your fire-gut center, and as per the more advanced shapeshifting breathe deeper and stronger, now low rumble-growling with each inhalation and exhalation, and let the energetic fires erupting from there expand and fill your body as it awakens, empowers and helps the Animalself to rise up through your body and spine.[82] It overwhelms the human consciousness which, with every exhalation-rumble-growl, slowly sinks into the deep shadows of your mind. Feel this tsunami of feral, primal power subsume and alter your consciousness, shutting down the constant ego-chatter and opening up your senses and calm beast-consciousness of simply being. Take as long as you need to attain this.

Now feel the fiery Animalself-werewolf energy warmly spread up and through your whole body, like a tingling awakening all nerves and senses that were asleep and this speeds the awakening of your wolf as you truly begin the shapeshifting process.

As your consciousness is subsumed by the animal consciousness, intensely visualize becoming who you see in your mind as your full werewolf self or persona, visualize and feel this as clearly as you can, body part by body part, fur, claws, fangs and so on. After several practice sessions it will come naturally. When it is clear and you actually feel your astral self transforming with the fiery will of the Animalself, begin to sway side to side, foot to foot, feel and vibrate to the now pulsing rhythm and the energy filling you from the Earth. Now begin to low up growl rumble deep in your chest in rhythm to the swaying.as before. Eyes semi-closed.

Now, feel your werewolf form arise as you shapeshift, energy from the fire center filling your new form, much as you have done many times before.

As you do so, slightly open your mouth so that your rumble-growling becomes up growling the vibration HA over and over in time with your swaying as you enter a trance. Go up slightly onto the balls of your feet, lean forward. Let arms relax and open shoulders, arms and your chest. Raise your lupine head, splay your claws with arms outstretched.

Now solidify the visualized shapeshift change to your werewolf form, as you have been practicing. See and feel all this with absolute clarity as the astral energy solidifies.

---

82. Sargent, Denny, *Werewolf Magick*, 101.

As the visualized shift expands through your will and power, increase the volume and intensity of the rocking/growling HA mantra and feel the warmth fill and transform you completely as you become your Animalself wolf! Finally, let your conscious mind and ego slide into the shadows and let your Animalself wolf-mind take over completely as you enter the trance state we call "being wer."

Once the Animalself wolf mind is firmly in control and you can clearly feel and "see" yourself as the werewolf you will to be, slow the swaying and let the HA growling fade but continue to rumble and do deep breathing.

Go up on the balls of your foot-paws, lean over, arms and claws outstretched.

Now, bend your upper torso down with every out-breath.

Reach up with your claws and slowly bring them down while visualizing pulling down the power of the moon into your body. Slowly and intently down-howl as you do so.

Reach down and let your claws touch the earth, visualize pulling up the power of Gaia, the Earth Mother, into your body and slowly and intently up howl as you do so. Do this three or more times as it solidifies your astral werewolf form.

When you are fully wer, that is, completely animalistic and werewolf as hell, take a deep breath and let the fiery primal energies coursing through you explode through your whole werewolf body and howl with everything you have, obliterating your conscious mind and completing the transformation. Howl as intensely as possible, your whole body tensing and then completely releasing all your physical, mental and emotional garbage and restriction. Afterward you'll feel a great weight fall off you, a great purge, and your mind should be open, still and the ego-yattering silent. Continue rumbling and swaying but the rumble-growling fades and slows as you adapt to your new herenow consciousness and this new, amazingly sensitive and powerful self. You may want to shake yourself to let go of the final bits of your human-self.

Now you are prepared to move on to any werewolf magick ritual or spell. When ready to end:

## PRAXIS RITE ENDING

After the rite or ritual, when you are ready to end this shifting trance state, do the following:

Raise your claws and up howl three times, releasing all the excess astral lunar power.

Bend down and touch your claws to Mother Earth and down-howl three times, releasing all the excess Earth power.

Sway side to side again, but this time down growl as you sway, with deep, long breaths in and out. Visualize and experience your transformation in reverse, slowly, step by step. The werewolf astral aura is contracting then fading with each sway as your human consciousness begins to awaken within and reassert itself as the now-tired Animalself wolf begins to grow sleepy and slides back down, down, down into the darkness where its lair is.

With every deep and long in and out growl-breath, feel and see the fiery etheric fiery energy of the primal wolf-power slowly withdraw from all your limbs and body core back into your gut-energy center with every inhalation and exhalation growl and fade to a small flame.

As you let the awakened Animalself wolf withdraw into your inner being, slowly your rational mind and human self returns. When mostly human, stomp your feet on the ground with several deep MA MA MA deep down growls and release what is left, then violently shake your whole body like any canine, your body's trunk turning side-to-side, thus shaking off the clinging feral consciousness and changes.

Then stand, breathe deeply in silence and offer silent thanks to the Lord of the Forest, the Earth Mother, the Moon Mothers and the Great Wolf Spirit.

End with a long, subdued out breath to center your true Self, growling AHhhhh-HAaaa.

Now, go forth as a recharged wolfish human.

# Pack Blessing Rite for Talismans and Tools: Revised and Expanded

This rite can easily be used for any werewolf magick talismans, tools or items used in werewolf magick that need purification and charging. Of course, any animal remains involved should be clean and safe to handle. Doing this as a pack is more powerful and allows several items to be blessed and charged together. This rite can be done within a larger ritual as well, such as the pack esbat or sabbat. All pack members are encouraged to bring items to be charged if this rite is held.

## Set Up

Find a quiet wooded natural place where you can be undisturbed. The pack rally grove would be perfect, but any place that is full of trees and positive energy is fine. Make sure you are clean with relaxed clothing.

Items needed for werewolf magick should be charged with this rite but many other possible items can be as well. Shapeshifting trigger talismans in this book (see Chapter 1) is a good example of something that may call for intensive charging.

For reference, every pack needs the pack tools charged up before they can be ritually used and the same for wers. All items must be from natural materials, made by hand is best. Each pack member can have their own versions of these items for solo work, but one set should absolutely be the pack tools. All items taken from trees or parts of wild animals must be gathered with honor and prayers and items in the shrine, such as the wolf or coyote skull, will be blessed in the shrine ritual. These are the items that would best be blessed and empowered with the full pack involved, since most are pack tools:

The stang, (from an oak tree). The sacred drinking cup or small bowl. The three staves crafted from appropriate woods each stained or painted with different natural pigments, one black, one red and one white, They should be fairly sharp at one or both ends and about one foot long. A ritual knife. A burning bowl. Candle holders or lanterns. Altar clothes and special werewolf magick clothing. Individual werewolf magick talismans. The scrying portal. The werewolf magick oracle. Any other appropriate items used.

Again, this can be done solo and in this case the ritual would be simplified a little and "scaled to fit" a solo working. The following is for a collective pack blessing:

## ITEMS NEEDED

A flat stone, stump or green cloth made of natural fabric to act as an altar.

Dried rosemary

A shell or natural bowl to burn them in

A tuft of hair from all participating

A small amount of sea salt

A sacred bowl or cup

A container of pure water

A green beeswax candle and holder.

Optional: A form of divination (Runes, tarot or I Ching are useful but use
   what you like or simply sit in silence and let the Lord of the Forest "speak"
   to you)

Do this at twilight on a near full or full moon

The pack sets up an altar and the items are laid out appropriately on the altar which is set in the center, to the north. The stang is stuck in the ground behind the altar, the rosemary is in the burning bowl. All items to be blessed are placed in the center. Items on the altar, like the burning bowl and candlesticks, will be blessed where they are.

## THE RITUAL

The pack stands in a circle about the altar and rumbles and sways in sync as a warm up, each wer "waking up" their Animalself. After a time, the alpha cues them to turn outwards and all do the Up Growl Banishing.

All then turn back to the center and again rumble and sway in sync as the alpha lights the candle and rosemary and walks about the outside of the circle while growling HA HA HA... and the pack picks up the growled chant.

All then stand in silence and together do deep breathing, as the power of nature fills. and the Animalself arises in each wer as the Lord of the Forest comes and all begin low growling HA HA HA and again swaying as the alpha sprinkles salt on the items being blessed and then a bit on every wer, walking clockwise. All visualize any negative or distracting energies dissipating.

All in silence then cut a bit of their hair.

### ALL NOW DO THE PRAXIS RITE (FIRST PART)

Then all direct all the power raised at the items being charged rite with paws outstretched and with a long low growled HAaaaaaaa while visualizing green power flowing into the items.

Now, on cue from the alpha, all do the following:

Each wer then places their snip of hair with the burning herb in the burning bowl. When done, the alpha takes the burning bowl and carefully censes the items being blessed while all are growling RA RA RA in sync while channeling the blessing of the Great Wolf Spirit directly from each wer's Animal self into items. During this all entwine their auras into and through the item and feel the wolf energy fill the items.

Then all are silent and the alpha joins them and cues all as follows:

Paws up to the moon, all growl AHhhhhhHHHH and see the energy of the Moon Mothers descend into the items being blessed.

Then all hold extended arms to either side, calling on the Lord of the Forest and all growl HAaaaaaaaa and see the energy of the Lord of the Forest flow from the woods into the items being blessed.

Then all come forward and extend paws and all touch the items being blessed, calling on Gaia and all growl MAaaaaa and see the energy of the Earth Mother flow up from the ground into the items being blessed.

Finally, all lock arms and loudly growl AHhhh-HAaaaa! with all their might, seeing the items now filled with a whirlwind of pure light that is absorbed.

When done, all step apart and begin to rumble continuously while each wer rubs their face and chest and other parts as they will and then, one at a time, each wer steps forward and rubs their scent and skin oil into the items being blessed. The alpha goes last. When this is done, all up howl with love and joy as these new sacred are part of the pack.

The now cool burning bowl is then taken up by the alpha and proffered to each wer who, one by one, takes some ashes, smears his or her forehead, heart and fire or sex center, then moves forward and sprinkles some ashes on the blessed items with a growled RAaaa! This is a final blessing of the Great Wolf Spirit.

Then, with low up growls, the alpha offers some ashes to the four quarters to honor the Earth Mother and then some above into the air honoring the Moon Mothers and some counter clockwise about the circle to honor the Lord of the Forest. Finally, the rest is buried before the altar to honor Gaia.

All howl and clap paws! The items are blessed!

Now is the time to do other ritual work if that is on the agenda. Alternatively, the last part of the Praxis Rite could be completed or the Up Growl Banishing is done.

More howls and a group hug are done to wrap it up.

From now on, these items are sacred. The items that are only for pack use are to be kept at the alpha's place. When the pack has crafted and blessed a pack shrine, the items can be kept about that shrine. All items, whether personal or pack, should be tended to as is appropriate for such sacred feral talismanic tools. Listen to your Animalself!

## APPENDIX B

# EXPANDED WEREWOLF MAGICK SYMBOLS AND THE ORACLE

Following are a number of symbols or glyphs that are described in *Were-wolf Magick*. More of such symbols have been added for pack magick as you'll see below, all together there are sixteen which offer symbols of werewolf magick that can be used for potent images on our tools talismans, tattoos and so on, but they can also be used for divination, see the Werewolf Magick Oracle Rite in Chapter 3. Note that the last seven newer symbols can be seen as more specific, less open and more personal. You are encouraged to manifest your own symbols that you receive from visions and the werewolf magick gnosis. These can be added to the pack oracle deck or drawn or carved on a set of small items made of bone, stones and so on, like runestones.

## Uses of Werewolf Magick Symbols

Aside from oracular use, such symbols can be painted, engraved, burned-on, carved, painted, tattooed in flesh, sewn on cloth or incorporated in other artistic ways to manifest the power of werewolf magick. This is especially true for magickal tools or other sacred items, ritual clothing, altar cloths, talismans, tools, and so on. Use your imagination! It is expected that experienced werewolf magick wers will create new, powerful symbols from received wolfish visions and gnosis as well and these can be added to the pack's magickal symbol stash.

Here are the symbols and meanings, many seen in *Werewolf Magick*, followed by a more recent set of werewolf magick symbols that have been received recently. Each has a description of the meaning as well as an omen or divination meaning. All can be used as potent symbols and talismans, for divination and in scrying as a focus as is explained in Chapter 4 or for any kind of astral ritual work. The Omens are open to interpretation depending on your query, as with most oracles. They can be pulled and used for simple, quick divination as well at any time. Once copied onto a set of cards or flat pieces of wood or on stones, any wer can simply draw one as an omen or to answer a question. This can be done amid any other werewolf magick ritual for a variety of reasons, it is good to bring the oracle to every ritual for this use. Again, be creative.

## Werewolf Magick Oracle Symbols

Triskele

**Meaning:** It represents the three aspects of the Moon Goddess Artemis, Selene, Hekate), and the three skills and powers: Wildness, the Wyrd, and the Way and Instinct, Intuition and Insight.

**Omen:** Balanced forces, immersion in the three-fold world, mystical experiences, visions and lunar powers.

Wolf Paw

**Meaning:** The feral power of werewolf magick, primordial sexuality, power, and shapeshifting. Such paws are often used to indicate a feral nature in social and sex-oriented communities.

**Omen:** Intense animalistic power, rush of feral and shapeshifting potency and experience, for good or ill. Sex magick and intensity that is positive or negative. Wild feral feelings.

Werewolf Fangs

**Meaning:** Banishing, protecting and even cursing those who disrespect or seek to harm or attack wers and the pack. This actively attacks any kind of bigotry, hate or anti-wer aggression.

**Omen:** Protect yourself, protect the pack and pack members, raise a force field of magick. Defend, set wards and be aware of possible enemies. Be prepared, be strong.

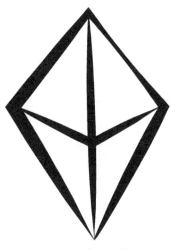

Eye of the Wolf

**Meaning:** The most powerful symbol of werewolf magick, representing the Great Wolf Spirit, our tutelary deity. It is the "third eye" of the Wolf God. A key focus of werewolf magick.

**Omen:** The Wolf Spirit is here. A direct gnosis and empowerment from the Great Wolf deity, a yes! Answer and promise that this is the right path and blessed by the Wolf God.

Claw Slash

**Meaning:** This symbol means: Hey! back off, our area, no bigotry or prejudice accepted here, our territory, PISS OFF! Bark Bark Bark!

**Omen:** Take action now! Put an end to bickering, toxic situations, resentments, stress and so on. Ban toxic people and situations. Now. Let things go and say NO when needed.

Pentagram in Paw

**Meaning:** An ancient cross-cultural sign also used when Witchcraft was deeply entwined with lycanthropy. Also called the "witch's foot," it represents the five elements and indicates our gods: The three Moon Goddesses, the Lord of the Forest and Gaia, the clawed hand being the Wolf God that united them. The pentagram was said to "appear" on werewolves indicating a shapeshifter.

**Omen:** Strength, unity, pride and power. Great regarding shapeshifting skills and expansion of magickal skills and trance work. Unity, honoring all the gods and keeping the pack united.

Lit Stang

**Meaning:** The stang is the Lord of the Forest, guardian and manifester of Wildness, and bearer of wisdom of Wyrd and Way. The Lord of the Forest has many names, exists in every culture and is often depicted as half beast like Pan or Faunus or as a forest god like the Green Man. The stang with a small flame between the horns indicates his presence and blessing.

**Omen:** Invoke or seek out the Lord of the Forest, his power is available now. Go into the wilderness and receive what he is waiting to give. Do direct work with him and his power and be open to hearing his voice and his message.

Triple Moon

**Meaning:** Our triple moon symbol is different in that all three Goddesses are entwined thus revealing the whole moon which empowers Shifting and visionary work. All the phases are one as are all lunar goddesses, thus the symbol shows the fully awakened lunar power in totality.

**Omen:** Pay attention to the moon, it's cycles and powers! Focus on visions, erotic magicks, feral and lucid dreams, spell work and all lunar magicks. Answers and intuition will guide you when you honor and invoke the Moon Mothers.

Wolf Triquetra

**Meaning:** This ancient and powerful symbol traditionally associated with werewolves is the ancient Celtic *Triquetra* origins are obscure, but signifies magicks of speed, strength, and quickness, like that of a wolf. It also here represents the Double or your astral/energetic self which is the stiff of shapeshifting and astral travel as well as familiars. In a deeper sense it represents the Wyrd or flow of life and death and the finding and following of one's true way within this flow.

**Omen:** Go with the flow! Get out and prowl and run. Stop intellectualizing and overthinking. Take a break from the human world of madness. Shapeshift more and unplug! Take long walks without headphones! Reconnect with the flow of nature about you. Open to your Animalself and become crazy-active! But, take time to meditate, have fun, get out of your head and channel all this energy into creative and life affirming projects! The following icons are new werewolf magick symbols:

These new symbols are more focused on more specific magickal actions or states as opposed to being divine icons of power. However, each can certainly be used in talismanic work and may be adopted as personal icons and used in all the ways the other werewolf magick symbols are used.

Wildness Powers

**Meaning:** The power of Wildness that arises within and around you, the manifestation of pure wild energy that comes from primal nature about you integrating with the arising Animalself within you. This potent image offers an intuitive way to unity with the local ecosystem.

**Omen:.** You are caught up in a mighty wave of wildness energy and are being pushed to get **out** and commune with nature and the ecosystem **now.** You and your impatient Animalself need this energy! Your Animalself is restless is letting you know it needs more wildness, play, sexuality and physical release in nature. This may also indicate that specific animal spirits are reaching out to you and your feral self is calling them to them, be open to this! Get out into the woods!

Wyrd Weaving

**Meaning:** The Wyrd has been described often as the vast multi-level web of energy, causality and interconnectedness within and about us, it is the active intelligence of all nature. Wyrd weaving is the art of our interconnecting with and becoming open to and proficient with weaving the powers we embody, embodied in the Animalself weaving the webs of Wyrd with our own growing power and magick. While naturally manifesting when being in deep nature, learning to work with and initiate this psychic weaving is called for.

**Omen:** You are beginning to experience liminal moments of *seeing* the Wyrd, the interconnectedness of all living things. You are feeling, and at times seeing, the vast web of life and the quantum universe about you. This is a bit scary but it echoes visionary experiences all wers have felt. Go with the flow, do not fear your new powers and perceptions, gently embrace them! You are becoming a seer and your shapeshifting is opening up the other world to you. Record your experiences, go to the woods often and be open to weaving your energies with that of the ecosystem as you open to Animalself.

Active work such meditation, shapeshifting, Tai Chi, Yoga and conscious standing within the woven matrix of all life about you is the key! Share your experiences, become the Wyrd.

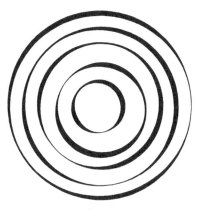

Being/Not-Being

**Meaning:** The Way experienced directly with no thought or duality. Apperceive consciousness, pure and open. When pure Animalself consciousness is attained within nature, the ego dissolves and one is as all animals are: Simply Being, in the moment, in the flow, with no past-future confusion. Here. Now. No thought. Ah! This is a kind of Samadhi.

**Omen:** You are being drawn into a more mystical state of being. Your shapeshifting work is opening up a meditative state of pure being, of losing yourself in the pure essence of nature and the universe. This Taoist-like state is new and opens you to the animal state of simply being, with no thought. Spend time in deep stillness in nature after shapeshifting work and just be silent, clear, open. Taoists call this "nothing doing nothing" (Wei Wu Wei) and in Tantra is called Dhyana or a non-ego bliss-state. Do as your Animalself bids you. Become a pure animal and just *be*. Carry this freedom with you in all your work.

Growing Cohesion

**Meaning:** The more you let Animalself arise, the more of a whole being you are, the more unified you are, you are becoming natural *you*. This manifests outwardly in your life and inwardly within the alchemical transformation of your Self. In the sense of the pack (or any group you belong to) naturally coalescing love and unity is a state always strived toward in that nothing important can be done amid dispersion or chaos in a group setting.

**Omen:** Work diligently at breaking through the walls within you that separate your human and Animal selves! Smash the false cultural, emotional and psychological barriers between your "normal" and wild personas, rescue. Now, nourish and own your true suppressed natural self! This is a time for removing the false separations of civilized misery and self-hate! You are one with nature, one with all life and you can now use this to unify your true Self so help unify the pack. Finding your appropriate place and creating calm interconnections between you and the others in your pack are crucial to anything positive. It is wise to examine your own actions and ego, especially in a shifted state and embracing unity, the goal of real work and real magick.

Conjure

**Meaning:** Getting out into nature and intuitively doing a magickal spell or rite to accomplish something. Conjure here means to bring together the appropriate energies, ideas, and items within your wild Animalself consciousness to actively make things happen through Wildness, Wyrd and Way. The dance of active magick within nature by the Animalself, guided by instinct, intuition and insight is the key to this feral magick. Conjure is a term for such intuitive and often unplanned magickal operations with the help of spirits. Conjure uses prior experience to guide intuition to accomplish things through magickal work.

**Omen:** You are pondering, dreaming and inspired by wild magick; now is the time to do it! Intuitively grab some items and hike into nature and begin! Open to working magick instinctively and intuitively as you discover within wildness insights for crafting real magick; authentic spells, and rituals. The sorcerer-artist Austin Spare defined magick as "The Art of Attracting without asking." Our feral magick is the gateway to this! You don't need books, videos, classes, no. Go into nature, shapeshift, and Gaia will reveal all to you who are ready! The trees will tell you their powers. Rivers, lakes and seas will unveil their magicks. Commune wordlessly with winds, fire, rain and storms and remember their wisdom. Rocks and flowers will call to you. Then, as a wer, with the howls of your Animalself, call the animal spirits to you! Later, write everything down! This is where magick came from! Rediscover true natural magick as shapeshifters, shamans and sorcerers have done for millennia! Now is the time, they are calling you.

Feral Ferocity

**Meaning:** The intense, aggressive, innate animal Intensity of your Animalself. We are primates. Your Animalself, being primal and primitive and full of your innate power can also be seen in our repressive, controlling culture in aggressive outbursts, territorialism and fights, especially when the Animalself on each of us is suppressed, enslaved and vilified. Our fearlessness, our animalistic side, is not inherently wrong, it keeps us alive in many ways, it empowers us to defend our autonomy and kin and what is ours. This omen offers us fire and backbone so we may assert our true will and not become influenced, corrupted or enslaved by predatory situations or humans. It is powerful and important, but also it needs to be fully comprehended, embraced and under control of the will of the shapeshifter.

**Omen:** The berserker intensity of the shadow-wolf side of the Animalself is making you agitated, but for a reason. Your wer-self is offering ways to work with these energies that need release! Time to *get out* of the civilized prison you're in and get out into the green of nature. Go running, hiking, swimming, climbing; anything physical and let the green peel away the false "human" darkness caused by repression, frustrations and resentments. Get lost in the pure joy and positive energy of nature. Shapeshift and empty your chattering mind, embrace the healing power that Gaia and the Lord of the Forest offer you. When you are clear, meditate on this in wer form until the real cause of this frustrated wolfish ferocity rises up. Contemplate the true issue. You must decide, as a balanced, crafty wolf, how to resolve it like an ulfsark wolf warrior. You need not confront or become angry, you are called now to use your feral power to let go of things, people or situations without overt conflict. It is time to make real, maybe difficult, decisions and changes in your life. This is the gift of the shadowolf.

Renewing/Healing

**Meaning:** Why unleash our Animalself? What is the true purpose of bonding deeply with nature, our ecosystem and the wild gods? How does the Wildness about us, the Wyrd that interconnects all living things and the Way of pure, open consciousness help us really heal from all the pains and suffering being in our civilized prison has done to us? Once we can remove all the lies and programming and remember our true natural being, we truly see and feel the personal and ecological disaster humans have caused. No animal besides us does this. As we become awake we begin to feel the pain of such destruction and horror. Yet nature ever offers to heal us and we can help heal nature. We can use our werewolf magick, our Animalself reunited with nature to heal ourselves and our pack brothers and sisters through our feral power, love and will. In our work we are called to heal our environment, heal each other, and heal ourselves on every level. nature, within and without, offers us everything we need.

**Omen:** It is time to heal yourself or seek healing within or from your pack. Meditate on what is hurting you, dig deep, even note them down unless they are painfully obvious. Go into the woods, find a pure and healing place, do the Praxis Rite or another and invoke intensely your Animalself. Once the human "skin" is gone and the jabbering ego-mind is stilled, simply be in nature and open to the truth of your suffering and pain. How much is self-inflicted, consciously and unconsciously? What would a wolf do? Is the suffering physical, mental or emotional? Listen to your Animalself! Ignore your ego! Push the past to the side, ignore future worries. Be *present*. What will you *do* now? Reach out to your pack for help! This is crucial! In your own "normal" life, calmly and directly take action. It may be a very truthful meeting with a coworker, hurtful friend or partner, or directly dealing with health or emotional issues. Seek and facilitate healing in an active way now. With every pack rhythmic growling we heal, with every drumbeat, our hearts become the heartbeat of Gaia. So may it ever be.

# BIBLIOGRAPHY

)(

Adkins, Lesley. *Dictionary of Roman Religion*. Oxford, UK: Oxford University Press, 2000.

Baring-Gould, Sabine. *The Book of Werewolves*. Independence, KY: Cengage Learning, 1981.

Brewer, E.C. *Dictionary of Phrase & Fable*. London: Wordsworth Editions, 2006.

Carr-Gomm, Philip. *The Book of English Magic*. New York: Hodder & Stoughton, 2014.

Cooper, J. C. *Symbolic & Mythological Animals*. Northampton, UK: The Aquarian Press, 1992.

Cunningham, Scott. *Encyclopedia of Magical Herbs*. St. Paul, MN: Llewellyn Publications, 1996.

Curran, Bob. *Werewolves: A Field Guide to Shapeshifters, Lycanthropes, and Manbeasts*. Newburyport, ME: RedWheel/Weiser, 2009.

de Blecourt, William, ed. *Werewolf Histories*. Hampshire, UK: Palgrave McMillian, 2015.

Fries, Jan. *Cauldron Of the Gods: a Manual Of Celtic Magick*. Oxford, UK: Mandrake, 2003.

Fries, Jan. *Seidways: Shaking, Swaying and Serpent Mysteries*. Oxford UK: Mandrake of Oxford, 2010.

Gary, Gemma. *Traditional Witchcraft: A Cornish Book Of Ways*. London, Troy Books, 2012.

Graves, Zachary. *Werewolves*. New York: Chartwell Books, 2011.

Griffiths, Bill. *Aspects of Anglo-Saxon Magic*. Norfolk, UK: Anglo-Saxon Books, 2012.

Izzard, Jon. *Werewolves*. New York: Spruce, 2009.

Jackson, Nigel. *Call of the Horned Piper*. Berks, UK: Capall Bann, 1994.

Jackson, Nigel. *The Compleat Vampyre: The Vampyre Shaman, Werewolves, Witchery & the Dark Mythology of the Undead*. Berks, UK: Capall Bann Publishing, 1995.

Jackson, Nigel. *Masks of Misrule*. Berks, UK: Capall Bann, 1996.

Knowles, Elizabeth. *Oxford Dictionary of Phrase and Fable*. Oxford UK: Oxford University Press, 2016.

Leach, Maria ed. *Funk & Wagnalls Standard Dictionary of Folklore Mythology and Legend*. New York: Harper Collins, 1972.

Lecouteux, Claude. *Witches, Werewolves, and Fairies: Shapeshifters and Astral Doublers in the Middle Ages*. Translated by Clare Frock. Rochester, VT: Inner Traditions, 2003.

Lupa. *Fang and Fur, Blood and Bone: A Primal Guide to Animal Magic*. Stafford, UK: Megalithica Books, 2006.

McHargue,Georgess. *Meet the Werewolf*. New York: Dell, 1983.

Morgan, Lee. *A Deed Without a Name: Unearthing the Legacy of Traditional Witchcraft*. Winchester, UK: Moon Books, 2013.

Ronnberg, Ami. *The Book of Symbols*. Cologne, Germany: Taschen, 2010.

Sargent, Denny. *Global Ritualism, Myth and Magick Around the World*. St. Paul, MN: Llewellyn Publications, 1994.

Sargent, Denny. *Book of the Horned One*. Richmond, CA: Concrescent Press, 2012.

Sargent, Denny. *Werewolf Magick, Authentic Practical Lycanthropy*. Woodbury, MN: Llewellyn Publications, 2020.

Spence, Lewis. An Encyclopaedia Of Occultism. NYC: Cosimo Classics, 2006.

Steiger, Brad. *The Werewolf Book, Encyclopedia of Shape-Shifting Beings*. Detroit, MI: Visible Ink Press, 2012.

Summers, Montague. *The Werewolf.* Secaucus, NJ: Citadel Press, 1973.

Telesco, Patricia. *Dog Spirit: Hounds, Howlings, and Hocus Pocus.* Rochester, Vermont: Park Street Press, 2000.

Vedhrfolnir, Shade. *Runespells, A Grimoire of Rune-Magick.* Richmond, CA: Concrescent Press 2021.

Walker, Barbara. *The Woman's Dictionary of Symbols and Sacred Objects.* NYC: Pandora, 1995.

Walker, Barbara. *The Woman's Encyclopedia of Myths and Secrets.* Harper & Row: New York, 1983.

## Websites

Anderson-Minshall, Diane. "Riveting Wolf Documentary Worth a Gay Gander." Advocate. Last updated August 15, 2012. https://www.advocate.com/arts-entertainment/film/2012/08/15/riveting-wolf-documentary-worth-gay-gander.

Colavito, Jason. "The Werewolf In Ancient Greece." Jason Colavito blog. Last updated June 2, 2012. https://www.jasoncolavito.com/blog/the-werewolf-in-ancient-greece.

Free Dictionary, The. "Esbat." Accessed August 2021. https://encyclopedia2.thefreedictionary.com/esbat.

Guardian writers. "10 traditional winter festivals in Europe." *The Guardian.* Last updated November 29, 2019. https://www.theguardian.com/travel/2019/nov/29/10-europe-winter-festival-traditions-christmas-new-year.

History.com editors. "Lupercalia." History.com. Last updated December 13, 2017. https://www.history.com/topics/ancient-rome/lupercalia.

Ingram,Simon, What makes Glastonbury so mystical? *National Geographic.* Accessed June 2019. https://www.nationalgeographic.co.uk/history-and-civilisation/2019/06/what-makes-glastonbury-so-mystical.

Pliny the Elder. "Natural History 1-11." Topos Text. Accessed June 2021. https://topostext.org/work/148.

Living with Wolves. "The Social Wolf." Accessed June 2021. https://www
.livingwithwolves.org/about-wolves/social-wolf/.

Lovgren, Stefan. "Chimps, Humans 96 Percent the Same, Gene Study Finds."
*National Geographic*, August 31, 2005. https://www.nationalgeographic
.com/science/article/chimps-humans-96-percent-the-same-gene-study-
finds.

McKenna, Terence. "The Ethnobotany of Shamanism." Last updated July 9,
2009 (text and podcast) http://erocx1.blogspot.com/2009/06/terence
-mckenna-ethnobot-any-of.html.

Thayer, Tom. "Russian Werewolf Spell." Learning Witchcraft. Last updated
April 9, 2018. https://learningwitchcraft.com/russian-werewolf-spell/.

Davis, Lauren. "Why Everything You Know About Wolf Packs Is Wrong,"
Gizmodo. Last updated November 29, 2014. https://io9.gizmodo.com
/why-everything-you-know-about-wolf-Packs-is-wrong-166430196.

McCoy, Daniel. *The Viking Spirit An Introduction to Norse Mythology and Religion*.
CreativeSpace, 2016. https://www.goodreads.com/work
/quotes/50867672.

Magnus, Olaus. *Historia de gentibus septentrionalibus*, 1555. Quoted *in Esto-
nian Werewolf History,* https://link.springer.com/chapter/10.1007
%2F978-1-137-52634-2_9.

Moreson, Ryan. "Gay behaviour 'is the norm for most animals'." Daily Mail.
Last updated November 2018. https://www.dailymail.co.uk/sciencetech
/article-7698117/Ancient-ancestors-modern-animals-humans-bisexual.html

Sargent, Denny. "Feral Magick." Denny Sargent Author. https://
dennysargentauthor.com.

The Free Dictionary. "Esbat." Accessed August 2021.
https://encyclopedia2.thefreedictionary.com.

## To Write to the Author

If you wish to contact the author or would like more information about this book, please write to the author in care of Llewellyn Worldwide Ltd. and we will forward your request. Both the author and the publisher appreciate hearing from you and learning of your enjoyment of this book and how it has helped you. Llewellyn Worldwide Ltd. cannot guarantee that every letter written to the author can be answered, but all will be forwarded. Please write to:

Denny Sargent
℅ Llewellyn Worldwide
2143 Wooddale Drive
Woodbury, MN 55125-2989

Please enclose a self-addressed stamped envelope for reply,
or $1.00 to cover costs. If outside the U.S.A., enclose
an international postal reply coupon.

Many of Llewellyn's authors have websites with additional
information and resources. For more information,
please visit our website at http://www.llewellyn.com.